Communications
in Computer and Information Science 2630

Series Editors

Gang Li, *School of Information Technology, Deakin University, Burwood, VIC, Australia*
Joaquim Filipe, *Polytechnic Institute of Setúbal, Setúbal, Portugal*
Zhiwei Xu, *Chinese Academy of Sciences, Beijing, China*

Rationale

The CCIS series is devoted to the publication of proceedings of computer science conferences. Its aim is to efficiently disseminate original research results in informatics in printed and electronic form. While the focus is on publication of peer-reviewed full papers presenting mature work, inclusion of reviewed short papers reporting on work in progress is welcome, too. Besides globally relevant meetings with internationally representative program committees guaranteeing a strict peer-reviewing and paper selection process, conferences run by societies or of high regional or national relevance are also considered for publication.

Topics

The topical scope of CCIS spans the entire spectrum of informatics ranging from foundational topics in the theory of computing to information and communications science and technology and a broad variety of interdisciplinary application fields.

Information for Volume Editors and Authors

Publication in CCIS is free of charge. No royalties are paid, however, we offer registered conference participants temporary free access to the online version of the conference proceedings on SpringerLink (http://link.springer.com) by means of an http referrer from the conference website and/or a number of complimentary printed copies, as specified in the official acceptance email of the event.

CCIS proceedings can be published in time for distribution at conferences or as post-proceedings, and delivered in the form of printed books and/or electronically as USBs and/or e-content licenses for accessing proceedings at SpringerLink. Furthermore, CCIS proceedings are included in the CCIS electronic book series hosted in the SpringerLink digital library at http://link.springer.com/bookseries/7899. Conferences publishing in CCIS are allowed to use our online conference service (Meteor) for managing the whole proceedings lifecycle (from submission and reviewing to preparing for publication) free of charge.

Publication process

The language of publication is exclusively English. Authors publishing in CCIS have to sign the Springer CCIS copyright transfer form, however, they are free to use their material published in CCIS for substantially changed, more elaborate subsequent publications elsewhere. For the preparation of the camera-ready papers/files, authors have to strictly adhere to the Springer CCIS Authors' Instructions and are strongly encouraged to use the CCIS LaTeX style files or templates.

Abstracting/Indexing

CCIS is abstracted/indexed in DBLP, Google Scholar, EI-Compendex, Mathematical Reviews, SCImago, Scopus. CCIS volumes are also submitted for the inclusion in ISI Proceedings.

How to start

To start the evaluation of your proposal for inclusion in the CCIS series, please send an e-mail to ccis@springer.com

Matthes Elstermann · Matthias Lederer
Editors

Subject-Oriented Business Process Management

Process Customer Satisfaction and Process Excellence

16th International Conference, S-BPM ONE 2025
Munich, Germany, July 2–3, 2025
Proceedings

 Springer

Editors
Matthes Elstermann ⓘ
University of Münster
Münster, Germany

Matthias Lederer
Technical University of Applied Sciences
Weiden in der Oberpfalz, Germany

ISSN 1865-0929 ISSN 1865-0937 (electronic)
Communications in Computer and Information Science
ISBN 978-3-032-04943-8 ISBN 978-3-032-04944-5 (eBook)
https://doi.org/10.1007/978-3-032-04944-5

© The Editor(s) (if applicable) and The Author(s), under exclusive license
to Springer Nature Switzerland AG 2026

This work is subject to copyright. All rights are solely and exclusively licensed by the Publisher, whether the whole or part of the material is concerned, specifically the rights of translation, reprinting, reuse of illustrations, recitation, broadcasting, reproduction on microfilms or in any other physical way, and transmission or information storage and retrieval, electronic adaptation, computer software, or by similar or dissimilar methodology now known or hereafter developed.
The use of general descriptive names, registered names, trademarks, service marks, etc. in this publication does not imply, even in the absence of a specific statement, that such names are exempt from the relevant protective laws and regulations and therefore free for general use.
The publisher, the authors and the editors are safe to assume that the advice and information in this book are believed to be true and accurate at the date of publication. Neither the publisher nor the authors or the editors give a warranty, expressed or implied, with respect to the material contained herein or for any errors or omissions that may have been made. The publisher remains neutral with regard to jurisdictional claims in published maps and institutional affiliations.

This Springer imprint is published by the registered company Springer Nature Switzerland AG
The registered company address is: Gewerbestrasse 11, 6330 Cham, Switzerland

If disposing of this product, please recycle the paper.

Preface

In an era when digital transformation is in rapid progress, companies and organizations are faced with the challenge of optimizing their business processes while ensuring the satisfaction of all stakeholders, both internal (employees, management) and external (customers, partners). Technological advances and the implementation of innovative tools and methods are opening up promising opportunities to redesign business processes, significantly increasing efficiency while also improving the user experience and thus creating significant added value.

Current discussions in academia and practice focus on how technologies – e.g., (generative) artificial intelligence, machine learning, cloud computing, and blockchain – are transforming the way companies operate and interact with customers and partners (actors). At the same time, companies must rise to the challenge of using these technologies effectively to meet the needs of all stakeholders and generate real value. Therefore, the question of the actual benefit for process excellence or satisfaction of process customers when using technology is at the center of the current debate in the IT and business world.

At S-BPM ONE 2025, we wanted to highlight the central role of technology and process optimization and explore how they can contribute to creating excellence in process management. The way organizations digitally transform their processes directly influences the satisfaction of all stakeholders, whether it is through improved internal communication, the implementation of agile methods, or the provision of customized services to customers. Our focus was not only on the technologies, but also on the actors involved in these processes, who ultimately experience the outcomes of this transformation.

We invited the participants to share their innovative approaches, insights, and case studies that highlight technology-enabled satisfaction and excellence in process management. Together, we explored new ways to address the challenges of digital transformation and maximize the value that processes can create for businesses and their stakeholders.

Topics for academic papers, presentations, workshops, and discussions covered (but were not limited to) areas of:

1. Technology-enabled processes, e.g., Usage of intelligent technologies, Data-driven approaches, and Automation
2. Stakeholder satisfaction in processes, e.g., Use of systems, Implementation of engagement tools, Focus on actors and their communication, and the Improvement of the customer experience
3. Innovative tools and methods in (S-)BPM, e.g., Use of new tools/ecosystems, Virtualization, and Traditional techniques like lean management and Six Sigma
4. Process excellence, e.g., Development of creative methods to promote creative solutions in process design or Implementation of KPI-based models to measure and manage process performance
5. Interdisciplinary approaches in (S-)BPM

6. Future trends, challenges and case studies in (S-)BPM

All submitted 29 papers were reviewed by at least two members of the international program committee. As a result of the double-blind peer review, 12 papers were accepted as full research contributions in this conference volume (acceptance rate of 47%). Additionally, 4 contributions could be accepted as Work in Progress and Reflections.

On another note, a successful conference is always based on the interaction of many contributors, whom we would like to thank at this point:

- All presenters and contributors of research reports, all of whom have advanced the knowledge of innovation in and with business processes.
- All reviewers, who checked the academic quality of the contributions and, with their many hints, increased it further.
- All participants on site in Munich for the constructive discussions at a high scientific level.
- The two keynote speakers, who offered highly topical and real-world process orientation.
- Finally, all readers of this conference series who strengthen the value of the discipline with their interest in questions of (subject-oriented) business process management.

Lastly, we would also like to thank mgm and the many helping hands who created a pleasant environment for the conference. Likewise, our thanks go to the Institute for Innovative Process Management, which provides the framework for the conference.

July 2025

Matthias Lederer
Matthes Elstermann

Organization

General Chairs

Matthias Lederer — Technical University of Applied Sciences Amberg-Weiden, Germany

Matthes Elstermann — University of Münster, Germany

Steering Committee

Albert Fleischmann — InterAktiv Unternehmensberatung, Germany
Werner Schmidt — Technische Hochschule Ingolstadt, Germany
Christian Stary — Johannes Kepler University Linz, Austria

Program Committee

Antunes, Pedro — Victoria University of Wellington, New Zealand
Becker, Jörg — Universität Münster, Germany
Betz, Stefanie — Hochschule Furtwangen, Germany
Dittmar, Anke — University of Rostock, Germany
Elstermann — Matthes, University of Münster, Germany
Fischer, Herbert — TH Deggendorf, Germany,
Fleischmann — Albert, InterAktiv Unternehmungsberatung, Germany
Forbrig, Peter — University of Rostock, Germany
Gadatsch, Andreas — Hochschule Bonn-Rhein-Sieg, Germany
Helferich, Andreas — ISM International School of Management, Germany
Hoppenbrouwers, Stijn — HAN University of Applied Sciences, Germany
Hvannberg, Ebba — University of Iceland, Iceland
Koch, Stefan — Johannes Kepler University Linz, Austria
Komarov, Mikhail — HSE University, Russia
Kurz, Matthias — Ministry for Schools and Education of NRW, Düsseldorf, Germany
Lamersdorf, Winfried — Hamburg University, Germany
Lederer, Matthias — Technische Hochschule Amberg-Weiden, Germany

Lawall, Alexander	IU Internationale Hochschule, Germany
Märtin, Christian	Hochschule Augsburg, Germany
Matzner, Martin	Universität Erlangen-Nürnberg, Germany
Neubauer, Matthias	University of Applied Sciences Upper Austria, Austria
Oppl, Stefan	Donau University Krems, Austria
Proper, Henderik	Public Research Centre Henri Tudor, Luxembourg
Schaller, Thomas	Hof University, Germany
Schieder, Christian	Technische Hochschule Amberg-Weiden, Germany
Schmidt, Werner	Technische Hochschule Ingolstadt, Germany
Stary, Chris	Johannes Kepler University Linz, Austria
Strecker, Florian	actnconnect, Germany
Turetken, Oktay	Eindhoven University of Technology, Netherlands
Winckler, Marco	Université Côte d'Azur, France
Zemaitaitiene, Gintare	Mykolas Romeris University, Lithuania

Contents

Subject-Oriented Modeling, Philosophy, and Technology

A Subject-Oriented Consideration of Object-Orientation 3
   Matthes Elstermann

Mapping of Agents to Subjects in S-BPM 19
   Thomas Schaller and Albert Fleischmann

Systematics Models for Understanding Declarative Description Concepts
and Approaches 35
   Matthes Elstermann and Andreas Krämer

Incremental Development of Multi-agent Systems Based
on Subject-Oriented Process Modelling and Validation 52
   Udo Kannengiesser

An Analysis and Tool for Converting PASS to BPMM for Execution 69
   Matthes Elstermann

Design Science Research Approach to Minimal Viable Product Validation
Using PASS Diagrams 91
   Sleiman El Bobbou, John Geiger, Jakob Bönsch, and Jivka Ovtcharova

webPASS: A Lightweight Web-Native, Collaborative PASS Editor
for Subject-Oriented Process Modeling 103
   Jakob Bönsch, Timo Lizak, Simon Heß, and Leon Patrick Okello

Human or Artificial Intelligence in BPM?

Describing and Analyzing AI Agents with the Tools We Already Trust:
A Comparative Study of PASS and BPMN 115
   Christoph Piller

From Process Designers to AI Facilitators: The Transformative Impact
of Agentic AI on Business Process Managers 137
   Saskia Schmid and Christian Schieder

Narrative Identities for Contextualized, Human-Centric Process
Knowledge Acquisition 146
   Christian Stary

Relating Design Rationale Representations: Concepts and Tool Support 161
   Anke Dittmar and Peter Forbrig

Staying Agile: A Process Lifecycle Model for Maintaining SCRUM
Practices in Software Development 179
   Katie Clark, Melanie Pufahl, and Matthias Lederer

A Systematic Literature Review on Business Process Automation
Frameworks and Technologies 198
   Lisa Rüeck, Thomas Auer, Stefan Rösl, and Christian Schieder

Empowering Experts in Data-Driven Process Design: A Reference Model
for Sales 214
   Matthias Lederer, Steevan Christopher Menezes, and Kris Dalm

Employee Retention as a Success Factor: Data-Based Optimization of HR
Processes in the Consulting Industry 223
   Theresa Zopke, Michael Hein, and Ana Moya

Many Rules, Many Roles, Few Bytes: The Public Sector IT Project Paradox ... 228
   Matthias Kurz

Author Index 237

Subject-Oriented Modeling, Philosophy, and Technology

A Subject-Oriented Consideration of Object-Orientation

Matthes Elstermann(✉)

Institute for Information Systems, University of Münster, Münster, Germany
matthes.elstermann@uni-muenster.de

Abstract. This essay presents a philosophical discussion and analysis of the modeling paradigm of object-orientation—viewed through the lens of the modeling paradigm of subject-orientation. One aspect of this investigation is the hypothesis that, from a subject-oriented perspective, there currently is no such thing as object-oriented process modeling. The work aims to explore and clarify the nature of object-orientation by examining what it means to model objects classically.

Through theoretical reflection, the goal is to better understand both object-oriented and subject-oriented modeling approaches in comparison and to identify the role object-orientation might play within a subject-oriented framework. This reflection includes a derivation of what can be meaningfully modeled using object-oriented concepts and leads to the formulation of requirements for object-oriented modeling within the subject-oriented paradigm. The work thereby contributes to the broader discourse by advancing a specific conceptual position and forms the basis for further discussions on integrating or aligning object-oriented constructs within the theory of subject-orientation.

Keywords: Subject-Orientation · PASS · Object-Orientation · process modeling

Nomenclature

FP functional programming paradigm
ITO input-task-output
OO object-orientation
SO subject-orientation

1 Introduction

This essay is a contemplation or philosophical discussion on the modeling paradigm of object-orientation (OO). It is also about discussing the hypothesis that there is no such thing as true *"Object Oriented Process Modeling"*—at least from a subject-oriented point of view. It is a theoretical reflection with the goal to better understand both modeling paradigms in comparison and to understand what role OO could take within the subject-oriented process modeling—about what can or should meaningfully be modeled in such a manner.

This reflection includes a derivation of what can be meaningfully modeled using object-oriented concepts and leads to the formulation of requirements for object-oriented modeling within the subject-oriented paradigm. The work thereby contributes to the broader discourse by advancing a specific conceptual position and forms the basis for further discussions on integrating or aligning object-oriented constructs within the theory of subject-orientation (SO).

2 Paradigms, Orientation, and Languages

As stated, this essay is on the analysis and comparison of modeling philosophy (in the context of description aspects of socio-technical process/process systems). Subject-Orientation and Object-Orientation, in this regard, both are *"modeling paradigms"* where *paradigm* is understood as the principal approach to description. As a paradigm is also *"a way of thinking"*, using it implies that the modeler has adopted this way of thinking and subsequently does modeling according to the principle. *"Orientation"*, in this context, can be understood as "what is at the center" of the description; it determines what is at the core of a stringed model and what other aspects are consequently derived or attached to that core.

Paradigms are often closely related to certain formal description, modeling, or programming languages, but they are not necessarily the same as a modeling language. E.g., even in an object-oriented programming language like JAVA, it is possible to do programming completely according to or with a procedural (Input-Task-Output - ITO - see Sect. 3.2) paradigm. On the other hand, even without formal support by modeling language, a modeler or programmer could use the thinking structure of a paradigm for their descriptions. E.g., in the non-object-oriented programming language C, object-oriented concepts could be applied conceptually, even though it would be tedious, using concepts like *"structs"* and methods exclusive to certain types of structs while lacking formal concepts like inheritance, instantiation, or encapsulation and binding it all together in formal within a class group. Similarly, in principle, it is possible to model a process according to the paradigm of subject-orientation using, e.g., the Business Process Model and Notation (BPMN)—by, a.o., exclusively using single lane pools—without that language being subject-oriented or providing support or restriction for it; BPMN is an ITO-paradigm language.

Programming vs. Process Description: A note on comparing *"programming"* with *"process modeling"* is necessary because OO predominantly exists as a programming paradigm: Both are not truly the same, but also not completely different. Both are activities of expressing processes. Programming languages are used exclusively to note down *execution instructions*, usually for computing machines. And in the context of multi-tasking enabled operating systems, the term *"process"* can be used as an alternative to describe a program being executed (see, e.g., the Task Manager within the Windows OS -> running processes). Programming languages, therefore, could be understood as a specific subset of process modeling languages.

Descriptions made with a process modeling language, on the other hand, could be taken as computational instructions for machines as well—if they are formal, syntactically correct, and written as instructions (compare the concept of workflow engines [4]). However, the purpose of a process model could also be to describe or document what does exist or is happening (AS-IS).

Furthermore, in contrast to general process modeling, any kind of programming no matter the underlying paradigm basically always comes with a base assumption or ground truth of what or who will execute the specified process - who or what is the active entity in the process - namely the central processing unit (CPU) of the computation machine that the program code is intended for.

3 Subject, Object, Task, and the According Paradigms

Now, as the title states, this work is an analysis from a subject-oriented point of view. Consequently, first, the quintessential idea of that approach is discussed in order to have a foundation for considering other paradigms that, in many cases, can be seen as sub-ideas within the paradigm of subject-orientation.

3.1 Subject-Orientation

Subject-orientation is a process (system) modeling paradigm originally conceived by Fleischmann in [8] and subsequently refined in works such as [9].

Following [4], it is *"a modeling or description paradigm for processes that is derived from the structure of natural languages [and] requires the explicit and continuous consideration of active entities within the bounds of a process as the conceptual center of description. Active entities (subjects) and passive elements (objects) must always be distinguished and activities or tasks(verbs) can only be described in the context of a subject."*

The natural language aspect stems from the explicit engagement of *subject*, *object*, and *verbs/predicates*, as they are the three base elements in standard complete active sentences in basically any natural language in the human world. SO requires all elements to explicitly occur, and all elements in the model fall under exactly one category and are not ambiguous in regards to their nature. The hypothesis here is that this distinction enables easier human understanding as these are also the standard categories in which humans think and the default relationship between them is fundamentally ingrained and understood by humans. This default relationship understanding is expressed in Fig. 1.

Arguably this is a relatively simple concept, but effective paradigm that changes the understanding of what a process is, away from the "classical" or DIN Norm [2] understanding of a process as *"a sequence of activities"* (see also the following Sect. 3.2) towards understanding a process as a system of interacting entities - that in turn might perform a sequence of activities. A slight but important difference that forms what is considered the subject-oriented view.

3.2 Input-Task-Output-Paradigm - The Classical Procedural Description Concept

At the core of (process) modeling according the input-task-output (ITO)-paradigm is the task or the activity, as is the case for basically all graphical

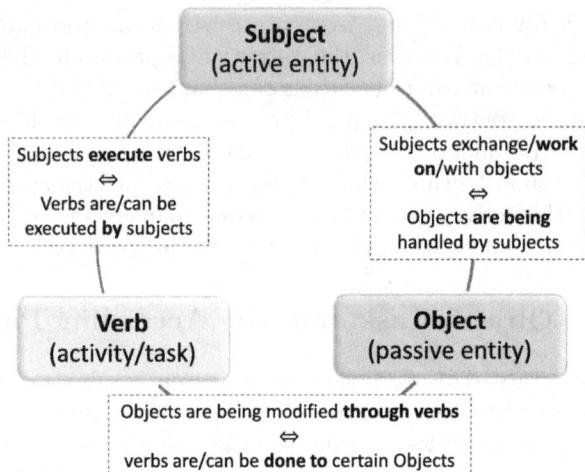

Fig. 1. Fundamental Description elements in Natural languages (and the Subject-Oriented Modeling Paradigm) and their (obvious) relationships

process modeling languages, be it Flowcharts, Petri-Nets, Event-Driven Process Chains, UML Activity Diagrams, or the Business Process Model and Notation (BPMN) [6].

As mentioned, it is the classical way of thinking and understanding the term "process"—as a *"set of interrelated or each other influencing* **activities** *which transforms inputs into outputs."*. These activities require resources such as people, materials, or information to achieve the intended results [2].

Consequently, the models created with this paradigm are centered around activities or tasks as the center of description. All other information (regarding subjects and objects) is an optional addition that can be left out without the model becoming syntactically incorrect. Most process modeling languages that follow this paradigm do include means to express information about active entities and passive entities—since they are naturally important, as any practitioner of this approach is likely to point out. However, the paradigm *does not require* their modeling or inclusion. Leaving them out simply means descriptions with less information, but not incorrect or incomplete descriptions. Furthermore, information about subjects and objects is attached to activity descriptions and is thus formally dependent on it, while, e.g., in SO it is the other way around, with task only being able to be modeled in the context of a subject and thus being dependent on that model element.

With a simple process, this might actually even be beneficial, reducing lengthy explanations and leaving out unnecessary aspects. E.g., in the context of a barber shop, the procedural process instructions of "wash", "cut", and "style" are a complete process description that is sufficient for the context in which it is given. The barber will not ask if this process is to be executed by him or her on your hair with their scissors.

In regards to programming, this description paradigm is equally predominant in process modeling and programming as the fundamental description concept is virtually the same as seen in Fig. 2.

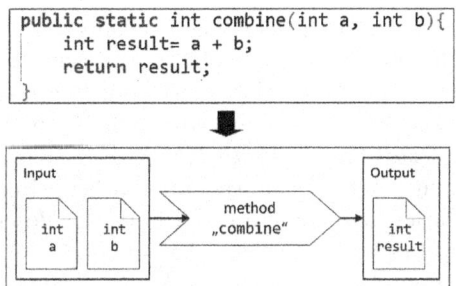

Fig. 2. Classical Task-Oriented Description. Same fundamental description approach in Procedural Programming (top) and Process modeling (below)

Obviously, this paradigm and modeling languages supporting it soley, by default, cannot be considered as *object-oriented*.

3.3 Side Note: Functional Programming

As a sight note, the functional programming paradigm (FP) should be briefly considered. It is a description approach with a mathematical abstraction concept behind it that does not easily fit into the subject-object-verb consideration. In FP, every element of a description is *"a function"*. There is no conceptual differentiation between data/values, computational tasks/algorithmic activities, or different active entities. Every description element is thus interchangeable and could be interpreted or used in every other way—making description elements kind of *"amorph"*. At the end, FP is still a means to give instructions to computing machines, aka process descriptions, while going away from simple concepts like computational steps as the default concept.

It could be argued that, on the one hand, this gives the programmer an ultimate amount of freedom, aka no restrictions regarding expressiveness. But on the other hand, it makes understanding the made descriptions much more complicated, as there is no simple understanding of ground truth that human description interpreters can base their intuition on. This becomes more true the less familiar and accustomed humans are with formal mathematical thinking.

From an ITO point of view, FP is a step into the opposite direction of subject-orientation −> total freedom for the party doing the description, as everything could be everything else. Subject-orientation, on the other hand, and as stated, requires an explicit distinction and usage of the three fundamental elements that cannot be interchanged.

Another way to consider or think about FP is to understand it as a kind of *"declarative"* approach to programming according to the ITO understanding.

3.4 Side Note: Imperative vs. Declarative

Often, the classical approach to programming introduced in the ITO section is referred to as an *imperative* approach. This is true, but a consideration on a different *"dimension"* from the *"Task-vs-Object-vs-Subject"* consideration.

With an imperative approach, modeling elements, e.g., the order of computational steps of a program/process or object elements, must, in principle, be completely expressed or specified – they must be imperatively given.

However, neither *subject-oriented* nor *object-oriented* is the opposite of *imperative*. The actual opposite of an *imperative* approach is a *declarative* approach to modeling/programming. With declarative approaches, circumstances are specified by their boundaries, leaving it up to a model or description interpreter - be it human or program - to work within the boundaries. Another name for the concept of declarative modeling is *Modeling by Restriction* as explained in [9].

For both approaches, imperative and declarative, there are examples within programming and/or process modeling. In task-oriented process modeling, the first thing that comes to mind would be the process modeling language, Declare, ConderSec, or case-based aspects. And as mentioned and depending on the strictness of consideration, Functional Programming can be considered to be a kind of declarative approach opposite to imperative ITO concepts. See, e.g. [16] or [14]—for declarative modeling in SO see [7]. An overview considering this circumstance can also be found in [5]

4 Processual Object-Orientation - from A Subject-Oriented Point of View

Now, after the previous section, the actual focus of this work shall be discussed: object-orientation (OO).

The basic idea has already been stated: the OO-paradigm, in principle is the idea that descriptions of programs or processes is centered around concept of *"objects"* or the according instantiable description artifact called *"classes"*[1].

4.1 Are Objects Subjects? - Sometimes Maybe?

Now what OO does not do is to differentiate between *active* and *passive* objects within this consideration. In programming, especially for single-core machines, this is not even necessary, as the active entity for which instructions are intended is always implicitly there: the CPU.

---

[1] As a side note on OO programming: one misconception especially beginners tend to make about the idea of classes in programming is that they confuse them with the *descriptive* class concepts that is being used to form taxonomies in many natural or biological science in order to *classify* what is existing and that needs to change if it is not a good fit with reality. In programming, the nature of classes is that of a *prescriptive* or instructional element. They describe what or how a computational system is to act and need to change if the output of the system is not as desired.

Sometimes object-oriented programming is taught as a programming of *"interacting objects"*. But this is not really true if no parallel programming with the assumption of multiple special thread objects is being used. Thread objects are indeed active entities that "act" on their own. According to standards in parallel programming (e.g., [10,13]), thread objects are supposed to be distinguished from data-holding objects and should not hold data on their own.

However, in this little differentiation in the sub-discipline of parallel programming, namely lies the, in this case non-formal, differentiation of active (threads) and passive (data object), fundamentally being subject orientation under a different name. If only the passive data holding objects are involved, their programming should be understood as describing first the intended structure of an entity, the attributes, and secondly the **activities that can be done to the object**.

But this is not understood by all authors. E.g. [11] sees that *"The object-oriented paradigm aligns with systems theory by treating objects as autonomous entities with states and behaviors. These objects interact to form complex systems, emphasizing modularity and reusability"*. This statement shows a need or want by its author to think and conceptually work with active entities, but not naming them as such, and rather considering everything to be an *object*. But if everything is an object, what is the difference between the active entities and the passive data objects that are actually playing a role in OO programming much more often? This statement is also an indicator of the hypothesis that there is logical convergent development towards subject-oriented thinking.

4.2 OO - the Passive Tense

Following the logic described before, there is a simple way to understand what OO actually could mean from a natural language point of view. For that purpose, let us consider the following Object-Oriented natural language description of a process: *"The Ball is being rolled (by X)"*. This sentence starts with the object and describes what is being done to it. As in all OO, description means the active entity could be given, but also be left out if deemed unnecessary.

But more importantly, this is a sentence in the *passive tense*. What consequences can be derived from this consideration? As the passive tense, OO is practical if well applied. However, the passive tense is not always easy to learn. The simple active sentence is much simpler and less error-prone to understand. E.g., reason, the passive is never learned as the first grammatical structure when learning any foreign language.

4.3 A Graphical Comparison of SO, OO, and ITO

To summarize the previous sections, Fig. 3 graphically depicts the typical relationships that exist in descriptions according to the respective paradigms. While SO and ITO descriptions are explicitly expressing processes, the understanding of OO here is referring to its application in programming (see Sect. 2)

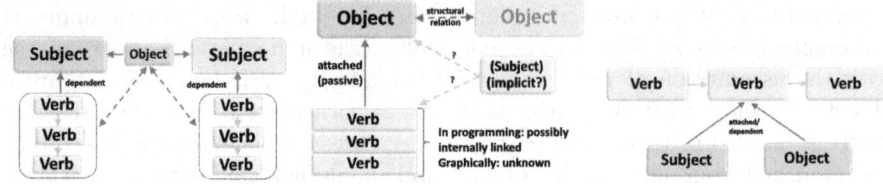

Fig. 3. Typical interrelation/dependencies of model-elements in SO(left), OO(middle), and ITO (right) description approaches

5 Related Work Analysis

While, as mentioned, OO is well established in programming, this work is written under the hypothesis that there is no such thing as OO process modeling.

Now, when researching the topic of *"object-oriented process modeling"*, there are at least three languages/approaches to be found, those being the Unified Modeling Language (UML) [12], the "Process Modeling Language" PML by Rassler and Anderl [15], which claims to be an *"Object Oriented Process Modeling language"*, and the *"Object Process Methodology"* by Dori [3].

However, all three do not seem to be methods to express processes from a true object-oriented viewpoint. Arguments on this claim will be given in the following subsections. Note, though, that due to the limited extent of this work, details about the approaches cannot be given in detail, and the reader is required to have or gain the required familiarity with those approaches.

5.1 Unified Modeling Language

The so-called "Unified Modeling Language" (UML) [12] is—contradictory to its name—not a singular modeling language but rather a collection of 14 different diagram types compiled from prior existing modeling approaches used especially in *software development* and modeling of software systems with an especially focus on the programming with object-orientated languages.

AS such, UML does not support the formal differentiation between active and passive entities, even though many of its diagram types understand certain objects to be active entities. Also, not every diagram type involves the description of processual concerns.

Due to there being 14 types, the analysis is done in Tables 1 and 2.

5.2 The (Object-Oriented) Process Modeling Language

The "Process Modeling Language" PML by Rassler and Anderl [15], by title, claims to be an *"object-oriented process modeling language"*, and has a *"complete object-oriented view to processes and the differentiation and linkage of and between processes and projects"*. But it simply is not that.

Table 1. Analysis of static UML diagram types and their limitations in regards to object-oriented process modeling

UML Diagram Type	Reason Not Useful for Object-Oriented Process Modeling
Static UML Diagrams (Class, Component, Object, Composite, Deployment, Package, and Profile)	The Static UML diagrams, by their very nature, while being essential to object-oriented description and representing that view par excellence, describe *static structures* and not dynamic process aspects. However, they may *implicate* processual aspects. E.g., the methods a class/object possesses. Methods are sometimes also deemed the *"behavior"* of a class/object. However within SO logic, entities that *have* a behavior are of an active nature and thus subjects, while passive objects are specified by describing the *activities that can be done to them* (by the processor or thread).

It is neither about the modeling of a process from an object's point of view, nor is the modeling centered around describing objects. As far as can be deemed, the process understanding or paradigm employed is that of the DIN norm/ITO principle.

The object-oriented consideration stems from the concept of classes and objects being used to describe the meta-model of the language and thus every model-element, when being modeled, is "an object" derived from a class that is defined in the meta-model - which is the same for SO models or any modeling language as all models by their nature are passive entities containing description elements. But, at the center, they describe processes in the meaning of activities with all other information attached to it.

5.3 Object Process Methodology

Dov Dori's Object-Process Methodology (OPM) [3] may be the closest to what OO process modeling could be. It proposes a *"holistic"* modeling approach that integrates the description of structure (object) aspects and behavioral (processual) aspects. But, by claim of the author, it is neither a pure procedural activity oriented, nor does it claim to be "purely" object-oriented (OO)——with OO being an approach where objects are the *"first-class citizens"* and behavior (i.e., methods) are subordinated to the objects - which indeed would be a true object-oriented point of view but one rejected outright. Rather, both approaches exist equally and in tandem with a focus on graphically modeling the links between them.

Consequently, in regard to the question of whether this is an object-oriented approach, this already gives the simple answer: no. The fundamental critique can be especially made because it considers the idea of process as in classical DIN-standard definitions, with process being basically activities that transform things. The activities are considered as "behavior" but since no differentiation

Table 2. Analysis of dynamic UML diagram types and their limitations for object-oriented process modeling

UML Diagram Type	Reason Not Useful for Object-Oriented Process Modeling
Use Case Diagram	Describes user interactions and goals at a high level; provides only a rough outline of process intentions, and is focused on users and the strangely hard-to-define thing that is *"a use-case"*. Since the logic is that a user is "bound to a use-case", a use-case is either a complex process scenario in need of a more detailed description that the user is *involved-in*, or it is simply an "activity" that the user supports. In both cases, the model is not conceptually oriented around objects.
Activity Diagram	Activity diagrams are basically a derivative of classical flow-charts and thus are oriented around the activity (imperative ITO) and therefore cannot be object-oriented process descriptions (if not limited to a singular object; which they are not required to be).
Sequence Diagram	Shows *"the interactions of instances over time"*. The conceptual problem, from a SO point of view, is that it implicates the understanding that instances are active entities. A model revolving around active entities is Subject-Oriented and not OO.
Communication Diagram	Similar to sequence diagrams, it focuses on *"object links"* and with the same basic implicated assumption that the communicating objects that interact are active entities and, therefore, subjects.
Timing Diagram	Focuses on time constraints in the interaction between "objects". They are considered specific variants of sequence diagrams, and the "objects" in them are implicitly considered active entities (e.g., Systems or Servers, etc.).
Interaction Overview Diagram	They are strange aggregates of interaction diagrams in a flow similar to activity diagrams, with the same base conception that this flow is going from one *"activity"* to the next. Passive objects play no role in this diagram type
State (Machine) Diagram	Describe the states that some entity is in and how or under what conditions these states can change. In contrast to all other UML diagram types, State Machines could conceptually be used for object-oriented process modeling, but only if the "object" that has certain states is being coherently described and considered as a single passive entity. This is not the case if the "states" are the states of a system that is considered to be active and executing something on its own, e.g., an elevator.

between multiple active entities is made in any kind, this behavior necessarily can only "belong" to an implicated *system* in which the description is embedded.

However interesting and indeed object-oriented is Dori's concept of "object state", which *"has meaning only in the context of the object to which it belongs"*, emphasizing that behavior is anchored in object context, but not dependent on object ownership, which does not seem to be a concern of the modeling here anyway. An object state is a particular situation classification of an object at some point during its lifetime. At every point in time, the object is in one of its states or in transition between two of its states—from its input state to its output state.

5.4 A Description Challenge for OO-Process Models

The previous sections analyzed three approaches and discussed in that context that at least those are not approaches for modeling processes object-orientedly. In addition to no known methodology truly being OO even if claiming to be, [4] also notes another conceptually challenging aspect, which is not insolvable, but makes using true OO in process modeling somewhat impractical, possibly being a reason for it not existing. According to [4], following OO logic, a process would need to be defined for the object. In a very strict OO approach, problems would arise when two or more objects need to be combined into a third object. As depicted in Fig. 4, the question arises as to what object-process the activity of joining should belong to, since in an OO world it needs to be defined somewhere in the context of one object—at least if double definitions are not wished for.

[4] also remarks that the *IS-A*-abstraction mechanism—also known as inheritance—is hard to formally incorporate for process descriptions.

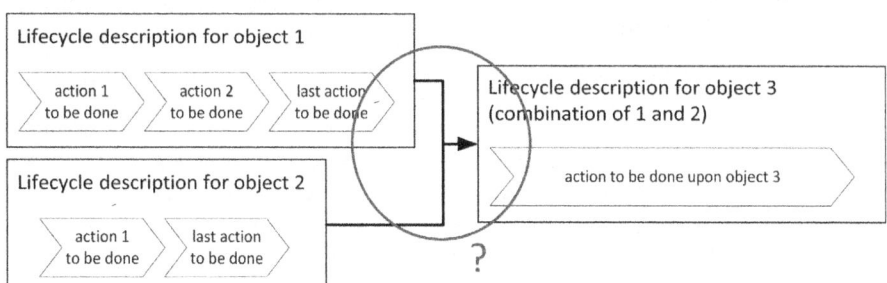

Fig. 4. Descriptional gap when considering OO process modeling: To which object do joining process descriptions belong when objects A and B are combined into C? from [4]

6 What Could OO Process Modeling be - in a Subject-Oriented Context?

6.1 Why Model (Data) Objects?

As was outlined in this work on multiple occasions, from a subject-oriented point of view, objects do not have a behavior and do not act on their own—because otherwise they would be subjects.

However, objects still play a crucial role in any process, so their description is necessary if a process is to be modeled holistically. The question is what can or should be modeled about them if processual aspects can be described actively with normal subject-oriented process modeling means, like, e.g., the Parallel Activity Specification Schema (PASS) language.

But what to model then? The following section tries to derive and structure some fundamental insight into what could be described about objects, first in general and then with regard to process aspects, with process aspects being about how an object is supposed to be handled.

6.2 What to Describe?

Structural Rules: When modeling/describing (data) objects, in a digital context, next to stating their simple existence, first and foremost, their structure or *structural rules* will be described classically, giving answers to the questions of:

- What objects (classes/datatypes) exist?
- What (data) elements does an object consist of?
- What are the data types for those elements?
- What are allowed data values/value ranges in general and independent from other values (incl. undef/null)?

Simple Processual Rules: So far, no procedural descriptions are involved, meaning action upon an instance of that data structure over time. Describing those simply starts by describing answers to the following questions:

- What actions (methods) can be done **to** the object?
  - In the simplest case, this is the writing and reading data from and to the object (getter and setter methods in programming)
  - Internally, sequences of activities or sub-activities could be described using basically a sub-process concept. They could also be hidden from outside consideration via an encapsulation concept. However, the "danger" with allowing something like that potentially lies in overspecification and hiding processual complexity in this passive version if everything in a process is centered around a single object—which should not be done.
- What are (data) input and output restrictions/promises (input pre- and post-conditions) for those activities?

– What are internal structural rules for data values of elements of the objects? E.g. in an order form for *"perishable"* and *"non-perishable"* goods, the delivery method must be *"express"* and not *"standard"* for perishable goods[2].
– What are dynamic structural conditions (in the sense of *dynamic data structures* like lists, trees, or graphs)? (See footnote 2)
– Who (what active entity) is allowed to do certain activities?[3],[4]

Complex Processual Rules (with States?): The above processual aspects are relatively easy to describe, as most of those are done in a standard way in most OO programming languages. However, the greater challenge regarding modeling processes from an object-oriented point of view comes if the rules regarding structure and allowed activities themselves are not static but change over time/under specific processual conditions. E.g., values may not be changed retroactively, or they are allowed to be undefined at the beginning of a process but need to be set after a while, or under certain conditions.

The most likely concept that allows us to make statements about such circumstances is that of having *(object)-state* definitions, which would allow to define that certain rules/activities are only active under specific conditions.

Note for emphasis: what is considered must be the states of a passive object and not the state of an active entity!

In general, an object's state is simply determined or understood as just a certain combination of values in its data fields at a certain point in time—making the *number of states indefinite* as soon as one unrestricted natural number is involved.

A simple approach would be to have explicitly *defined states*. This practically means to simply have another data element "current state" as part of the object's structure with an enumeration of imperatively defined values. E.g., a project proposal document being in the state of "Draft" vs. "Turned-In", "Denied", "Approved", etc. Defined states could be easily modeled with all rules *"within"* them implicitly given the condition that this state is the current state of the object. For each object-state, it could be individually allowed to state which activities are available. Certain activities are likely to change the data value of the "current state". With a defined state concept, it is possible to express that in certain states, certain activities are possible or impossible.

---

[2] This is very similar, if not the same as post-conditions, but not regarding the output of the activity, but rather the internal structure of the object.

[3] In order to state information about active entities, an object-oriented model needs a connection to—ideally, a dependency on—a model that defines those. Basically, an SID for PASS.

[4] In a distributed environment, the problem is naturally that at one point in time, the data may be in the possession of an active entity but without a central coordinating entity (aka. central workflow system, or a form of distributed database like a blockchain) it will be hard to enforce certain restriction in regards to permissible actions on subject basis.

An alternative to a *defined states* concept is an *abstract state concept* similar to Abstract State Machine (ASM) methodology of [1][5]. Simply speaking, abstract state modeling would mean stating for every activity individually what the value conditions are to be met in order to allow or forbid execution. Abstract states are also a declarative approach rather than imperative. But in both cases, abstract or defined states, the base idea will be to express when/under what conditions, activities can be done upon the object and internal structural rules should apply.

One challenge, especially in the context of subject-orientations, is how to include descriptions - "possession" changes /data ownership concerns/ acceptance of data validity, which again involves the idea of active entities or actors to be included in the consideration or to express the corresponding rules.

6.3 How to Use

The summary in the previous section sketched the general concept of how to approach modeling objects in a processual context: a definition of what could be stated about a data object: a definition of structural rules, combined with rules of what is considered correct about the structure, and how to handle them.

Such rules could be used in two different ways: First, during the runtime execution of a process model that includes such an OO procedural rule definition. Given a sophisticated *interpreter*, it could be possible to directly execute such a description. But it would need excessive assumptions about the execution context. The advice here would be to leave imperative definitions to standard PASS/SID/SBDs, but come up with an idea of how or where.

The second usage scenario is the use of OO procedural rule definitions during the creation of an SO process model. The idea is that the structural rules of an object-process are created where useful and supplied to the SO modeler as *specification*. In order to be useful beyond simply informing humans, a tool would be needed that another model can use. Such a tool would function as a kind of rule checker that could verify whether the SO model that claims to handle a certain object is addressing or contradicting the handling concerns as a kind of specification confirmation.

Both scenarios are informally sketched in Fig. 5

However, a WARNING in regards to both versions: Even if such OO process modeling possibilities would exist, do not overuse them and exclusively model a process from an individual object viewpoint...this will lead to people thinking without embracing subject-orientation at all and just thinking in the concept of a single object category, vastly limiting their idea. Creating means to do so is explicitly not the intention of this work. What is intended is a concept for creating a modeling approach that may have its niche usage, but should not allow people to avoid using SO.

---

[5] Note, however, that ASMs are not object-oriented as they are used to describe state machines in the sense of an active entity, not a passive one.

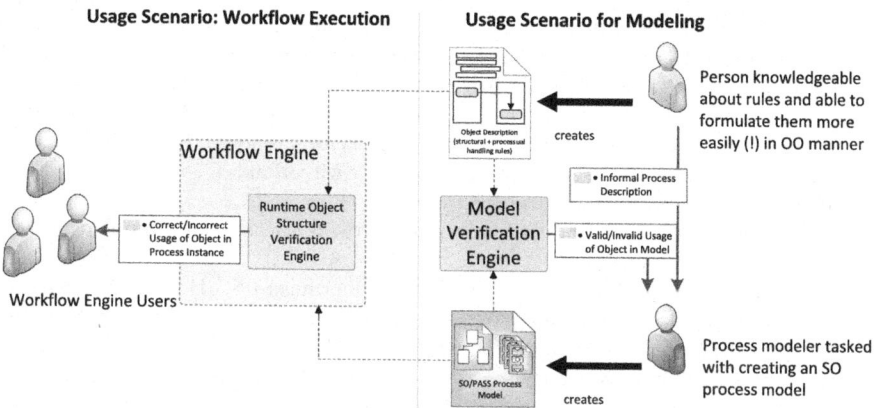

Fig. 5. Informal sketch for two usage concepts of object-process descriptions within SO modeling

7 Conclusion and Outlook

This work was a theoretical reflection on comparing the fundamental idea behind object-oriented and subject-oriented modeling approaches and tried to identify the role object-orientation might play within a subject-oriented framework.

The made observations and derived concepts can be used as the foundation for an actual modeling tool that allows using these ideas practically. Creating such a tool, including the appropriate graphical notation and verification engines that can make use of object-oriented descriptions, is future work. Following this, and based on this tool, including the development of application scenarios and example models. With this, the question should be to investigate when and for whom it would truly be a useful tool if created.

References

1. Börger, E.: The abstract state machines method for high-level system design and analysis. In: Boca, P., Bowen, J.P., Siddiqi, J. (eds.) Formal Methods: State of the Art and New Directions, pp. 79–116. Springer London, London (2010). https://doi.org/10.1007/978-1-84882-736-3_3
2. DIN e.V.: DIN EN ISO 9000:2015-11, Quality management systems – Fundamentals and vocabulary (2015)
3. Dori, D.: Object-process methodology. In: Knowledge Management: Concepts, Methodologies, Tools, and Applications, pp. 421–434. IGI Global Scientific Publishing (2008)
4. Elstermann, M.: Executing strategic product planning. KIT Scientific (2019). https://doi.org/10.5445/KSP/1000097859
5. Elstermann, M., Andreas, K.: Systematics models for understanding declarative description concepts and approaches. In: S-BPM ONE 2025. Springer Nature Switzerland (2025)

6. Elstermann, M., Fleischmann, A., Moser, C., Oppl, S., Schmidt, W., Stary, C.: Ganzheitliche Digitalisierung von Prozessen. Springer (2023)
7. Elstermann, M., Ovtcharova, J.: Revisiting the ALPS - an investigation of abstract layered PASS. In: Elstermann, M., Dittmar, A., Lederer, M. (eds.) Subject-Oriented Business Process Management. Models for Designing Digital Transformations, vol. 1867, pp. 263–283. Springer Nature Switzerland, Cham (2023). https://doi.org/10.1007/978-3-031-40213-5_19
8. Fleischmann, A.: Distributed Systems - Software Design and Implementation. Springer Verlag, Berlin (1994)
9. Fleischmann, A., Schmidt, W., Stary, C., Obermeier, S., Börger, E.: Subject-oriented business process management. Springer Berlin Heidelberg, Berlin, Heidelberg (2012). https://doi.org/10.1007/978-3-642-32392-8
10. Herlihy, M., Shavit, N., Luchangco, V., Spear, M.: The Art of Multiprocessor Programming, Second Edition. Newnes (2020)
11. Newman, W.A., Hendrickson, A.R.: The object-oriented paradigm as an implementation of systems theory in is. J. Int. Inf. Manage. **5**(2), 7 (1996)
12. OMG: Unified Modeling Language® (OMG UML®). An OMG® Unified Modeling Language® Publication (2017)
13. Pacheco, P.: An Introduction to Parallel Programming. Morgan Kaufmann (2011)
14. Pesic, M., van der Aalst, W.M.P.: A Declarative Approach for Flexible Business Processes Management. In: Eder, J., Dustdar, S. (eds.) BPM 2006. LNCS, vol. 4103, pp. 169–180. Springer, Heidelberg (2006). https://doi.org/10.1007/11837862_18
15. Raßler, J., Anderl, R.: Pml, an object oriented process modeling language. In: Computer-Aided Innovation (CAI): IFIP 20th World Computer Congress, Proceedings of the Second Topical Session on Computer-Aided Innovation, WG 5.4/TC, pp. 145–156. Springer (2011)
16. Watson, I., Woods, V., Watson, P., Banach, R., Greenberg, M., Sargeant, J.: Flagship: a parallel architecture for declarative programming. In: [1988] The 15th Annual International Symposium on Computer Architecture. Conference Proceedings, pp. 124–130. IEEE Comput. Soc. Press (1988).https://doi.org/10.1109/ISCA.1988.5221

Mapping of Agents to Subjects in S-BPM

Thomas Schaller[1](✉) and Albert Fleischmann[2]

[1] Hof University, Alfons-Goppel-Platz 1, 95028 Hof, Germany
`thomas.schaller@hof-university.de`
[2] Interaktiv Expert, Pfaffenhofen, Germany
`albert.fleischmann@interaktiv.expert`

Abstract. This paper presents an extension of the Subject-oriented Business Process Management (S-BPM) methodology to integrate organizational structures and agent assignment mechanisms. While S-BPM offers a robust framework for modeling business processes based on the Parallel Activity Specification Schema (PASS), it lacks explicit constructs for associating organizational agents—such as humans, machines, or services—with process subjects. To address this gap, we propose an enhancement of the S-BPM methodology by incorporating an external organizational model and an Organizational Query Language (OQL) interface. This extension enables fine-grained specification of process initiation permissions, dynamic assignment of agents to subjects, and direct derivation of access rights to business objects from process models. Our approach leverages an organization model server to evaluate OQL expressions at runtime, supporting context-sensitive and rule-based agent selection. We demonstrate how these enhancements facilitate advanced organizational scenarios, such as context-dependent approval processes and multi-agent assignments. By embedding access rights directly into process models, our solution eliminates the need for traditional access control lists. This integration significantly improves automation, compliance, and maintainability in enterprise environments.

Keywords: Subject-oriented Business Process Management (S-BPM) · Organizational Modeling · Agent Assignment · Access Control · Process Automation · Multi-Agent Systems

1 Embedding of Agents in S-BPM

The integration of organizational structures into enterprise process modeling and automation frameworks remains inadequately addressed in many approaches [2, 3, 6]. For instance, BPMN 2.0, a widely adopted standard, provides only basic constructs such as pools, hierarchically structured swim lanes, and the concept of additional participants to model organizational roles. These constructs are limited to representing simple organizational hierarchies and lack support for multidimensional structures, delegation mechanisms, or skill-based specification of task ownership [2]. In process automation, this shortcoming necessitates manual selection of responsible agents[1] for subsequent

---
[1] In this contribution, the terms agent, actor and subject-carrier are used synonymously.

workflow steps or reliance on complex scripting logic to define task assignees - a practice prone to errors and compliance risks [19, 20].

Similarly, the formal design of the Subject-oriented Business Process Management (S-BPM) methodology exhibits a definitional gap in assigning the appropriate human or machine-based task executor to a subject. We would like to analyze this a little more closely. The S-BPM idea is described with three concepts [10]:

The PASS (Parallel Activity Specification Schema) is a modeling language for business processes based on the paradigm of subject orientation. Its central concept involves active entities called "subjects," which communicate with each other and perform operations on objects. A PASS model, therefore, consists of two primary components: the Subject Interaction Diagram (SID), which depicts the communication relationships between subjects, and, for each subject, a Subject Behavior Diagram (SBD) that specifies its individual behavior. A subject transitions between states starting from an initial state and progressing toward terminal states based on message inputs, temporal events or Boolean condition evaluations. Unlike conventional workflow paradigms, this approach does not enforce predefined execution sequences, simplifying modeling by eliminating the need for exhaustive a priori path specification.

The formal definition (meta-model) of the static structure of PASS models is defined using the Web Ontology Language (OWL). The meta-model specifies which elements are permitted in a PASS model—such as subjects, messages, and message exchanges—as well as the relationships between them, independent of the process dynamics.

The execution semantics of PASS process models is described with Abstract State Machines[2] (ASM). Specifically, these specifications determine how the processes described in PASS are to be carried out—including the mechanisms for message exchange between subjects and the transition logic between states within SBDs. What is missing is the binding of agents, as elements of the organizational model, to subjects, as elements of the process model.

As mentioned, and with PASS being a process modeling language, it does not contain any means for modeling organizational structures, agents, or resources. However, what it does contain are placeholders to dock or link such a concept (Fig. 1).

Subjects remain abstract actors, representing pure behavioral logic. During execution, they must be mapped to concrete organizational agents to enact the modeled behavior [8]. For this mapping a docking element `SubjectExecutionMapping` and the specializations `StaticSubjectExecutionMapping` and `DynamicSubjectExecutionMapping` can be found in the meta-model of PASS (Figs. 1 and 2). These placeholders are meant to include definitions or query strings that could link a subject to elements of an organizational model. We will discuss the difference between static and dynamic mapping later in this article.

---

[2] Since 2023 a description of a PASS interpreter in PASS is also available [21].

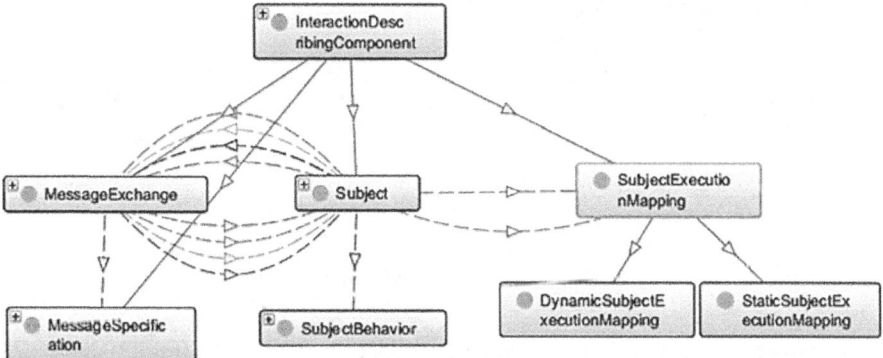

Fig. 1. Part of the Meta-Model of the Subject Interaction Diagram (SID) in PASS

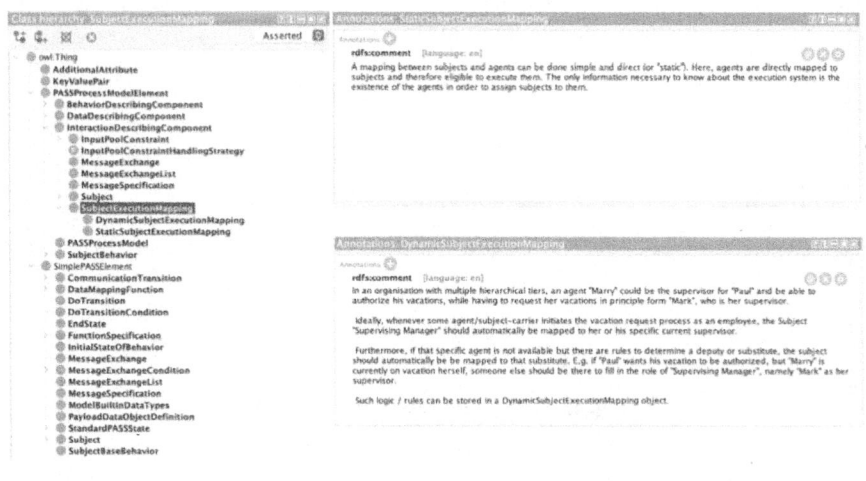

Fig. 2. Subject Execution Mapping

2   Mapping of Agents – Status Quo and Challenges

In software systems, organizational models comprising the structure and resources of an organization are primarily required for two purposes: access control and the assignment of tasks in the context of process-oriented solutions. These models should represent reality as accurately as possible, yet in a targeted manner, to subsequently select the appropriate agents or to ensure the security of IT systems in case of access control. This can only be achieved if the underlying meta-model provides adequate modeling constructs.

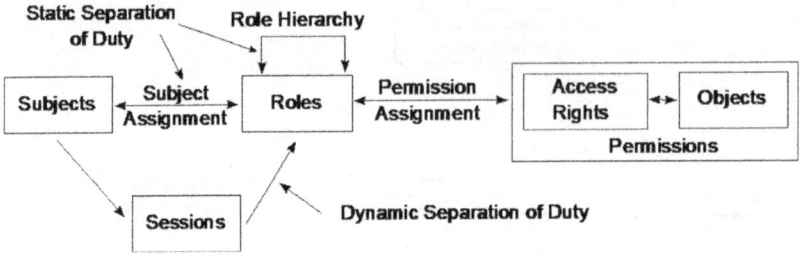

Fig. 3. Role-Based Access Control [1]

Approaches based on Role-Based Access Control (RBAC) [5] (Fig. 3) are widely used. In this context, users[3] can be assigned to roles. The roles themselves can be organized within a role hierarchy and are linked to access rights or tasks. Although this approach is widespread, there are few studies investigating whether it is suitable for adequately representing an organization (see [2]). One point of concern could be that only simple tree structures can be represented.

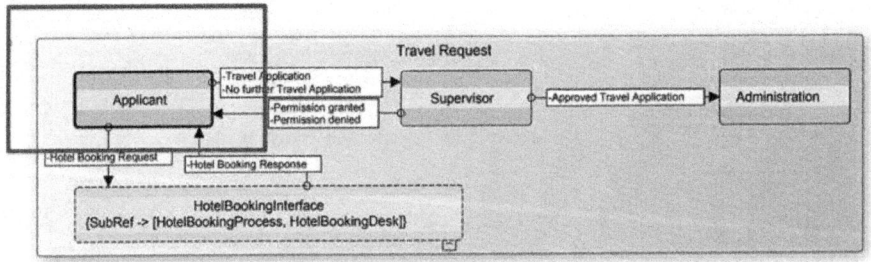

Fig. 4. SID of a Process Travel Request

As an example, the subject-interaction diagram shown in Fig. 4 illustrates the process of applying for a business trip at a university. When instantiating this process an agent will need to be assigned to each subject, which can be very tricky:

In our example, the applicant is a professor. The professor named Weidraweil is, on the one hand, a member of a faculty (Faculty Computer Science (CS)), leads a research group at an institute (Working Group Information Management (IM)), and is also the head of that institute. The selection of the appropriate agent for the subject "Supervisor" depends on the role in which the professor submits the application. If the trip is undertaken in the context of the faculty, the dean would be responsible for approval. In the context of the institute, however, the situation is different: here, the institute head would be responsible. Since in this case the applicant and the approver would be the same person, an alternative approver must be found (e.g. the vice president).

---

[3] Unfortunately, these are called subjects.

The following diagram (Fig. 5) shows an excerpt from the associated organizational model, with the dashed lines showing the possible approvers of the travel request depending on the role of the applicant.

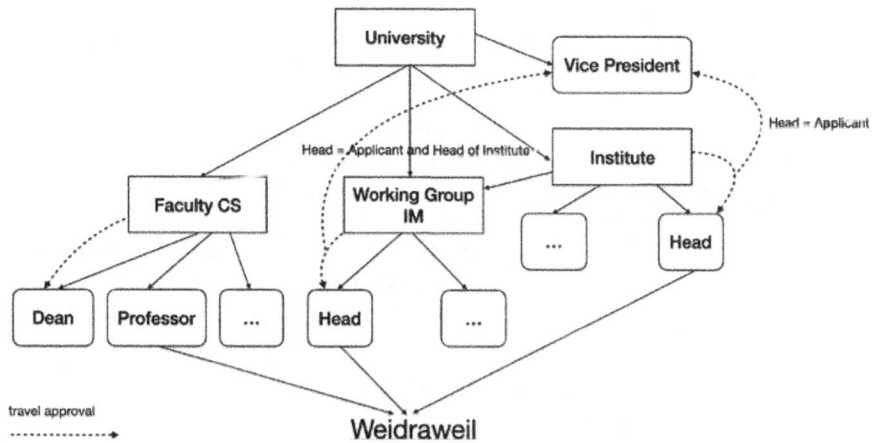

Fig. 5. Part of the Organization Model of the Example

In companies, these context-dependent responsibilities are described using rules, but these cannot be easily adopted into existing approaches for organizational modelling and process execution. On execution a common pragmatic solution is to require the user to select the agent for the next workflow step themselves. The "policy resolution" or "user dispatchment" [9] is thus delegated to the user. Another common practice is to specify a program that determines the agent or possible agents for the next process step. Scripting languages such as Groovy are often offered for this purpose. The following Figure shows a simplified excerpt of a script used in a Process Model of the Bonita Workflow Engine that finds the correct approver based on the applicant's role of the travel request example. While this approach may be practical, it is error-prone, requires significant maintenance effort, and is difficult for business departments to understand (Fig. 6).

```
// Get process initiator's information
var processInitiator = apiAccessor.processAPI.
    getProcessInstance(activityInstanceId).startedBy;
var user = apiAccessor.identityAPI.getUser(processInitiator);

// Retrieve applicant's role from process data
var applicantRole = context.applicantRole;

if (applicantRole === "FACULTY_MEMBER") {
    // Find dean of the applicant's faculty
    var faculty = user.getCustomAttributeValue("faculty");
    var deanUsers = apiAccessor.
                    identityAPI.
                    getUsersInRole("Dean", 0, 10).
                    filter(u => u.getCustomAttributeValue
                        ("faculty") === faculty);
    return deanUsers.map(u => u.id);
}
else if (applicantRole === "RESEARCH_GROUP_LEADER" ||
         applicantRole === "INSTITUTE_LEADER") {
    // Find vice president
    var vpUsers = apiAccessor.
                  identityAPI.
                  getUsersInRole("VicePresident", 0, 10);
    return vpUsers.map(u => u.id);
}
```

Fig. 6. Example of a Script in Bonita Workflow

In the following section, we present an example of a meta-model that can be used to adequately model the resources of an organization. We also show how such models can be used within S-BPM.

3 Graph-Based Management of Agents and Selection Using OQL

Schaller describes in [2] the development of a graph-based meta-model for the representation of organizations and their resources, which was derived from business organization theory[4]. For the purpose of sketching the approach, a simplified version will be employed in the following discussion.

---

[4] The description of the core model in English can be found in [3].

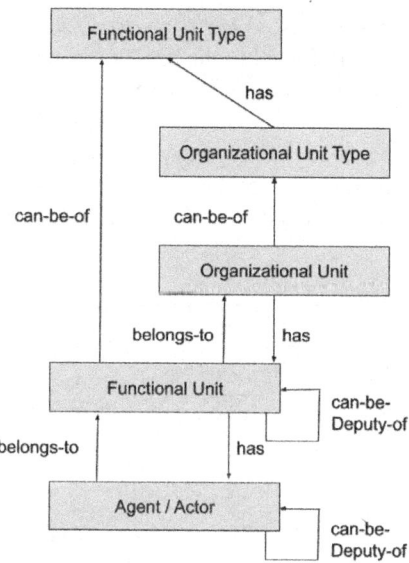

Fig. 7. Basic building blocks of the meta model

Figure 7 illustrates the core components of that meta-model, comprising a type level and an instance level. At the instance level, personal or machine-based actors can be assigned to functional units, which in turn belong to at least one organizational unit. These actors, functional units (FU), organizational units (OU), and the edges connecting them can be freely attributed. Furthermore, the meta-model allows the definition of arbitrary edge types, like "reports_to" or "can_repair", enabling the representation of highly complex organizational structures.

To facilitate the reuse of organizational knowledge, the meta-model introduces organizational and functional unit types (type level). The latter allow abstract modeling of typical positions such as department heads or the abstraction employee along with their attributes and relationships, which can then be assigned to concrete functional units. With the assignment the FU inherits the properties of the type. Let's assume a FU type employee contains a personnel number property. The connection of the FU professor with the FU type employee then means that the professor must also have a personnel number.

OU-types and OUs initially operate in the same way as FU-Types and FUs. However, OU-types and FU-types can be bundled into templates. These represent standardized organizational structures, such as the general composition of a faculty consisting of dean, vice dean, professors, dean's office, etc. and their different relationships to each other (e.g. the vice dean represents the dean). The connection of an OU Faculty Computer Science to the OU-type Faculty then causes it to inherit the structures from the template.

Figure 8 exemplifies this idea as an organizational model. Here, two OUs are depicted, namely the claims departments Car Damages and House Damages. These

OUs are connected to their respective FUs Manager, Clerks, Lawyers and Secretary. The FUs, in turn, are linked to the agents assigned to them. In the example, user-defined relations are restricted to deputyship relations. Unconstrained deputyship relations exist between the agents Smith and Winter, between the FUs Manager and Secretary, as well as between the two Lawyers (bidirectional edge). Additionally, there is a type-level deputyship relation between Manager and Lawyer. The nodes Smith and Hinton are connected by a constrained relation.

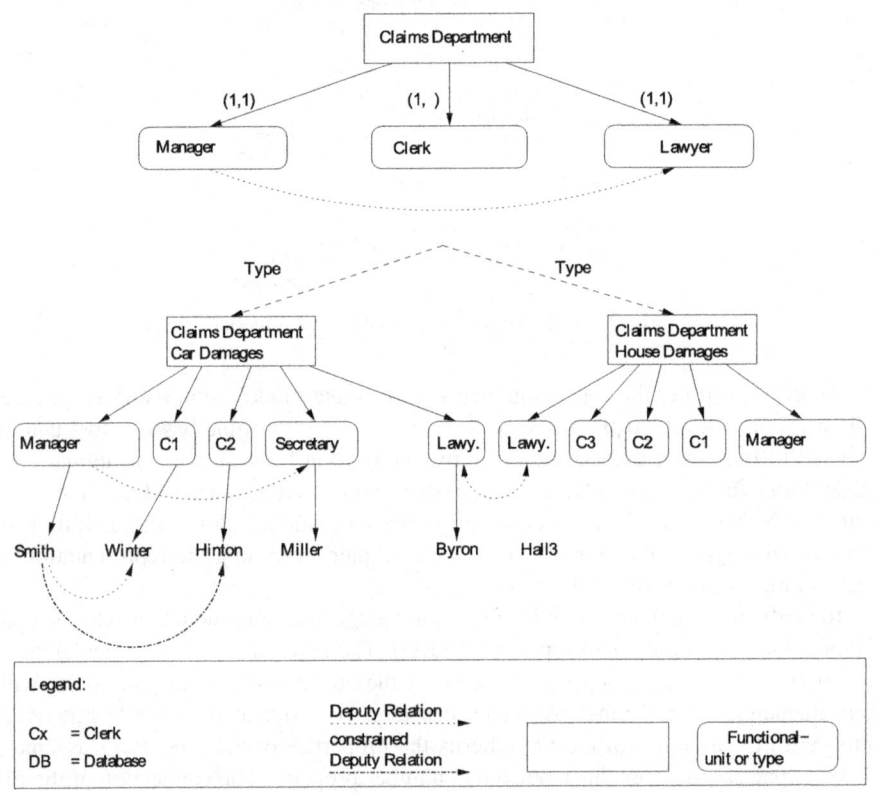

Fig. 8. Example of a Model of an Organization [13]

The meta-model presented was implemented as software called C-Org using Java and the graph database management system Neo4j. It was validated by modelling the organizational structure of Hof University and linking C-Org with several software systems (Fig. 10), such as the Bonita Workflow Engine. Figure 9 shows a part of the university's model in C-Org.

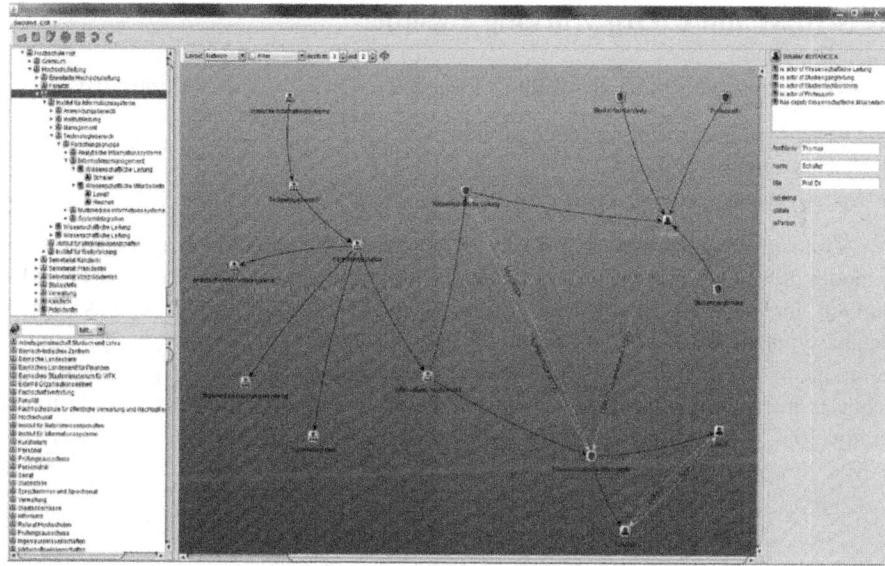

Fig. 9. Organizational Model in C-Org

In the original approach agents can be selected using a relational algebraic language [2]. Because expressions in this formal language are difficult for modelers to understand, a facade called Organizational Query Language (OQL) [11, 15, 17] has been created to provide easy-to-read languages that do not have the full range of functionality, but are easier to understand, like.

- *Professor(FacultyCS)*: all professors of organizational unit FacultyCS,
- *Head(*)*: all heads of organizational units or
- *Institute*: all members of the institute.

A more sophisticated variant of such an OQL in the context of secure manufacturing environments[5] is defined in [12]:

- *(Turner OR Mill)(*).ATT.(workpieceLength $\geq$ "40cm" AND workpieceKind = "octagonal")*: all turners or mills that can process workpieces with a length of 40 cm and an octagonal shape.
- *DEPUTYOF(Assembly(Manufacturing Company).ATT.(workpieceLength $\geq$ "30"))*: all deputy production systems that can process workpieces of a length greater than or equal to 30 cm.

The idea of OQL is like the use of SQL in database management systems as an alternative to relational algebra or languages like Datalog. As implementation C-Org accepts OQL-Terms (for example, from Bonita Workflow) and returns a set of agents fulfilling the specified requirements.

---

[5] The requirements of this domain are discussed in [15, 16].

4 S-BPM and C-Org Working Together

This chapter presents three possibilities for using C-Org's concepts within S-BPM:

- Define permissions for initiating processes
- Assign agents to subjects.
- Specify access rights to business objects.

A fundamental prerequisite involves employing a software component that maintains a model of an organization and its agents. This organization manager/server provides an OQL interface. An S-BPM / PASS process engine alongside other systems such as database management systems, email platforms, telephony infrastructure, and similar components [13] can submit OQL queries to this server. The server processes these requests and returns a result set of agents that satisfy the query parameters, as illustrated in Fig. 10.

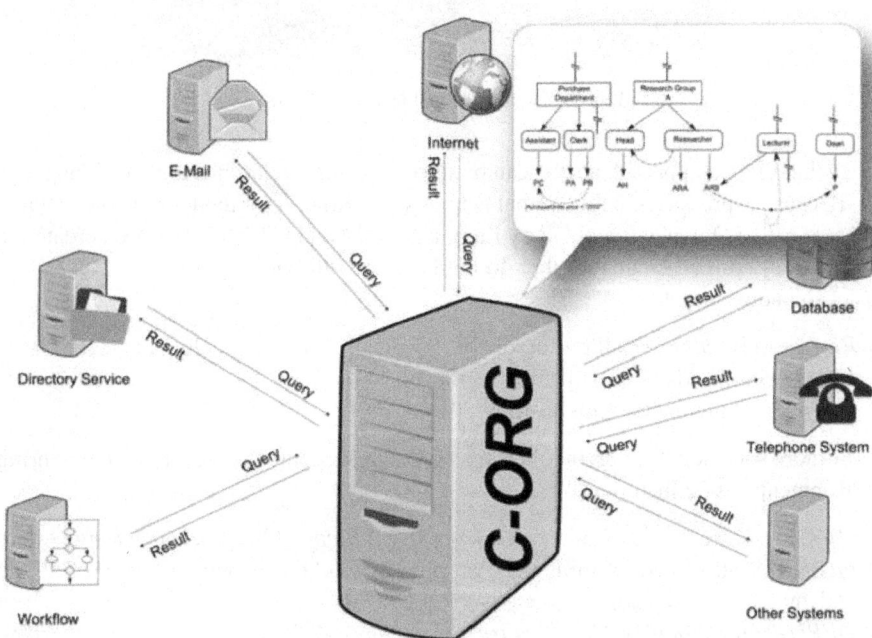

Fig. 10. Communication with the Organization Server

The principal combined application and usage concept is illustrated in Fig. 11. The starting point is the graph-based meta-model for the description of organizations described in Sect. 3. This also defines the syntax and semantics of the organization query language (OQL). A modeler uses the meta-model to create a model of an organization. This model is managed in an organization model manager such as C-Org. A process modeler uses the organizational model to formulate OQL terms. These describe the mapping of subjects and agents and are attached to the respective subjects via the

SubjectExecutionMapping class. The PASS model enriched with OQL terms is interpreted by an execution engine, whereby the OQL expressions are passed to the organization model manager, which returns a list of agents to the engine. The engine then decides on the assignment of agents to subjects.

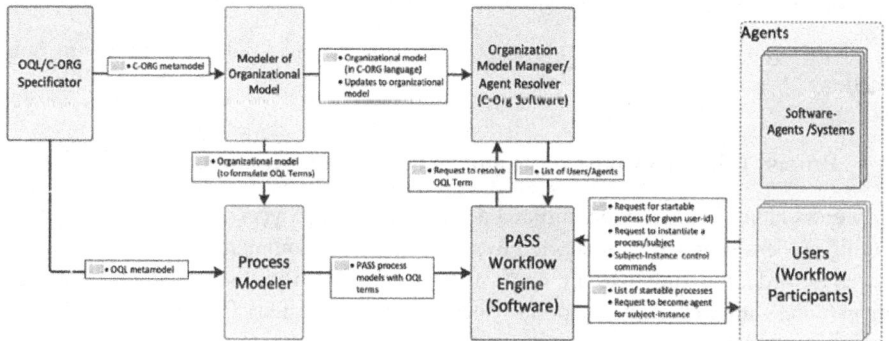

Fig. 11. C-Org and PASS Workflow Engine working together

The current PASS editor already contains the option to include OQL terms into the PASS process model, albeit only as a simple string as shown in Fig. 12.

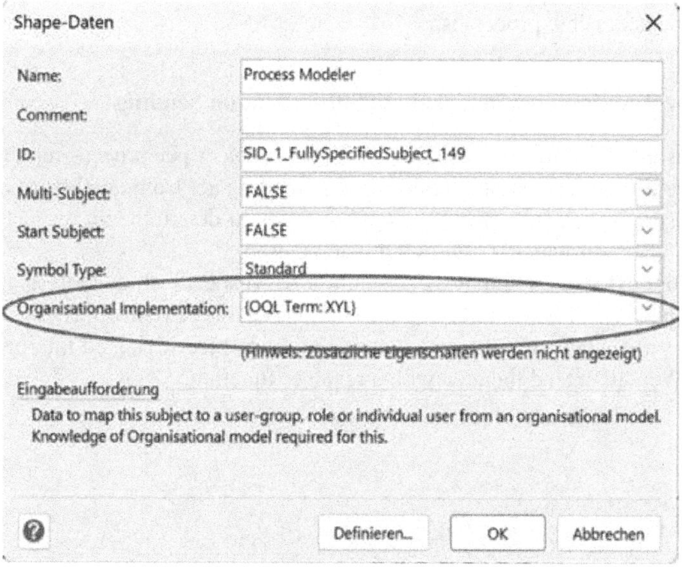

Fig. 12. Mapping with OQL-Terms

OQL-expressions leveraging functional units, organizational units or attribute-based criteria offer fine-grained mappings of agents to subjects:

- Functional Units: map agents to a subject based on their assigned FUs (e.g. "all agents that are accountants").
- Organizational Units: map agents to a subject based on their association with specific organizational units (e.g., "all agents of claims department car damages").
- Attribute-based criteria: map agents to a subject using properties (e.g. "all agents from the claims departments who have completed the IT security training").

This setup would allow for the usage scenarios sketched out in the following subsections.

4.1 Process Initiation Constraints and Authorization Mechanisms

Processes cannot typically be initiated arbitrarily by employees. For instance, the budgeting process is generally restricted to personnel in the commercial department, while purchase orders to suppliers are conventionally triggered by the procurement department (unless automated reorder point systems are implemented). Permissions for process initiation can be granularly defined using the OQL.

When an employee attempts to initiate a process, the organization server evaluates whether the employee satisfies the OQL expression of the startsubject's execution mapping. If the employee is included in the query's result set, process execution is authorized.

An alternative is to show the user only those processes on his interface that he is allowed to start. This requires evaluating the docked OQL expressions of all StartSubjects to determine accessible processes.

4.2 General Assignment of Agents to Subjects upon Sending

As there usually is only one initializing or start-subject per process model, all other subjects are usually instantiated upon the first sending act from an already instantiated subject. At that moment, a workflow engine needs to determine an agent for the new subject-instance, for which, C-Org/OQL can be used.

An earlier extension to the PASS execution ASM specification addressing this issue was developed in [17]. The underlying idea in [17] is based on replacing the assignment of the `receiver` in the communication action of the Subject-Oriented Interpreter Model (Fig. 13). We will extend the idea with a resolver function.

$TRY_{ComAct}(subject, state) =$

    choose $m \in MsgToBeHandled(subject, state)$
        $MARKCHOICE(m, subject, state)$
        if $ComAct = Send$ **then**
            let $receiver = receiver(m), pool = inputPool(receiver)$
                if not $CanAccess(subject, pool)$ **then**
                      $CONTINUEMULTIROUND_{Fail}(subject, state, m)$
                else $TRY_{Async(Send)}(subject, state, m)$
        if $ComAct = Receive$ **then**
            if $Async(Receive)(m)$ **then** $TRY_{Async(Receive)}(subject, state, m)$
            if $Sync(Receive)(m)$ **then** $TRY_{Sync(Receive)}(subject, state, m)$
    where
        $MARKCHOICE(m, subject, state) =$
            $DELETE(m, MsgToBeHandled(subject, state))$
            $currMsgKind(subject, state) := m$

Fig. 13. Original Communication Action of the Subject-Oriented Interpreter Model [14]

Redefining the receiver assignment `let receiver= receiver(m)` with an OQL resolving function such as `let receiver= resolveOQL(extractOQLTERMfromReceiverspec(receiver(m))` introduces dynamic role resolution into S-BPM/PASS execution. The OQL term of the target subject is first read out and then resolved into a set of matching agents.

4.3 Further Possibilities

The connection of the subjects with the agents of an organization via OQL expressions also offers the possibility of deriving access rights to data objects directly from the subject interactions and the corresponding Subject Behaviour Diagrams. An example of the application for a severely handicapped pass at the Bavarian Centre for Families and Social Affairs (ZBFS) is given in [18]. In the article the concept of so-called Shared Business Objects (SBO) is presented. These are data objects that are not exchanged between the participants in a process but are used jointly. The respective access rights to these objects are derived directly from the process model. SBOs are managed by Business Object Governance (BOG), which manages all business objects and operates an S-BPM process engine. For the concept of SBOs to work, the S-BPM framework must be extended accordingly. As SBOs are created, read and changed within the states of a subject, the PASS state definition must be supplemented with information on the SBOs concerned and the required access rights. If an agent is assigned to a subject, it automatically receives all necessary access rights to the respective SBOs in order to be able to fulfill the tasks of the subject. In case an agent requires access to an SBO, it sends a request to the BOG via its workflow client. If it is a read authorization, the BOG retrieves the SBO and makes it available to the agent (see Fig. 14). In the case of a write request, the SBO is created or updated in the data memory.

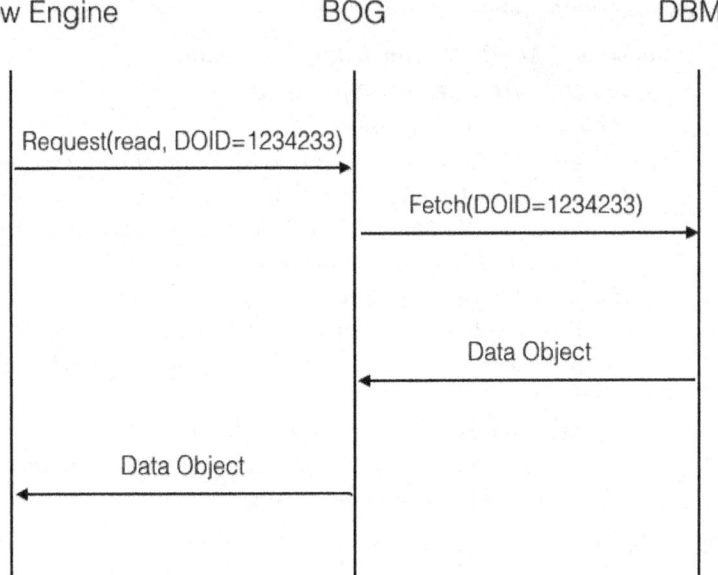

Fig. 14. Read Request to an SBO [18]

An important aspect of this approach is that no classic access control list is required in the BOG data storage system, as the access rights are derived directly from the process model. However, the prerequisite for this is that the process model is correct, and the appropriate agents are assigned to the respective subjects via OQL expressions.

5 Conclusion

This work has presented a comprehensive extension to the Subject-oriented Business Process Management (S-BPM) methodology and its modeling language PASS, addressing a gap in the assignment of organizational agents—such as humans, machines, or services—to process subjects. By integrating an external organizational model and an Organizational Query Language (OQL) usage concept into the S-BPM meta-model, we enable the dynamic and context-sensitive mapping of agents to subjects, as well as the direct derivation of access rights from process models. This approach not only enhances the expressiveness and flexibility of S-BPM but also bridges the divide between abstract PASS process specifications and their concrete organizational implementations.

After C-Org has already been tested with Bonita, a "typical" workflow engine, a coupling with a PASS process engine would be desirable. The idea would thus receive practical feedback and could be further developed.

Finally, we would like to expressly thank our reviewers for their detailed feedback and constructive comments.

References

1. Ferraiolo, D. F., Sandhu, R., Gavrila, S., Kuhn, D. R., Chandramouli, R.: Proposed NIST standard for role- based access control. ACM Trans. Inf. Syst. Secur. (TISSEC) 224–274 (2001)
2. Schaller, T.: Organisationsverwaltung in CSCW-Systemen, PhD Thesis, Universität Bamberg (1998)
3. Lawall, A., Schaller, T., Reichelt, D.: Enterprise architecture: a formalism for modeling organizational structures in information systems. In: 10th International Workshop, CAiSE 2014, Thessaloniki (2014)
4. Lawall, A., Schaller, T.,Reichelt, D.: An Approach towards Subject-oriented Access Control S-BPM One - Scientific Research, pp. 33–43. Springer, Heidelberg (2012)
5. Chen, L.: Analyzing and Developing Role-Based Access Control Models, PhD thesis, University of London (2011)
6. Klizenthas, A.: In Search of a Perfect Access Control System. https://goteleport.com/blog/access-controls/. Accessed 24 Apr 2025
7. DeTreville, J.: Binder, a logic-based security language. In: Proceedings 2002 IEEE Symposium on Security and Privacy, Berkeley, CA, USA, 2002, pp. 105–113 (2002)
8. Zehbold, C.: Controllingansatz für S-BPM, Arbeitsberichte – Working Papers, No. 25, Hochschule Ingolstadt - University of Applied Sciences, Ingolstadt. https://nbn-resolving.de/urn:nbn:de:bvb:573-2438. Accessed 23 Apr 2025
9. Bussler, C., Jablonski, S.: Policy resolution for workflow management systems. In: Proceedings of the Twenty-Eighth Annual Hawaii International Conference on System Sciences, Wailea, HI, USA, vol. 4, pp. 831–840 (1995)
10. Elstermann, M., Wolski, A., Fleischmann, A., Stary, C., Borgert, S.: the combined use of the web ontology language (OWL) and abstract state machines (ASM) for the definition of a specification language for business processes. In: Raschke, A., Riccobene, E., Schewe, K.D. (eds.) Logic, Computation and Rigorous Methods. Lecture Notes in Computer Science, vol. 12750. Springer, Heidelberg (2021)
11. Lawall, A., Schaller, T., Reichelt, D.: Cross-organizational and context-sensitive modeling of organizational dependencies in C-Org. In: S-BPM ONE (Scientific Research), pp. 89–109. Springer, Heidelberg (2014)
12. Lawall, A., Schaller, T.: Secure resource management in smart factories. Int. J. Cryptog. Inf. Secur. (IJCIS) (2022)
13. Lawall, A., Schaller, T.,Reichelt, D.: Propagation of agents to trusted organizations. In: 2014 IEEE/WIC/ACM International Joint Conferences on Web Intelligence (WI), Intelligent Agent Technologies (IAT), Brain Informatics and Health (BIH) and Active Media Technology (AMT), pp. 433–439 (2014)
14. Fleischmann, A., Schmidt, W., Stary, C., Obermeier, S., Börger, E.: Subjektorientiertes Prozessmanagement, Mitarbeiter einbinden, Motivation und Prozessakzeptanz steigern (2011)
15. Lawall, A., Schaller, T., Reichelt, D.: Role and rights management In: S-BPM in the Wild - Practical Value Creation, pp. 171–185. Springer, Cham (2015)
16. Kannengiesser, U.: Agents Implementing subject behaviour: a manufactoring scenario In: S-BPM in the Wild - Practical Value Creation, pp. 171–185. Springer, Cham (2015)
17. Lawall, A., Schaller, T., Reichelt, D.: Integration of dynamic role resolution within the S-BPM approach. S-BPM One – Sci. Res. 21–33 (2013)
18. Schaller, T., Obermeier, S.: Shared business objects for paperless public management processes. In: Proceedings of the 8th International Conference on Subject-Oriented Business Process Management. ACM (2016)

19. Kumar, A., Van der Aalst, W., Verbeek, E., Dynamic work distribution in workflow management systems: how to balance quality and performance. J. Manag. Inf. Syst. **18**(3), 157–193 (2002)
20. Schefer-Wenzl, S., Strembeck, M.: Modeling support for role-based delegation in process-aware information systems. Bus. Inf. Syst. Eng. **6**, 215–237 (2014)
21. Elstermann, M.: Proposal for a recursive interpreter specification for PASS in PASS. In: Elstermann, M., Dittmar, A., Lederer, M. (eds.) Subject-Oriented Business Process Management. Models for Designing Digital Transformations. S-BPM ONE 2023. Communications in Computer and Information Science, vol. 1867. Springer, Heidelberg (2023)

Systematics Models for Understanding Declarative Description Concepts and Approaches

Matthes Elstermann[1]( ) and Andreas Krämer[2]

[1] Institute for Information Systems, University of Münster, Münster, Germany
matthes.elstermann@uni-muenster.de
[2] Karlsruhe Institute of Technology, KIT, Karlsruhe, Germany

Abstract. This work is a study and overview intended to investigate commonalities and differences between various modeling approaches that are either explicitly referred to as *'declarative'*, follow the same principle, or share a very similar idea.

Consequently, a unifying comparison concept in the form of three classification models is developed in order to have a system that allows for a better overview, understanding, and comparison of the investigated approaches.

The main goal behind this work was orignally the investigation of the research question of whether there already is or is not an explicit approach for using declarative *process* models as formal specification for less abstract or imperative process models outside a very specific application concept in the domain of subject-oriented modeling. As a side effect, this work also provides a domain overview and a systematic approach to better understand the underlying concepts.

Keywords: declarative modeling · overview · process modeling · declare · PASS · subject-orientation

1 Motivation

This contribution was initiated to investigate a specific research question regarding declarative process modeling.

Namely, that question or assumption is that there does not exist an approach for using declarative *process* models as specification for less abstract or imperative process models, in the same way as it is the intend of a specific concept in the domain of subject-oriented modeling (see Sect. 3.6). The original motivation, therefore, was to investigate and find related works for that approach, barring the question of how useful and practical such approaches are. The research gap found unintentionally was that there are many approaches that are similar but also different, requiring a systematic approach to understand them and truly see if others have already conceptualized something similar.

To antedate the results, no examples for the pre-existence of such a concept could be found. However, the steps towards this conclusion first led to the question of what is or what can be considered a kind of "declarative" modeling approach and what are possible usage concepts.

Methodologically, all identifiable modeling or description approaches that could be found with standard means of research and that vaguely fit that description, either by wording or conceptual similarities with obvious candidates, were analyzed. However, due to the diverse nature of the identified approaches, another problem arose: the question of how to relate the approaches, understand their differences and similarities, and/or classify them in order to consider their relevance for the initially stated research question.

The result of that effort is a classification system that allows a comparison and ultimately gives a systematic overview of what is being considered or understood as *declarative modeling* and for what purposes declarative descriptions are being used.

Contrary to the standard structure of a research paper, first, the summarizing result and comparison structure for understanding are presented and used as the introduction to the topic (Sect. 2). Afterwards, in Sect. 3, the various sources and concepts used as the development foundation for that classification system are discussed in detail. This deliberate choice has been made with the intention to ease understanding for readers unfamiliar with this topic while at the same time conserving space.

2 A Comparison Systematic for Declarative Modeling

To define the idea or concept of *declarative modeling*, first, a definition of modeling in general and what is considered as *non-declarative modeling* is necessary, as that contrasting juxtaposition is crucial in understanding declarative modeling itself.

2.1 A Simple Understanding of Modeling

Instead of trying to find a suitable universal definition for *'modeling'* among a plethora of existing ones and subsequently bound to fail to satisfy any reader, here, a rather pragmatic understanding of modeling will be given as a guide for understanding the arguments in this work. It is made with the knowledge that this is not and simply cannot be a penultimate definition.

Following the principles of the Dimension Concept [7], modeling can be understood as an act of *describing* reality, usually to use the created description for communication or planning purposes, together with other humans or technical systems.

Following that *dimenSions* idea, what can be described is actually rather limited to fundamentally *objects*, *environments*, *processes/activities*, and *people/actors*[1], and or a mixture of all of these.

Now, naturally, models never can describe reality in its entirety, but must be simplifications or abstractions. Describing all aspects of reality at once would mean recreating it in another context, a god like task that is assumed to be impossible. Also, while philosophically an interesting idea, creating a model and using it for its intended purpose should usually be much more time and resource-efficient for human stakeholders in contrast to creating or experimenting in reality.

Regarding the question of "How?" to describe, there is a multitude of means and language to create descriptions—all with various focuses and benefits or drawbacks in a given situation. For this work, the two general modes that need to be defined further are the aforementioned *declarative modeling approach* and its opposing counterpart, the *imperative modeling approach*.

2.2 Imperative Modeling

Usually, declarative (modeling) approaches are seen as counterpart to more classical description concepts that straightforward describe how something is composed, made-up-of or consists of—this can be called imperative modeling [21] [22]. For objects and environments, that would mean stating exact dimension specifications of objects or how they are positioned in a space in relation to other objects. For processes, it would be, e.g., the classical control flow description of which activities exist and their conditional occurrence one after another. For actors, it would be, e.g., a list of their capabilities as well as their appearance. In the words of van Roy, imperative modeling tries to express "how to do something" rather than "say what is required and let the system determine how to achieve it" [24]. Originating from imperative programming, imperative process modeling specifies all execution possibilities before finally executing the process. Common imperative process modeling languages are the Business Process Model and Notation (BPMN) or Petri Nets. Pichler et al. conducted research on the advantages and disadvantages of imperative and declarative process modeling languages by testing the understandability of both paradigms on test participants. According to their work, imperative languages tend to be "more comprehensible than declarative process models, irrespective of the type of task involved" [21]. Still, due to the unfamiliarity of the test subjects with declarative approaches, the results have to be "handled with care".

2.3 A Basic Concept of Declarative Modeling

But what is declarative modeling or description in contrast to imperative?

---

[1] The special consideration of persons/actors as individual description dimension rather than as objects is akin to the concept of subject-orientation that explicitly requires differentiation of actors (subjects), activities (verbs) and objects. See also [4]. Debatable would be, furthermore, whether *objects* and *environments* should truly be seen as separate description dimensions or not.

There are multiple names for very similar concepts. The basic idea is always that of indirect or implicit description. The classical imperative modeling approaches are descriptions of circumstances along the lines of *"this is exactly like this or that"*. In contrast, declarative modeling approaches are *indirect* descriptions of things that should and especially should not occur or appear. This is done with a mixture of definitions of outcomes, e.g., for process descriptions of intervals or allowable tolerance, the setting of limits, restrictions, or boundary conditions instead of step-by-step instructions. *Modeling by restriction* as described, e.g., by Fleischmann [10], is therefore a valid descriptor for the concept.

Another interpretation for declarative modeling is that of intentionally *incomplete* descriptions[2], that leaves space to be filled out at a later state in a more detailed model or by the creator of the real entity (object, process, actor) when enacted. In all cases, the goal of declarative modeling is always similar: a modeler should be enabled to reduce the work that is necessary for specifying every detail of a model/program. Also, the way something is executed should remain flexible, be it a generator in programming or a process instance of a process model.

The actual means to the above-stated depend on *what* is being modeled and what modeling language is being used, as will be discussed in Sect. 3. However, to give some general examples for indirect descriptions here:

Requirements as part of requirements analysis are, in principle, indirect descriptions—models, so to speak—of various things. They could be determining what will later become a product or an information system.

Assumed needs or preferences of human beings usually describe or model not a specific actor but are a *generalized* assumption covering a larger group.

Boundary Condition or Restrictions in general, but especially for process descriptions, might not state what exactly is to happen in the given chain of events or how an object might be shaped, but they state what must not happen and therefore are usually an integral part in declarative modeling.

2.4 Usage Concepts Models for Declarative Description Approaches

When trying to understand declarative modeling, an important question is, how the description/model is being used. Like any model, in principle, a declarative model can be used to facilitate human-to-human communication.

However, among the investigated approaches, that seems to be rarely the case. More often, declarative models are intended to be used as input for programs of which there are two principal types.

Generators. The first category of programs takes declarative descriptions and restrictions as instructions to create or generate an output. This outpsut is then to be used by another program or IT system as sketched in Fig. 1.

The nature of the output depends on the nature of the targeted environment. For example, with descriptions of digital objects, the generator could create a concrete model of an object following the given specification to be tested in a

---

[2] From the point of view of an imperative modeler.

simulation software. As later seen, these objects could be 3D assets in e.g. a video game or CAD models of physical parts to be produced on a 3D printer.

On the other hand, with declarative process descriptions or functional program code, the generated output can come in form of execution instructions meant for a targeted execution environment, such as specific programs called workflow engine or a specific CPU with a specialized instruction set[3].

In both cases, the generator is bound to conditions and allows input for the targeted environment. Furthermore, the creators of the generator usually define the modeling semantics and additional external concepts that implicitly guide a generator. A modeler needs to be aware of these—a part of which is *speaking the modeling language*—in order to create declarative models that will lead to an intended execution.

The actual nature or description of the *generator* is ambivalent - it could be a "compiler", it could be an "interpreter", or any other general piece of software. Stretching the definition, it could be a physical machine. In theory, though unlikely, it could also be a human being.

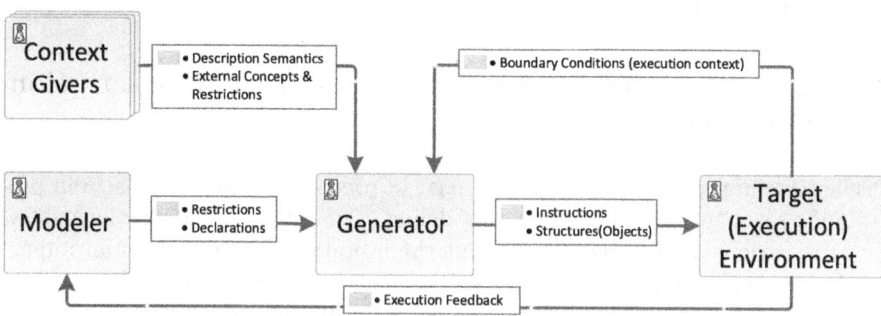

Fig. 1. Usage Scenario for Declarative Descriptions as input for Generators (Generator Concept)

Validators. The second category of entities that may receive declarative descriptions are validators that fulfill two principle activities (Fig. 2).

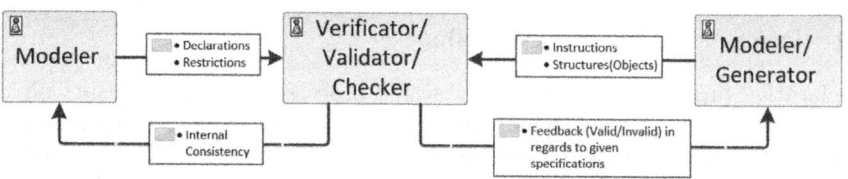

Fig. 2. Usage Scenario for Declarative Descriptions as input for Generators (Generator Concept)

---

[3] In this case *generation* basically is synonym with *compilation*.

Firstly, entities fall under this category that check whether a given declarative description is intrinsically coherent and non-contradicting in itself and in the context of the given boundary conditions and restrictions.

Following standard modeling denominations, this would correctly be defined as verification and separated from the activity of validation, where a description/model of structures or a set of instructions is first being generated and then checked whether it contradicts or breaks the rules of pre-established declarations or restrictions. If it does not break the rules, it is said to be valid.

In the context of this work, both activities are considered almost the same, as their only essential difference is the question of where the restrictions and declarations stem from. If all model elements stem from the same source, the check is called verification (Is it coherent in itself). If a model is checked on whether it fulfills the restrictions and definitions of a pre-existing description from a different source than the model itself, then this second model is said to be valid in regard to the earlier definition.

In some contexts, this differentiation is useful. However, in this work, given the stark contrast to the functionality of the generator concept, both validation and verification tasks are close enough to consider them together.

3 An Overview of Declarative Modeling and Description Approaches

Declarative approaches can be found, e.g., in process modeling, but also in programming semantics and graphical modeling. The following sub-sections showcase the various approaches throughout the literature that have had an impact on the created taxonomy. As the resulting taxonomy has shown, the involved disciplines are rather diverse and heterogeneous, and therefore, the subjects are considered to be stand-alone overviews of the individual domains.

Since the origin of the research stems from the domain of process modeling and management the first sub-section of declarative process modeling is the most elaborate followed by the approaches regarding procedural generation and design of 3D assets for simulations or productions and ending with an overview over similar concepts in the domains of programming and the indirect definition of data structures.

3.1 Declarative Process Modeling

Declarative process models try to describe processes without focusing on the individual activities and with more focus on the outcome. Classical approaches in Declarative Process Modeling are, e.g., ConDec [19,20], DecSerFlow [20], but also an extension to the subject-oriented modeling language PASS (Parallel Activity Specification Schema) [5].

Generally, this style of modeling should lead to more flexibility when executing said models, especially in regards to alternatives in the control flow [19].

These modeling approaches try to make process descriptions more flexible in the sense that process instances that do not break any given conditions/rule sets are valid. This ensures process flexibility and does not require the modeler to formulate every single detail of a process. This especially makes dealing with extensive and intertwined models easier. A complete overview and comparison of the different existing declarative *process* modeling approaches can be found in [11].

While a variety of concepts exist, none of these are targeted at verifying or specifying less abstract or imperative models. Aside from the research of Prescher et al. [22], who developed an approach to derive or generate imperative Petri nets from declarative constraint language, the other modeling languages have no semantic framework for this use case.

Case-Based Modeling/Case-Based Reasoning. Case-based reasoning (CBR) is an approach that tries to solve problems with human-like behavior. A subtype of CBR is Process-Oriented Case-Based Reasoning (PO-CBR) that uses this approach in the context of process management [18].

The general approach tries to solve problems case-based. In other words, it tries to find similar problems and use those to solve the current problem. This should resemble the approach humans would also choose in a real-life environment. Following the CBR cycle according to Aarmodt and Plaza [1], there are four main activity stages that CBR uses: **Retreive**: A search for the most similar problem case is conducted. A similarity measure has to be introduced that defines the similarity of the problem and the stored cases. **Reuse**: The found solution is applied to the chosen problem. If necessary, the solution is modified to suit the problem statement better in the form of an *adaptation stage*. **Revise**: The found solution is verified on how well it solved the presented problem statement. Finally, **Retain**: The problem statement paired with the found solution and the degree how well it performed are stored as a case and can now be used to solve further problems.

Implicitly given with this approach is the necessity to *model or describe cases*. However, many works on this problem do not go into detail about how to approach this. By CBR logic, a 'case' could be considered to be an incomplete, but similar, description of an existing problem, and the similarity measure, which is necessary to retrieve the instructions, is very similar to the concept of a validator engine. In this case, however, the validity is used as a measurement to determine similar cases.

3.2 Declarative Procedural Modeling

Declarative Procedural Modeling is a concept for virtual world designers (e.g. video game developers or visual effect artists), that uses the declarative flexibility to make the creation of virtual objects significantly faster and easier [23]. With a layer model for different landscape aspects and constraints for those layers, virtual landscapes can be generated and modified by the modeler. This process is also called "procedural sketching". With the given constraints, a landscape gets generated with adjustment options for the user afterwards.

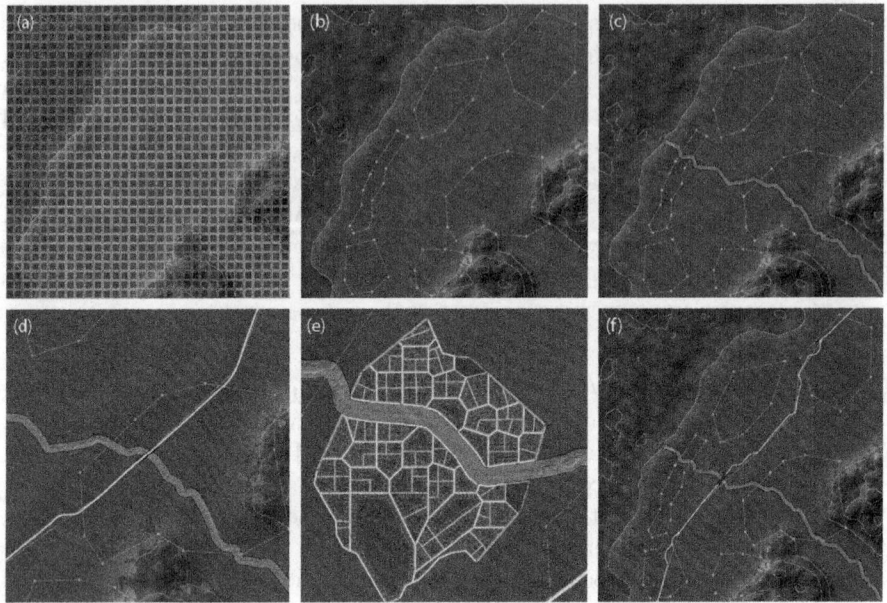

Fig. 3. Example of Procedural Landscape Generation [23]

Similarly to the work of Goedetier et al. [11], an imperative instruction for the generator is derived from the declarative constraints the modeler is initiating. But in the current state, there is no possibility for verifying an imperative execution instruction with the (abstract) constraint model (Fig. 3).

3.3 Generative Design and Convergent Modeling

More systematic than the generation of virtual objects and environments for video games are the techniques of constraint/converging/feature based modeling and the subsequent application of *generative design* application in the domain of mechanical engineering and usage of Computer Aided Designing (CAD)/ Computer Aided Engineering (CAE) [17].

Here, instead of creating a finalized model for a mechanical part, only a rough basic description and boundary conditions of application (stress) of a part are modeled. Subsequently, a generator together with simulation tools automatically creates a final model that fulfills all requirements given by the modeler, but is optimized with regard to stress, e.g., see Fig. 4.

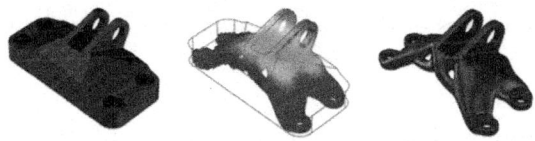

Fig. 4. Example for Application of Generative Design in Mechanical Engineering from [17]

3.4 Declarative Programming

We argue here that, on a fundamental level, programming can be seen as modeling as program code is basically a *description*—and therefore a kind of model—of a process that a computing machine is to execute.

Declarative programming is commonly used to get rid of control-flow logic by those who consider that style of programming to be hindering. Due to almost all physical computers still being Turing machines, they rely on underlying imperative concepts while not using imperative elements like loops or if/then conditions. The target is the focus for the developer on solution creation, rather than step-by-step instructions for a compiler. The user can specify certain constraints and use logic to get a result data set as an output[4].

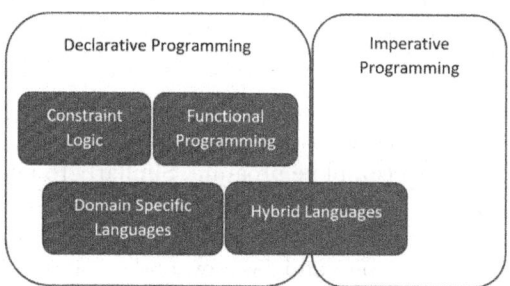

Fig. 5. Overview over paradigms considered declarative (own depiction)

Declarative Programming often summarizes other programming paradigms that have declarative properties. Often they are referred to as logic programming, functional programming, and constraint programming. Also, hybrid solutions between those fields are possible and already exist. Domain-Specific Languages (DSLs) like the Structured Query Language (SQL) or the HyperText Markup Language (HTML) are usually seen as declarative too, since they mainly target non-programmers and are output-focused without specifying every step for execution (Fig. 5).

---

[4] Note however, While the query is formulated via declarative semantics, with the current generation of computers, the underlying execution is still imperative (compare Sect. 2.4 Generators).

The main approaches of this domain are discussed in the following subsections:

Logic Programming. Based on influences that can be tracked back as early as 1960 (summarized in [14,15]) logic programming was introduced as a way to express program statements in formal expressions. These declarative expressions should help the programmer by structuring the expressions. The most commonly used logic programming language is Prolog [2] (Fig. 6).

```
+FLIGHT(<departure city>,<arrival city>,
        <departure time>,<arrival time>,<flight identifier>)
```

Fig. 6. Example of Prolog Queries [3]

An interesting variant for our use case is Constraint Logic Programming (CLP). Constraint Logic Programming (CLP) was introduced 1987 by Jaffar and Lassez [13] and tried to capture all programming languages that let the user manipulate data via declarative constraints. While using a similar constraint-based semantics to keep the real execution flexible, there is no reference point or even implication in both Logic Programming and Constraint Logic Programming for an existing imperative-declarative cross-validation.

Functional Programming. We argue that Functional Programming can be seen as a sub-category of declarative programming. It is composed of multiple functions, which generate a complete program. Similarly to Logic Programming, Functional Programming works without specifying imperative states. Instead, functional programming takes advantage of the modularity of functions. Hughes describes higher-order functions and lazy evaluation as the new "glue", that holds the modular pieces of a program together [12]. Higher-order functions are functions that return a function or take a function as an input. Lazy evaluation describes an approach, in which the evaluation of an expression is delayed, up until the moment it is explicitly needed. One of the first implementations and proposals of Functional Programming was presented by McCarthy in the form of LISP [16].

Again, the programming paradigm of Functional Programming does not seem to hold implications for a declarative-imperative verification solution. While Functional Programming possesses various declarative elements that allow the programmer to leave out a state-by-state description of the execution, verification is currently not possible nor the target of a programming paradigm. The usage of the generator to derive machine code remains the main purpose.

3.5 Data Structures

A data structure model, often only denoted *data model*, is, as the name suggests, a description of how data elements belong together or how the structure of data objects is supposed to be. There are examples of rather strict models, such as the concept of creating classes in standard object-oriented programming or modeling, where each data object is more or less strictly defined to have a fixed structure.

However, data structure definitions concepts like the formal XML Schema Definition (XSD) [26] —Developed by the World Wide Web Consortium—or the Resource Description Framework Schema (RDFS) [25]—Developed and recommended by the World Wide Web Consortium —, in principle, contain the option to only or partially define restrictions and limits for data structures—in this case XML or RDF documents. Thus, they do not model the structure of a specific collection of data, but rather put restrictions on what valid documents are or are not.

Being closely related to computing, these XSD or RDFS models can either be used in verification to assert whether a given concrete data structure adheres to the restrictions given. Alternatively, programs that are required to create data objects can use such abstract data structure models as templates to generate valid objects automatically, e.g., when translating from one data context to another.

3.6 The ALPS Concept

As initially mentioned, the research context of this work is an extension to the subject-oriented modeling process paradigm and its modeling language Parallel Activity Specification Schema (PASS) [8,9].

The *Abstract Layered PASS (ALPS)* extension was first envisioned in [5] and elaborated in [6]. It consists of concepts to extend PASS with declarative process modeling elements similar to those used for ConDec and Declare; however, it is not a standalone declarative process modeling language, but rather gives a modeler the option to use a description technique (imperative or declarative) fitting to her or his needs.

Furthermore, while direct execution of ALPS models containing declarative elements is also conceptually possible, the main focus is to create a modeling system where a declarative model can function as the specification for a more concrete or imperative process model.

The principle is visualized in Fig. 7. The idea is to formally support modeling endeavors that are spatially as well as temporally distributed. To validate if Modeler 2 and 3 truly create descriptions that formally adhere to the shown model A, a validator software as described in Fig. 2 would be needed. Figure 8 shows an example of a declarative ALPS process model and its valid imperative implementation. While visually seeming very similar, especially the transitions in the upper process flow are of various declarative concepts, be in only *advice* that can be ignored during actual process enactment, be it a *precedence transition* requiring that, before you can get an answer, you must have made a request, or be it a *trigger transition* requiring here that the process must not end that there must be at least on follow-up state and the messages specified should be received.

Figure 9 gives an overview of declarative ALPS SBD elements and which implementation a validator software should consider as valid or invalid.

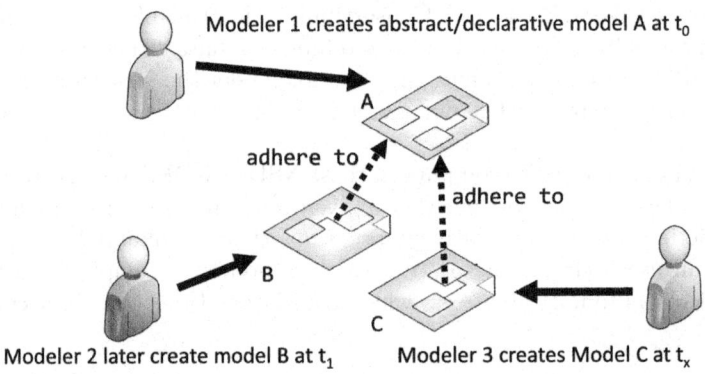

Fig. 7. Concept visualization for using declarative models as a guideline for other modelers

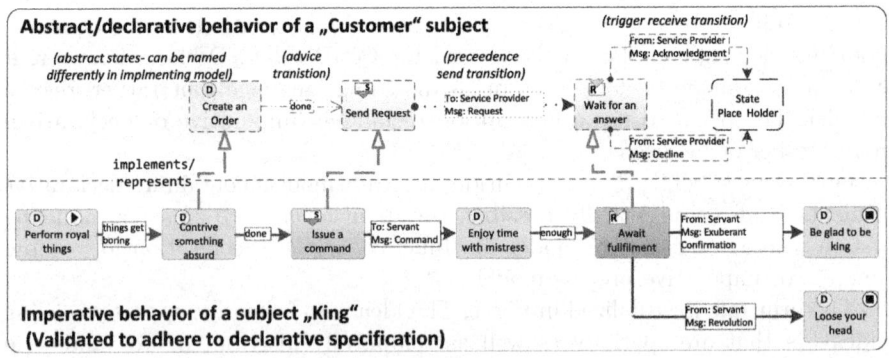

Fig. 8. Example for ALPS: declarative subject behavior diagram (top) and a verified imperative implementation (below) (Subject interaction diagrams not shown)

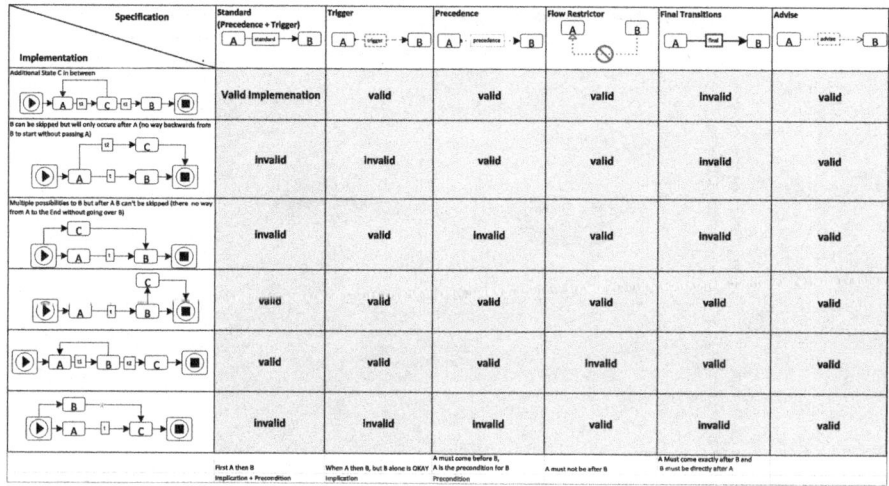

Fig. 9. Overview over ALPS declarative specifications (X-Axis) and valid or invalid imperative implementations (Y-Axis) From [6]

4 Comparison Model

All mentioned declarative approaches that were identified and investigated as part of this research have been found to fit into either of two categories and the corresponding process system models for the application described in Sect. 2. Naturally, and as explained, the order of development was inverted, with first identifying and analyzing the different approaches, their usage concepts, and trying to derive a systematic understanding from the various concepts, with the presented models being the result.

However, the usage comparison is not the only possible comparison dimension. Another aspect to consider is the aspect of what is being described, with all approaches being intended for the description of either objects, be it virtual or physical, or activities.

This led to the development of a combined classification schema, trying systematically to locate and compare the investigated approaches in, first, the dimension of intended usage and second, the dimension of intended description object. This classification understanding is conceptualized in the schematic of Fig. 10.

The Y-axis of Fig. 10 differs between objects and activities, while the X-axis is used to differentiate between the intended usage purposes as described in Sect. 2.

Instructions to do things/Description of (possibly physical) objects: Each of the approaches has the goal to either give instructions to a generator that get translated into machine code or to describe (physical) objects through constraints. Programming languages, by nature, are aimed at execution and

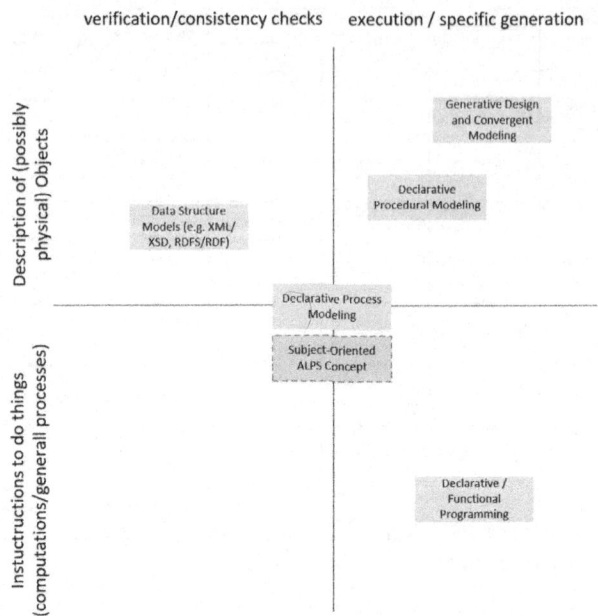

Fig. 10. Combined Overview Systematic of introduced declarative approaches

therefore function as instructions to do things. Declarative modeling languages, on the other hand, can function as instructions as they specify execution activities, but also are used as descriptive means to visualize processes.

Verification or Consistency Checks/Execution or Specific Generation: Either the input of the user is aimed at validation or execution by a generator. Declarative programming languages clearly inherit their primary function in the form of execution. Modeling Languages move between the two worlds and take into consideration elements of both verification and, consequently, execution.

5 Final Thoughts

The consequence of a declarative style of description is a possible loss of control over the exact means of execution or created details. This may not be acceptable for every modeling endeavor. In general, where exact details may not matter to a certain degree or where the details are to be filled by other modelers or executors at a later time.

As shown, there exists a heterogeneous multitude of modeling approaches under the umbrella of the term *declarative* modeling.

Declarative or implicit modeling is a tricky domain with at least some question marks regarding its usefulness and ease of application. However, we did not consider that aspect. Rather, as a result of our analysis, we created a generalized comparison systematic (the models of Sects. 2.4 and 4) that allow to understand the general idea and how all explored examples differ or relate to each other.

Based on that and the considered approaches, the following statements can be summarizingly made about declarative modeling:

- declarative approaches appear in various different domains (programming, 3D asset generation)
- it can be understood as kind of *incomplete* description, or not necessarily "completely connected" modeling.
- often understanding of the boundary conditions necessary to understand the declarative descriptions
- often intended for execution/generation, less for description/human-to-human interaction
- All investigated concepts can be fit into and understood in the context of the developed classification system

As initially stated, this research endeavor was originally initialized to identify related works to a concept, where declarative or abstract process models are used as formal specification for models that *implement* the source model in a less abstract/imperative way, with the main purpose to support distributed and collaborative modeling of complex process systems (see Sect. 3.6 - The ALPS concept).

However, for process modeling, no similar approach could be found in existing declarative semantics. Consequently, future research to further develop the ALPS concept will be conducted with the overall goal to create a usable modeling environment and tool suite, including a functional verificator that can verify independent models on an abstract source model to ensure semantic and logic coherence and to support the distributed creation of declarative process models.

Meanwhile, the presented overview, generalizations, and comparison models of this work can help new modelers and students to better understand similarities and differences between the various declarative approaches to either adopt them for their needs or use them as guidance for further developing their own applications.

References

1. Aamodt, A., Plaza, E.: Case-based reasoning: foundational issues, methodological variations, and system approaches. AI Commun. **7**(1), 39–59 (1994)
2. Colmerauer, A., Kanoui, H., van Caneghem, M.: Prolog, theoretical principles and current trends. Tech. Sci. Inf.; (France) **4** (1983)
3. Colmerauer, A., Roussel, P.: The birth of prolog. ACM SIGPLAN Notices **28**(3), 37–52 (1993)
4. Elstermann, M.: A missing concept? a short postulation about the need for human understanding and an often only implicitly given, fundamental aspect of modeling efforts. In: ER Forum, Demo and Posters 2020: Co-located with 39th International Conference on Conceptual Modeling (ER 2020). Ed.: J. Michael, volume 2716 of *CEUR Workshop Proceedings*, pp. 115–124. RWTH Aachen (2020)

5. Elstermann, M., Ovtcharova, J.: Abstract layers in PASS - a concept draft. In: Zehbold, C., ed., S-BPM ONE - Application Studies and Work in Progress - 6th International Conference, S-BPM ONE 2014, Eichstätt, Germany, April 22-23, 2014. Proceedings, vol. 422 of Communications in Computer and Information Science, pp. 125–136. Springer (2014)
6. Elstermann, M., xOvtcharova, M.: Revisiting the alps-an investigation of abstract layered pass. In: International Conference on Subject-Oriented Business Process Management, pp. 263–283. Springer (2023)
7. Elstermann, M., van Husen, C., Häfner, P.: Dimension concept - approaching service prototyping from a multi-aspect description perspective. In: Proceedings of the QUIS15 International Research Symposium on Service Excellence in Management (2015)
8. Fleischmann, A.: Distributed systems: software design and implementation. Springer Science & Business Media (1994)
9. Fleischmann, A.: Subjektorientiertes Prozessmanagement: Mitarbeiter einbinden. Motivation und Prozessakzeptanz steigern. Hanser Verlag, München (2011)
10. Fleischmann, A., Schmidt, W., Stary, C.: Subject-oriented business process management. In: Handbook on Business Process Management 2: Strategic Alignment, Governance, People and Culture, pp. 601–621 (2015)
11. Goedertier, S., Vanthienen, J., Caron, F.: Declarative business process modelling: principles and modelling languages. Enterprise Inf. Syst. (2015)
12. Hughes, J.: Why functional programming matters. Comput. J. **32**(2), 98–107 (1989)
13. Jaffar, J., Lassez, J.-L.: Constraint logic programming. In: Proceedings of the 14th ACM SIGACT-SIGPLAN symposium on Principles of programming languages, ACM Conferences, pp. 111–119. ACM, New York (1987)
14. Kowalski, R.A.: The early years of logic programming. Commun. ACM **31**(1), 38–43 (1988)
15. Lloyd, J.W.:Foundations of Logic Programming. Springer Science & Business Media (1987)
16. McCarthy, J.: Lisp: a programming system for symbolic manipulations. In: ACM '59: Preprints of Papers Presented at the 14th National Meeting of the Association for Computing Machinery, pp. 1–4. ACM (1959)
17. Molitch-Hou, M.: Frustum topology optimization integrated into siemens nx for 3d printing (2017)
18. Workflow Modeling Assistance by Case-based Reasoning. Springer, Wiesbaden (2018). https://doi.org/10.1007/978-3-658-23559-8_9
19. Pesic, M.: Constraint-based workflow management systems:shifting control to users (2008)
20. Pesic, M., van der Aalst, W.M.P.: A Declarative Approach for Flexible Business Processes Management. In: Eder, J., Dustdar, S. (eds.) BPM 2006. LNCS, vol. 4103, pp. 169–180. Springer, Heidelberg (2006). https://doi.org/10.1007/11837862_18
21. Pichler, P., et al.: Imperative versus declarative process modeling languages: an empirical investigation, pp. 383–394. Springer, Berlin, Heidelberg (2011)
22. Prescher, J., Di Ciccio, C., Mendling, J.: From declarative processes to imperative models (2014)
23. Smelik, R., Galka, K., de Kraker, K.J., Kuijper, F., Bidarra, R.: Semantic constraints for procedural generation of virtual worlds. In: Proceedings of the 2nd International Workshop on Procedural Content Generation in Games - PCGames '11. ACM Press, New York (2011)

24. van Roy, P., Haridi., S.: Concepts, Techniques, and Models of Computer Programming. MIT Press (2004)
25. W3C. Rdfs. https://www.w3.org/TR/rdf-schema/, Accessed 07 Mar 2022
26. W3C. Xsd. https://www.w3.org/TR/xmlschema11-1/, Accessed 07 Mar 2022

Incremental Development of Multi-agent Systems Based on Subject-Oriented Process Modelling and Validation

Udo Kannengiesser(✉)

Department of Business Informatics – Communications Engineering, Johannes Kepler University Linz, 4040 Linz, Austria
udo.kannengiesser@jku.at

Abstract. The multi-agent paradigm provides models of autonomous, interacting entities capturing the complexity many of today's software systems. The design of multi-agent systems remains a challenge, involving high project risk due to insufficient, late understanding of system behaviours and poor consideration of stakeholder requirements. Concepts from agile software development approaches, including incremental development and early prototyping, have been proposed to address these issues. Yet, most agent-oriented development approaches have not integrated these principles. In this paper, an incremental methodology for developing multi-agent systems is proposed based on the integration of subject-oriented process management (S-BPM) and a generalised approach for developing multi-agent systems. A toolchain has been implemented for demonstrating the methodology.

Keywords: Multi-Agent Systems · Agent-Oriented Software Engineering · Incremental Development · Agile Development · S-BPM

1 Introduction

Multi-agent models provide the foundation of many distributed, adaptive systems such as in smart manufacturing, logistics and energy management. This is because they capture autonomous, goal-directed actions of individual system components and their mutual interplay from which effective system behaviour can emerge.

While multi-agent models can facilitate complex systems engineering, important challenges remain. Many development projects run late, out of budget, or fail to meet the customer's expectations. To cope with these problems, the adoption of concepts from agile software development has been proposed for various systems engineering domains including IoT systems [1], (smart) service systems [2–4] and industry 4.0 [5–7]. Key ideas of agile development include increased incremental approaches and early validation [8]. Yet, there is little work on integrating such ideas into multi-agent modelling [9, 10]. This paper proposes an incremental approach for developing multi-agent systems (MAS) based on subject-oriented process management (S-BPM) [11].

The approach includes a procedural model and a mapping of S-BPM concepts onto agent-oriented constructs. A prototype implementation of a transformation tool from S-BPM to MAS is presented and applied to the example of a multi-agent-based food delivery service.

The paper is organised as follows. The foundations of agent-based systems and development approaches for multi-agent systems are reviewed in Sect. 2. The key ideas of the S-BPM methodology are presented in Sect. 3. A conceptual framework for integrating S-BPM in a generalised methodology for MAS development is proposed in Sect. 4. A prototype implementation of a tool for transforming S-BPM into MAS models is described in Sect. 5. A demonstration of the methodology and tool is provided in Sect. 6. A summary of the results and a discussion of future work conclude the paper in Sect. 7.

2 Developing Multi-agent Systems

2.1 Foundational Concepts

Agents are commonly understood as autonomous entities situated in an environment, such as the physical world or software, which perform actions according to their goals and knowledge [12]. They are typically employed in dynamic, unstable environments that may change in unpredictable ways. Agents are able to adapt to these changes by using different ways of achieving their goals, or even by abandoning previous goals and adopting new ones. Agents have sensors and effectors that allow them to interact with their environment and with one another.

Most agents have been conceptualized as cognitive agents following the Belief-Desire-Intention (BDI) paradigm [13]: Beliefs (B) represent the agent's knowledge about the world, Desires (D) represent states of the world that the agent wants to bring about, and Intentions (I) represent those desires that the agent commits to pursuing. Desires (D) and Intentions (I) are often referred to as (possible or pursued) goals. Examples of possible goals of an agent in the context of marine warfare, according to [14], include to "destroy submarine", to "assign escorts to sectors" and to "adopt zigzag pattern". BDI agents are equipped with a library of alternative plans for achieving a particular goal. Plans specify sequences of steps to be performed, typically represented using a formal process modelling language such as statecharts [15], UML [16] and BPMN [17]. Plans are selected based on the agent's current goals and beliefs. In the example of the agent in a warfare situation [14], a plan associated with the goal "navigate waypoints" may be applicable only if the agent believes that it is not under threat and the battery level is above 20%.

Plans may contain not only individual actions but also goals. These goals are associated with their own plans, which must be executed before the original plan can proceed to the next step. The recursive nature of goals and plans can lead to hierarchical goal/sub-goal structures at arbitrary depth. Goals may be delegated to other agents.

Systems in which multiple agents interact to coordinate their actions, cooperate or collaborate as a team, are referred to as multi-agent systems (MAS) [12, 18]. For effective team behaviour, it is often seen necessary for the agents to form joint intentions (or joint goals) [19]. In most approaches joint goals are modelled as part of the intentions of individual agents, so that the agents' autonomy remains unrestricted. Forming joint goals among autonomous agents requires communication, which often follows pre-defined interaction protocols [20]. Another social construct that supports teams or organisations of agents is the role concept [21]. Ferber et al. [18] define a role as "the abstract representation of a functional position of an agent in a group". Roles support the decomposition of joint goals into separate responsibilities that can be assigned to individual agents or sub-teams of agents.

2.2 Multi-agent Development Approaches

A number of methodologies for developing MAS have been proposed, particularly in the early 2000s. The most known approaches are briefly introduced in this section.

The Gaia methodology [22] comprises 2 phases: It begins with an analysis phase in which agent roles (including responsibilities, permissions and internal or "private" activities) and the ways in which they interact are specified based on given requirements. It then continues with a design phase in which details of the agents are defined, including the agent types to be associated with the roles, and the services to be provided by the agents. Gaia is described as a top-down approach moving from the abstract to the concrete, by focusing firstly on a conceptual view of the agent organization (in the analysis phase) and then on its realization by runtime components (in the design phase).

MaSE [16] resembles Gaia in that it consists of analysis and design phases. Yet, it contains more detailed steps within the two phases. Analysis has steps concerned with specifying goals (including non-functional goals) and their relationships, use cases and roles. Design has steps specifying agent types, communications, intra-agent components and deployments. MaSE is an extension of common software development methodologies, using similar types of diagrams including use case diagrams, sequence diagrams and class diagrams.

Tropos [23] places increased emphasis on the requirements stages and the notion of goals. Here, goals comprise not only the common "achievement" goals in most agent approaches but also "soft goals" in terms of non-functional requirements. The architectural design stage in Tropos includes the specification of human and software actors, their roles and capabilities, and agent types. The detailed design stage subsequently specifies details of the agents and their communication, based on the specific implementation platform chosen. Tropos uses Agent UML (AUML) as a modelling language.

Prometheus [24] includes a three-phase procedure beginning with system specification, followed by architectural design and detailed design. System specification deals with describing system goals, scenarios and the interfaces of the system in terms of inputs (percepts) and outputs (actions). Architectural design defines the overall system structure, by deciding on the agent types and the interactions between agents. Detailed design is about specifying the internal capabilities of agents including their plans. The models resulting from detailed design are taken as input for implementation. The authors of Prometheus propose a direct mapping of these models to the Java-based agent platform JACK which uses the BDI paradigm.

PASSI [25] comprises five consecutive stages, each of which produces a different model of the agent system: system requirements, agent society, agent implementation, code, and deployment model. The original methodology was later extended into Agile PASSI [26], aiming to reduce the time required for producing and testing agent code.

It is based on the automatic generation of documents and code, the reuse of previous projects (patterns), and the use of a unit testing framework. However, the testing phase remains the final step in Agile PASSI.

Most of the approaches surveyed focus on the sequential execution of requirements definition, architecture, design and coding phases. While some of them [16, 24] mention that iterating between different phases can be useful, their descriptions in the literature still have a strong waterfall character and typically view testing as a downstream rather than a continuous activity [27]. There have been only few proposals for extending existing methodologies with iterative, incremental approaches. For example, one approach [9] introduces the general idea of decomposing the overall system functionality into partial functionalities that are developed using separate iterations of the Gaia phases. The description of this approach remains at a fairly abstract level, without providing much guidance for MAS developers. Another approach [10] proposes a test-driven development framework for MAS development. As its focus is limited to the coding phase, it does not support iterations across the earlier phases.

3 Subject-Oriented Process Management

Subject-oriented process management (S-BPM) has been developed as an approach for business process management (BPM) [11]. It is based on the notion of subjects that are defined as process-centred functionalities [28]. Every subject encapsulates a behaviour. It interacts with the behaviour of other subjects via messages. The formal foundations of S-BPM are based on the calculus of communicating systems [29], communicating sequential processes [30] and abstract state machines [31]. S-BPM differs from other approaches in that its simple notation, modular structure and instant executability lead to faster and more effective process modelling, which was demonstrated in experimental settings [32] and industry practice [33, 34]. In particular, S-BPM was found to support incremental approaches to process modelling [34, 35].

In S-BPM, a process model consists of two kinds of diagrams:

- Subject Interaction Diagram (SID): specifies the subjects and the messages they exchange. Every process has exactly one SID.
- Subject Behaviour Diagrams (SBDs): specify the behaviour of a subject. For a set of N subjects in a SID, there will be N SBDs (except for so-called interface subjects, which will be neglected in this paper). Every SBD is a directed graph that defines a sequence of states. There are three kinds of states: Function states (representing actions), Receive states (representing the receipt of messages from other subjects), and Send states (representing the dispatch of messages to other subjects).

An example of a SID is shown in Fig. 1, representing an *Order Handling* process of a food delivery company. As SIDs are to provide a simple overview of who is talking to whom, there is no process logic embedded such as sequences or conditions related to the messages.

The process logic is encapsulated in the internal behaviour descriptions of individual subjects, which are specified by SBDs. An example of an SBD is shown in Fig. 2, representing the behaviour of the *Food Preparation* subject. Function states (orange

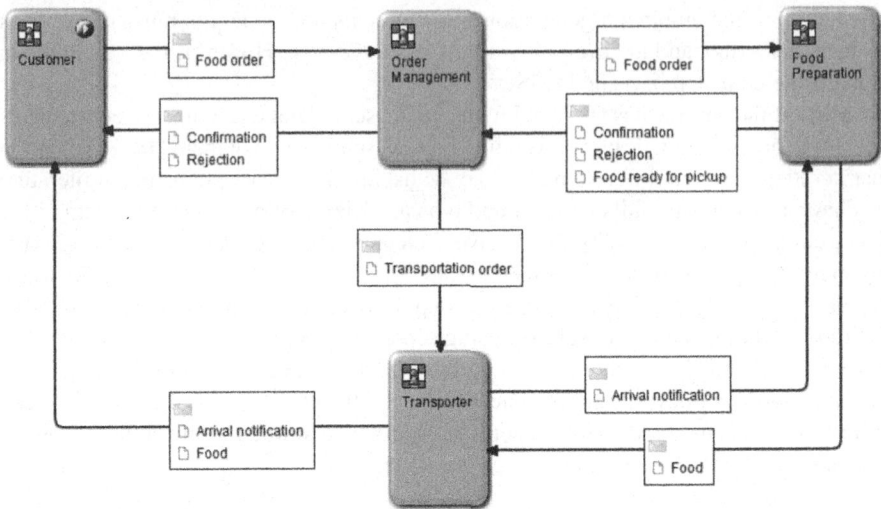

Fig. 1. Subject Interaction Diagram (SID) of an *Order Handling* process in the food delivery industry

boxes in Fig. 2), Receive states (green boxes) and Send states (red boxes) are connected by state transitions that specify conditions for proceeding to the next state. XOR branching in an SBD is represented by more than one outgoing transitions (with disparate conditions) from a state, such as in Fig. 2 where the process path is split in two branches. There is no parallel (AND) branching allowed within SBDs.

Based on their abstract state machine syntax, S-BPM models can be directly executed without requiring any coding. This is used for early validation of the models, supported by automated support. Here, stakeholders simulate (i.e., walk through) the individual steps defined in the SBDs of subjects they are responsible for. This allows them to "experience" their own behaviour, their communication with other stakeholders and the emerging system behaviour. S-BPM validation differs from common agent-oriented methodologies which require coding prior to validation and generally do not involve stakeholders.

There is some previous work on integrating subject-oriented and agent-oriented models. Most notably, Fleischmann et al. [28] propose an extension of the Agent/Group/Role (AGR) model [18] to combine the core constructs of S-BPM and MAS models. In particular, they show that the connection between subjects and agent roles is a many-to-many relationship. Roles are defined as aggregations of subjects, and subjects can be embodied (executed) by one or more roles. Fleischmann et al. [28] conclude that S-BPM models can add a process-oriented abstraction layer to the organisationally oriented concepts in MAS, leading to enhanced flexibility of implementation and execution of processes by multi-agent systems. While that paper lays important foundations for bringing subject-oriented process models and MAS models together, it does not include a subject-oriented methodology for designing MAS. In addition, it remains unclear how S-BPM models can be integrated in the internal structures of computational agents, using the agents' intentional constructs such as beliefs, desires, intentions and plans.

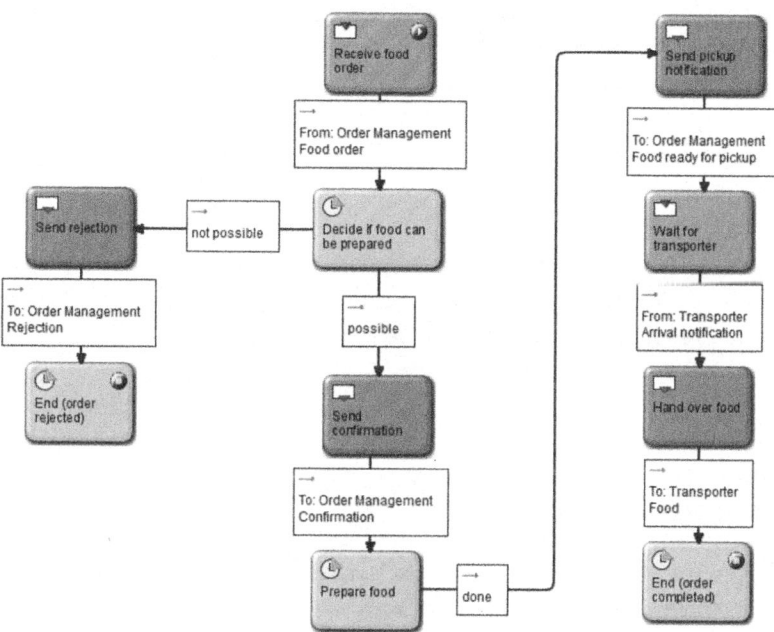

Fig. 2. Subject Behaviour Diagram (SBD) of the *Food Preparation* subject

4 Integrating Subject-Oriented Modelling in MAS Design

The main idea for the subject-oriented agent design methodology proposed in this paper is based on the many-to-many relationship [28] between processes and multi-agent systems, as shown in the UML class diagram in Fig. 3. When we design a particular MAS, we want it to execute a set of N processes, as shown in the UML object diagram in the top right of Fig. 4. The cycle of activities related to modelling and validation of each of these processes could be thought of as an increment in the development of the MAS. Once a process model is complete and validated, it is integrated in the MAS model. In this way, the MAS design emerges by incrementally integrating process models that constitute the delta between different versions of the MAS model.

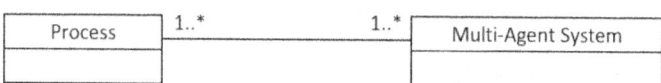

Fig. 3. Many-to-many relationship between processes and multi-agent systems (based on [28])

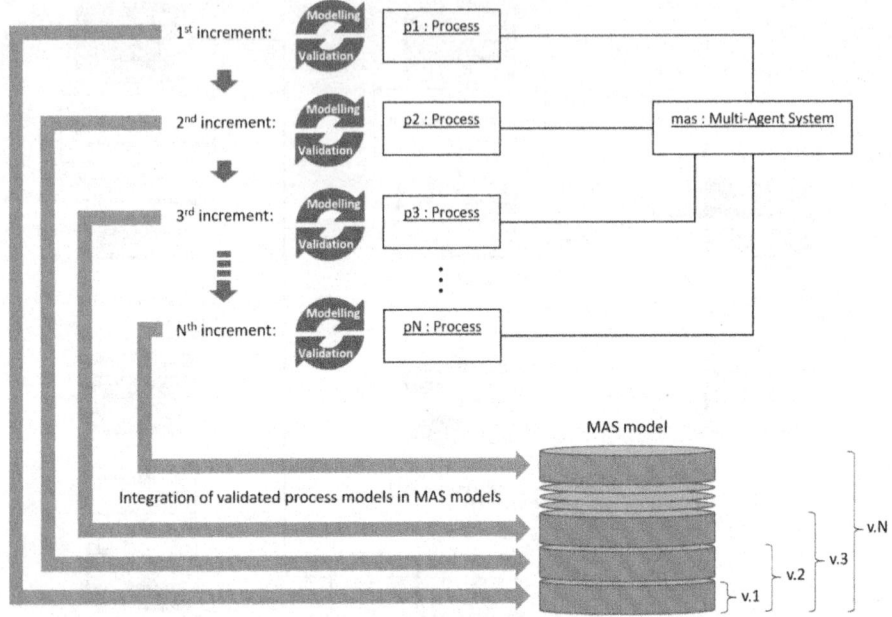

Fig. 4. Basic conception of an incremental, subject-oriented methodology for designing MAS

This approach shares some similarities with the notions of "feature slicing" and minimum viable products (MVPs) in agile software development. The general idea is to break down a system's functionality into manageable chunks that can be developed and tested independently and within short timeframes, allowing for early feedback and providing immediate value to users.

The individual cycles of modelling and testing within this methodology can be done entirely using existing S-BPM methods and tools. The integration of S-BPM models into MAS models requires mappings between key concepts of each approach, which are shown in Fig. 5. A process in S-BPM is assumed to have a one-to-one mapping to a joint goal. This is because a process can be viewed as a system functionality, whose execution becomes a joint goal for the agents in the system. Processes in S-BPM consist of at least two communicating subjects. Subjects have one-to-one mappings to the agent goals that compose the joint goal, as the execution of a subject becomes the goal of an agent. Agent goals are aggregated into different roles within the agent organisation. Subject behaviour is mapped onto one or several plans associated with an agent goal. This one-to-many mapping is based on the possibility to include multiple paths into an SBD, each of which can be viewed as an alternative plan to fulfil the goal represented by the subject.

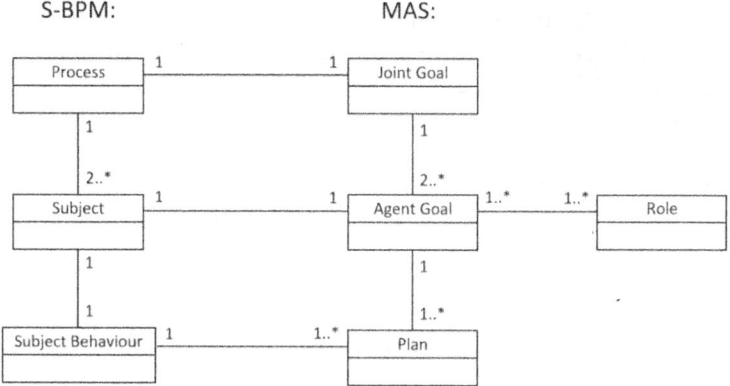

Fig. 5. Mappings between S-BPM and MAS concepts

More mappings are needed for effective model transformations, but these are dependent on the particular MAS methodologies selected, as each methodology comes with its own meta-models and ontologies. In this section, we will concentrate only on the most generic mappings that apply to most MAS models.

To add more detail to the conceptual approach presented so far, a generic methodology is defined based on the existing MAS development approaches. As concluded at the end of Sect. 2.2, most approaches use the phases of requirements definition, architecture, design and coding. The two phases that can be most directly supported by S-BPM include architecture, which is about defining the agents' joint and individual goals, roles and interactions, and design, which is about defining the agents' individual behaviour and data. The architecture phase would benefit mostly from the SIDs, and the design phase mostly from the SBDs created by S-BPM modellers.

A procedural model of the approach is shown in Fig. 6. It is represented in BPMN to provide a high-level overview of the MAS development process without encapsulating essential parts of the process. The process is partitioned into four BPMN Pools that represent requirements definition, MAS modelling, S-BPM modelling, and MAS coding. MAS development commences with the *Requirements Definition* Pool defining system requirements including a set of desired joint goals. Based on the requirements, the *MAS Modeller* Pool selects a joint goal to become the basis for incremental modelling and validation in S-BPM. The joint goal becomes the process to be modelled by the *S-BPM Modeller* resulting in a SID and associated SBDs (in any order, as indicated by the expanded BPMN Subprocess that has no internal sequence flows; see [36, p. 37]). These models can instantly be validated using S-BPM walkthrough techniques, allowing early feedback whether they fulfil expectations, or whether changes are required in the models. Validated S-BPM models are provided to the *MAS Modeller* Pool to proceed with extending the architecture (derived mostly from the SID) and agent design (derived mostly from the SBDs). This may involve adding MAS information not captured in S-BPM models (e.g. belief models and roles), refactoring (e.g. renaming elements, decomposing goals, and turning individual paths in an SBD into separate plans), transforming model elements to align with the chosen MAS coding platform, and integrating the current MAS models with previous model versions. A new increment can then start by looping back within the *MAS Modeller* Pool to selecting a new joint goal to be modelled and validated, creating a new instance of the *S-BPM Modeller* Pool. When all joint goals have been modelled and validated, the aggregated MAS model is provided to the *MAS Coder* Pool for coding and testing.

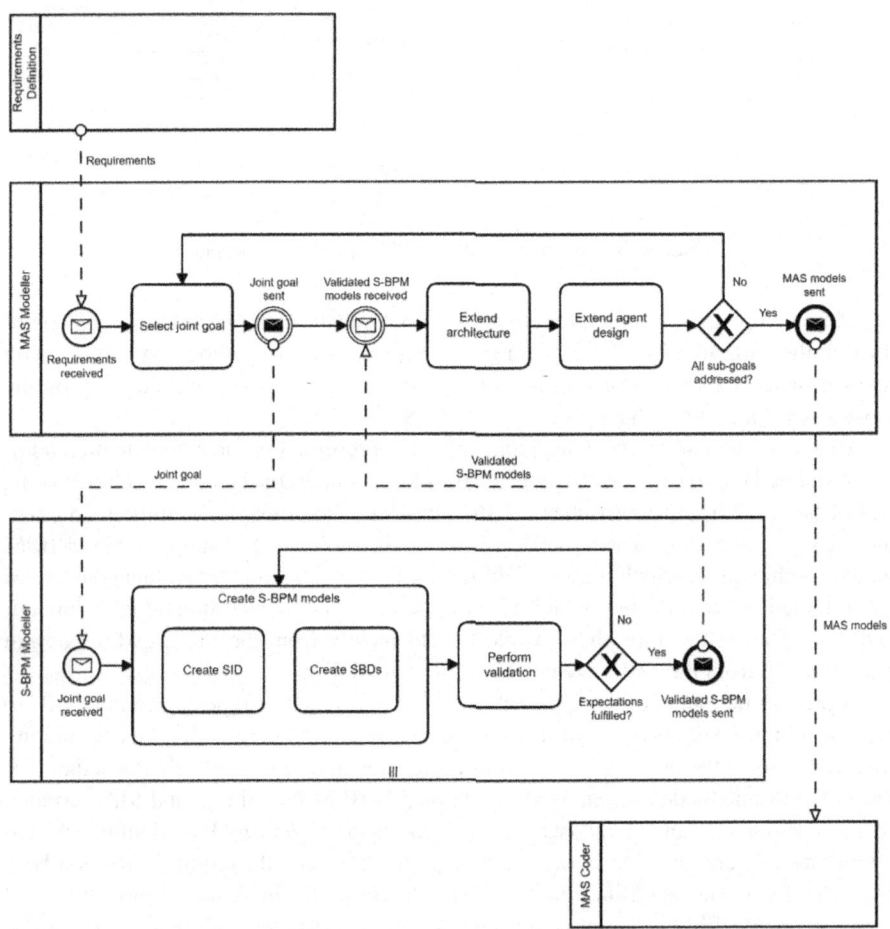

Fig. 6. Procedural approach for integrating S-BPM and MAS modelling

Requirements Definition and *MAS Coder* are modelled as black-box Pools in Fig. 6 to hide up- and downstream details that are not the focus of this paper. This simplifies the presentation of MAS development processes that are likely to include continuously changing requirements, and rework on the MAS model after coding has started.

5 Prototype Implementation

A prototype of an integrated toolchain for the proposed MAS development approach has partially been implemented [37]. It concentrates on the transformation of validated S-BPM models into MAS models. The transformation of joint goals into S-BPM processes has not be implemented, nor has been the transformation of MAS models into MAS code as there already exist tools for this.

The two main components of the toolchain are the Metasonic Suite (version 5.4.1) and the TDF (Tactics Development Framework) Tool (version 0.3). The Metasonic Suite supports S-BPM modelling and validation. It was the first commercially available S-BPM tool and has been used by various companies. The TDF Tool supports MAS modelling according to the proposed approach shown in Fig. 6. It is based on an extension of the Prometheus methodology [14, 24].

The two tools represent their respective modelling output in different formats: XML for Metasonic models, and JSON for TDF models. Therefore, a software program was developed to transform the models from Metasonic's XML to TDF's JSON files. The program was coded using Python and includes the following functionalities:

- Import of Metasonic's XML files (i.e., the S-BPM models)
- Transformation of S-BPM into TDF information according to Fig. 5 and more specific mappings on the diagram level, as will be presented later
- Export of TDF's JSON files representing MAS models, in one of two modes: (1) stand-alone mode: a new JSON file is generated to capture a new MAS from scratch; and (2) integration mode: an existing JSON file is augmented with information provided by a S-BPM model, which is used for integrating model increments $i \geq 2$ in an existing MAS model (cf. Fig. 4).

A simple graphical user interface (GUI) was developed to allow users to select one of the two export modes. The implementation of mappings from S-BPM focuses on two TDF diagrams:

1. *Architecture Overview*: can be viewed as a principal output of the architecture phase and includes a set of agents, the messages they exchange, the actions they perform, among others. This diagram does not include any information about process logic.
2. *Plan Diagram*: can be viewed as a principal output of the design phase and includes plan descriptions using a notation similar to UML activity diagrams, extended with additional elements including goals, agents, messages, actions, and others.

The mappings required to generate these diagrams are shown in Table 1. It can be seen that not all information for elements in the TDF diagrams is available in S-BPM models. In addition, there a few ambiguities in the mappings, as the same S-BPM concept could be mapped onto several TDF concepts, and several S-BPM concepts could be mapped onto the same TDF concept. Here, meaningful mappings would depend on a semantic understanding of the application context. A few workarounds have been implemented, but it is unavoidable that the automatically generated TDF models still need to be extended and refactored manually by MAS modellers. For more information on the meaning of particular modelling elements in TDF and S-BPM, readers are referred to the respective literature [11, 14].

Table 1. S-BPM-to-MAS Mappings for two major diagram types in TDF.

TDF Diagram type	TDF Diagram element	S-BPM concept
Agent Overview	Agent	n.a. (use Subject name as proxy)
	Team	n.a.
	Message	Message
	Goal request	n.a. (use Message name as proxy)
	Percept	n.a. (Receive state or Function state)
	Action	Function state
Plan Diagram	Action	Function state
	Belief set	n.a.
	Decision/merge node	Outgoing/incoming transitions in SBDs
	End node	End state
	Fail node	End state
	(parallel) Fork/Join node	n.a.
	Goal	Subject
	Interruption	Message guard
	Message	Message
	Percept	n.a. (Receive state or Function state)
	Start node	Starting state
	Wait node	Transition condition

Both Metasonic and TDF store graphical layout information in their models using x and y coordinates, which are included in the implemented transformation.

6 Example Application

In this section an application of the proposed methodology using the prototype is presented. Following the process example introduced in Sect. 3, a multi-agent system is to be developed for a food delivery enterprise that is able to handle and deliver food orders, prepare and execute marketing campaigns, maintain its fleet of delivery drones, onboard new employees, expand its partner network, and perform a number of other system functionalities.

All of these functionalities can be viewed as joint goals of the MAS, specified in the requirements definition phase. Some of them may be further decomposed into more specific joint goals. Using the incremental development approach, one of these goals is selected for the first increment of S-BPM modelling and validation. Let us choose *Order Handling* as the first joint goal (or S-BPM process).

The SID of that process was already shown in Fig. 1. All of its subjects have been modelled too, one of which was depicted in Fig. 2. The validation step in the Metasonic

Suite is assumed to be successfully completed, so that the S-BPM model can now be transformed into TDF diagrams. The *Architecture Overview* that was generated and refactored is shown in Fig. 7. Actions (green icons in Fig. 7) were generated from the Function states specified in the SBDs, and agents (red icons) and messages (purple icons) were generated from the SID. It can be seen that agents carry the labels of subjects in the SID, which is a workaround because agents (i.e., the concrete actors executing the subjects in a process) are not directly specified in S-BPM. Refactoring was necessary to optimize the graphical layout and to overcome a technical constraint in the TDF tool that the same element type cannot occur more than once in the same diagram. As a result, a few message names had to be manually modified (e.g. "food order c" was used for the food order message from the customer, and "food order o" for the food order message from the order management).

One of the *Plan Diagrams* generated in the first increment is the one for the *Food Preparation* agent, shown in Fig. 8, based on the corresponding SBD (see Fig. 2). Firstly, a goal (yellow symbol in Fig. 8) is inserted preceding the start node, to indicate that this goal is the precondition for invoking the plan. Actions are generated from S-BPM Function states and Receive states, while messages sent are generated by S-BPM Send states. A decision node (white diamond) is generated from S-BPM states with more than one outgoing transition; in this case, for the state "Decide if food can be prepared" (see Fig. 2). Refactoring was needed to optimize the graphical layout and to ensure consistency with the refactored elements in the *Architecture Overview* (here, by renaming the "Food" message to "Food t", see Fig. 7).

After extending the architecture and design of the MAS model, the next increment is carried out. In the example, the joint goal of *Maintenance Application* for the Transporter agent is selected as a new S-BPM process to be modelled and validated. The SID of this process is shown in Fig. 9. It contains the Transporter and a new "Maintenance" subject. After producing the SBDs and validating the interplay between the two agents, the S-BPM model is transformed and imported in TDF. The integrated *Architecture Overview*, resulting from augmenting the previous version (see Fig. 7) with the information extracted from the new S-BPM model, is shown in Fig. 10. The added information is located on the bottom left of the figure. It includes the new Maintenance agent, the messages it exchanges with the existing Transporter agent, and the two agents' actions related to the new process.

This example demonstrates how the S-BPM based approach incrementally builds up the MAS, by producing and validating individual process models for every joint goal, before integrating them in the MAS model.

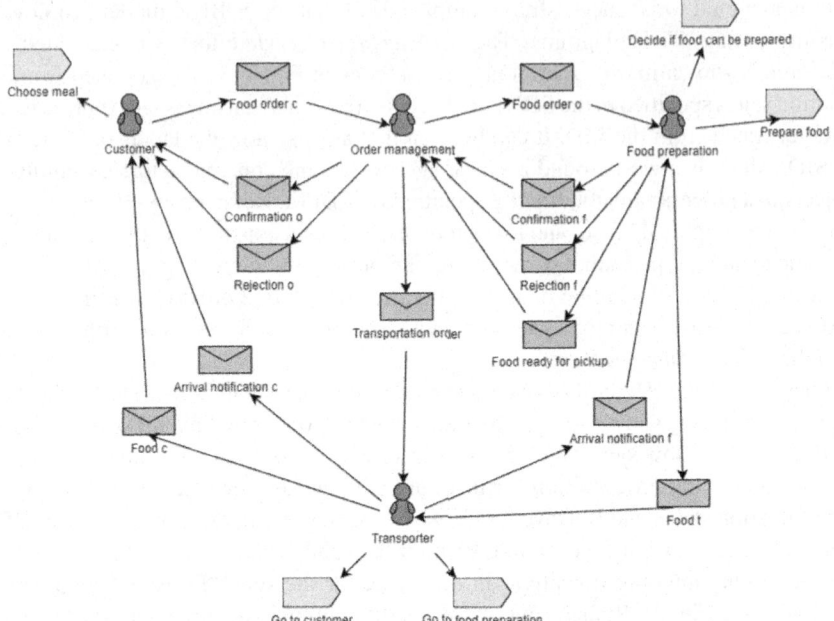

Fig. 7. *Architecture Overview* in TDF (after refactoring) generated from S-BPM: Agents (red symbols), messages (purple symbols), actions (green symbols) and their interconnections

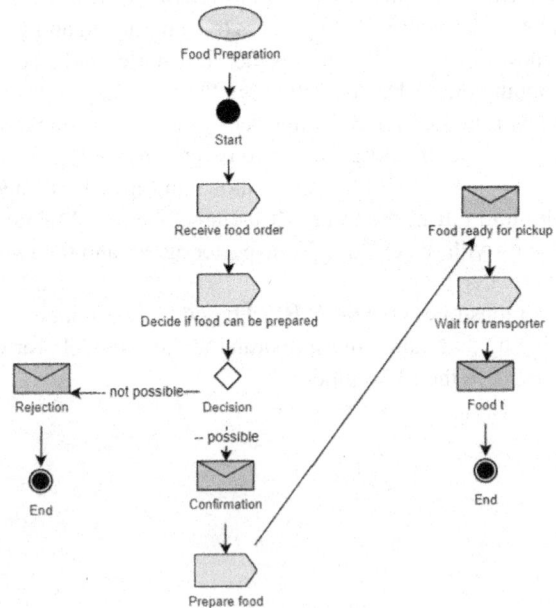

Fig. 8. *Plan Diagram* for the *Food Preparation* agent in TDF (after refactoring) generated from the SBD (cf. Figure 2)

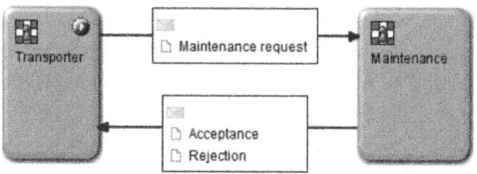

Fig. 9. Subject Interaction Diagram (SID) of the *Maintenance Application* process

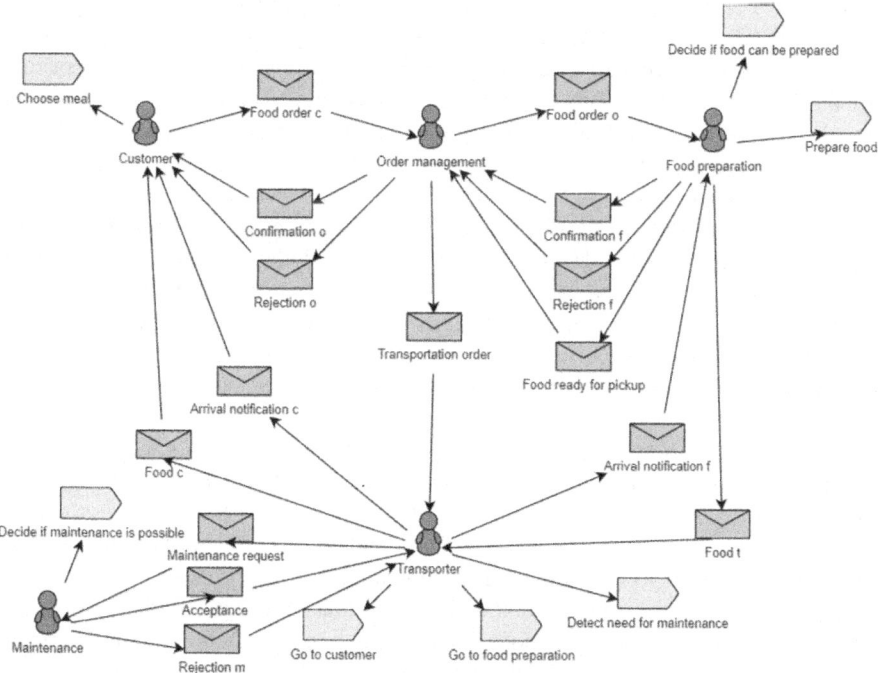

Fig. 10. Integrated *Architecture Overview* in TDF (refactored), generated by augmenting its previous version (Fig. 7) with information from the *Maintenance Application* process in S-BPM

7 Conclusion

This paper proposed a methodology for incremental development of multi-agent systems (MAS), based on subject-oriented process modelling and validation. Increments consist of selecting a joint goal in the MAS, producing and validating S-BPM models for it, and integrating them as part of the MAS architecture and agent design. The MAS model thus emerges step by step, with every step (or increment) contributing a validated set of agent goals and plans for the selected joint goal. This work has the potential to facilitate the development of large, complex multi-agent systems, particularly in multidisciplinary projects such as cyber-physical systems engineering. Here, MAS developers would no longer represent a bottleneck in the agile project team when their colleagues from other disciplines (e.g. software engineering or mechatronics) need access to MAS models at earlier stages in the project.

The approach combines two schools of thought that share a common way of looking at distributed systems, namely, as systems of autonomous entities that interact to achieve a common (or joint) goal. The foundations for bringing S-BPM and MAS together were laid by Fleischmann et al. [28], by identifying and characterising the connection between them. This paper goes a step further in that it focuses on model transformation, by embedding the process models, created in S-BPM, in the agent's internal cognition [38]. Design-ontologically speaking, it is about synthesizing an agent's (cognitive) structures based on expected (process) behaviour [39].

Experiences gained from the prototype implementation presented in this paper indicate potential directions for further research. One of the experiences concerns the considerable need for refactoring after model transformation. This was partially due to specifics of the selected MAS modelling notation and tool. However, it may be worth considering whether the S-BPM notation could provide a viable alternative for the UML-like diagrams used in most MAS modelling platforms. This would not only avoid gaps and errors in the transformation of S-BPM into MAS models, but could also help generate code from MAS models for the downstream phases of implementation and deployment. Any information that MAS developers may want to include apart from the executable S-BPM models could still be added as annotations. As can be seen in Fig. 10, some of the MAS diagrams can become quite large, potentially reducing their understandability. Using fragmented models, i.e., a subset of models for every joint goal, such as provided by S-BPM, rather than a single model for all joint goals, may be beneficial for human comprehension.

This work also provides food for thought for the (S-)BPM community. The focus of most process modelling researchers and practitioners has often been just "the process". Viewing process modelling in the context of MAS shows us that a process may be only one increment in the development of a complete system, and that there may be many more processes to be added and integrated. Different processes interact as they share resources, and interrupt each other as they ultimately depend on the dynamically changing desires, beliefs and intentions of the agents executing them. The single-process perspective in (S-)BPM does not fully capture the richness of organisational behaviour, whether it be executed by human or computational agents. It may be useful to broaden the view of process modelling as not only a key activity in BPM but also a technique for behaviour modelling in system design [40].

References

1. Guerrero-Ulloa, G., Rodríguez-Domínguez, C., Hornos, M.J.: Agile methodologies applied to the development of Internet of Things (IoT)-based systems: a review. Sensors **23**(2), 790 (2023)
2. Abramovici, M.: Engineering smarter Produkte und Services (Plattform Industrie 4.0 Studie). acatech – Deutsche Akademie der Technikwissenschaften, Munich, Germany (2018)
3. Jussen, P., Kuntz, J., Senderek, R., Moser, B.: Smart service engineering. Procedia CIRP **83**, 384–388 (2019)
4. Willmott, T.J., Hurley, E., Rundle-Thiele, S.: Designing energy solutions: a comparison of two participatory design approaches for service innovation. J. Serv. Theory Pract. **32**(3), 353–377 (2022)

5. VDI: Testing of Networked Systems for Industrie 4.0. Verein Deutscher Ingenieure, Düsseldorf, Germany (2018)
6. VDMA: Guideline Industrie 4.0: Guiding Principles for the Implementation of Industrie 4.0 in Small and Medium Sized Businesses. Verband Deutscher Maschinen- und Anlagenbau, Frankfurt, Germany (2016)
7. Wiesner, S., Hauge, J.B., Sonntag, P., Thoben. K.D.: Applicability of agile methods for dynamic requirements in smart PSS development. In: Ameri, F., Stecke, K., von Cieminski, G., Kiritsis, D. (eds.) Advances in Production Management Systems: Production Management for the Factory of the Future (APMS 2019). IFIP Advances in Information and Communication Technology, vol. 566, pp. 666–673. Springer, Cham (2019)
8. Fowler, M., Highsmith, J.: The agile manifesto. Softw. Dev. **9**, 28–35 (2001)
9. Gonzalez-Palacios, J., Luck, M.: Extending Gaia with agent design and iterative development. In: Luck, M., Padgham, L. (eds.) Agent-Oriented Software Engineering VIII. AOSE 2007. Lecture Notes in Computer Science, vol. 4951. Springer, Heidelberg (2008)
10. Tiryaki, A.M., Öztuna, S., Dikenelli, O., Erdur, R.C.: SUNIT: a unit testing framework for test driven development of multi-agent systems. In: Padgham, L., Zambonelli, F. (eds.) Agent-Oriented Software Engineering VII. AOSE 2006. Lecture Notes in Computer Science, vol. 4405. Springer, Heidelberg (2007)
11. Fleischmann, A., Schmidt, W., Stary, C., Obermeier, S., Börger, E.: Subject-Oriented Business Process Management. Springer, Berlin (2012)
12. Jennings, N.R., Sycara, K., Wooldridge, M.: A roadmap of agent research and development. Auton. Agent. Multi-Agent Syst. **1**, 7–38 (1998)
13. Rao, A.S., Georgeff, M.P.: Modeling rational agents within a BDI-architecture. In: Allen, J., Fikes, R., Sandewall, E. (eds.) Proceedings of Knowledge Representation 91 (KR- 91), pp. 473–484. Morgan Kaufmann (1991)
14. Evertz, R., Thangarajah, J., Ly, T.: Practical Modelling of Dynamic Decision Making. Springer, Cham (2019)
15. Spanoudakis, N.I.: Engineering multi-agent systems with statecharts: theory and practice. SN Comput. Sci. **2**, 317 (2021)
16. DeLoach, S.A., Wood, M.F., Sparkman, C.H.: Multiagent systems engineering. Int. J. Softw. Eng. Knowl. Eng. **11**(3), 231–258 (2001)
17. Endert, H., Küster, T., Hirsch, B., Albayrak, S.: Mapping BPMN to agents: an analysis. In: Baldoni, M., Baroglio, C., Mascardi, V. (eds.) Agent, Web Services, and Ontologies Integrated Methodologies, pp. 43–58 (2007)
18. Ferber, J., Gutknecht, O., Michel, F.: From agents to organizations: an organizational view of multi-agent systems. In: Giorgini, P., Müller, J.P., Odell, J. (eds.) Agent-Oriented Software Engineering IV, LNCS 2935, pp. 214–230. Springer, Heidelberg (2004)
19. Cohen, P.R., Levesque, H.J.: Teamwork. Nous **25**(4), 487–512 (1991)
20. Poslad, S.: Specifying protocols for multi-agent systems interaction. ACM Trans. Auton. Adapt. Syst. **2**(4), 15 (2007)
21. Odell, J.J., Parunak, H.V.D., Fleischer, M.: The role of roles in designing effective agent organizations. Software Engineering for Large-Scale Multi-Agent Systems, LNCS, vol. 2603, pp. 27–38. Springer, Heidelberg(2003)
22. Wooldridge, M., Jennings, N., Kinny, D.: The Gaia methodology for agent-oriented analysis and design. J. Auton. Agents Multi-Agent Syst. **3**(3), 285–312 (2000)
23. Bresciani, P., Perini, A., Giorgini, P., et al.: Tropos: an agent-oriented software development methodology. Auton. Agent. Multi-Agent Syst. **8**, 203–236 (2004)
24. Padgham, L., Winikoff, M.: Developing Intelligent Agent Systems: A Practical Guide. John Wiley and Sons, Chichester (2004)

25. Cossentino, M., Sabatucci, L.: Agent system implementation. In: Paolucci, M., Sacile, R. (eds.) Agent-Based Manufacturing and Control Systems: New Agile Manufacturing Solutions for Achieving Peak Performance, pp. 153–192. CRC Press, Boca Raton (2005)
26. Chella, A., Cossentino, M., Sabatucci, L., Seidita, V.: Agile PASSI: an agile process for designing agents. Int. J. Comput. Syst. Sci. Eng. **2**, 133–144 (2006)
27. Cernuzzi, L., Cossentino, M., Zambonelli, F.: Process models for agent-based development. Eng. Appl. Artif. Intell. **18**(2), 205–222 (2005)
28. Fleischmann, A., Kannengiesser, U., Schmidt, W., Stary, C.: Subject-oriented modeling and execution of multi-agent business processes. In: 2013 IEEE/WIC/ACM International Conferences on Web Intelligence (WI) and Intelligent Agent Technology (IAT), Atlanta, GA, pp. 138–145 (2013)
29. Milner, R.: Communicating and Mobile Systems: The Pi-Calculus. Cambridge University Press, Cambridge (1999)
30. Hoare, C.A.R.: Communicating sequential processes. Commun. ACM **21**(8), 666–677 (1978)
31. Börger, E., Stärk, R.: Abstract State Machines: A Method for High-Level System Design and Analysis. Springer, Berlin (2003)
32. Moattar, H., Bandara, W., Kannengiesser, U., Rosemann, M.: Control flow versus communication: comparing two approaches to process modelling. Bus. Process. Manag. J. **28**(2), 372–397 (2022)
33. Neubauer, M., Stary, C.: S-BPM in the Production Industry: A Stakeholder Approach. Springer, Berlin (2017)
34. Moser, C., Kannengiesser, U., Elstermann, M.: Examining the PASS approach to process modelling for digitalised manufacturing: results from three industry case studies. Enterp. Model. Inf. Syst. Arch. J. **17**(1), 1:1–24 (2022)
35. Moser, C., Kannengiesser, U.: Incremental implementation of automated guided vehicle-based logistics using S-BPM: experience report of a digitalization project at ENGEL Austria. In: S-BPM ONE, pp. 3:1–3:6. ACM (2019)
36. Silver, B.: BPMN Method & Style, with Implementer's Guide, 2nd edn. Cody-Cassidy Press, Aptos (2011)
37. Schoissengeier, T.: Using Business Process Modelling for Developing Agent Systems. Master Thesis, Johannes Kepler University. Linz, Austria (2024)
38. Kannengiesser, U., Wegmann, A.: Three stances in enterprise system design. In: Elstermann, M., Lederer, M. (eds.) Subject-Oriented Business Process Management. Models for Designing Digital Transformations. S-BPM ONE 2024. Communications in Computer and Information Science, vol. 2206, pp. 279–298. Springer, Cham (2025)
39. Gero, J.S., Kannengiesser, U.: The situated function-behaviour-structure framework. Des. Stud. **25**(4), 373–391 (2004)
40. Kannengiesser, U., Stary, C., Heininger, R., Jost, T.: Behaviour-entred design of IoT systems. In: Fortino, G., Mecella, M. (eds.) Internet of Things Meets Business Process Management: A Synergistic Integration. Springer Nature Switzerland AG (2025)

An Analysis and Tool for Converting PASS to BPMM for Execution

Matthes Elstermann(✉)

Institute for Information Systems, University of Münster, Münster, Germany
matthes.elstermann@uni-muenster.de

Abstract. Process modeling with the PASS language is, due to its stringent adherence to the paradigm of subject-orientation, a potentially advantageous alternative to today's predominantly activity-oriented process modeling approaches. Despite its potential benefits, PASS has faced adoption challenges, one being the limited availability of workflow engines. This work explores the possibilities and limitations of converting PASS models into executable BPMN models with matching execution semantics. This approach allows organizations to leverage the advantages of PASS while benefiting from BPMN's well-established ecosystem and industry-proven workflow engines. A systematic analysis and comparison of the two languages reveals significant insights into their fundamental conceptual and structural differences. The development of conversion rules demonstrates that while a substantial portion of the PASS standard can be effectively translated, certain elements and semantic nuances remain difficult to reproduce. Notably, the precise execution semantics of End States, Input Pools, and specific behavioral constructs of Guard Behaviors cannot be fully replicated using standard BPMN constructs. To facilitate this, a prototype tool was developed based on the theoretical conversion rules, enabling the automatic transformation of PASS models into BPMN.

Keywords: Subject-Orientation · PASS · Object-Orientation · BPMN · Workflow Execution

1 Introduction

The modeling paradigm of subject-orientation is an approach to process modeling, which positions active entities at the center of attention [13]. It requires the explicit and continuous consideration and differentiation of active entities (subjects) and passive elements (objects), while tasks can only be described in the context of a subject [5]. The interaction between subjects is particularly important and must be explicitly defined as an exchange of information that cannot be omitted. The Parallel Activity Specification Schema (PASS), originally proposed by [12], is a process modeling language that adheres to this subject-oriented paradigm. It consists of only a select few elements for modeling processes without compromising expressive power, as shown in [9] and with possible modeling advantages [16,19] over the current de-facto standard, that being the Business Process Model and Notation (BPMN) in its current 2.0 incarnation.

With its extensive repertoire of over 160 elements, BPMN is one of the most expressive and powerful languages available and supported by a vast ecosystem of tools [11,20,22]. However, and in contrast to PASS, this expansive set of elements also introduces significant complexity and a steep learning curve. Research by [17] reveals that only a small subset of BPMN's available elements is actually used in practice. More concerning, [21] found that a staggering 81% of 172 analyzed BPMN-based business process models contained syntactic or control-flow-related errors. Furthermore, [1] highlights additional issues with BPMN, including numerous ambiguities in the descriptions and under-specifications of semantically relevant concepts.

Despite its potential benefits, PASS remains significantly less popular than BPMN and struggles with broader adoption. A primary factor limiting PASS adoption appears to be the scarcity of available tooling and workflow engines. In fact, the most notable workflow engine for PASS, the *Flow* module from the Metasonic Suite [15], has been discontinued and seems to be no longer available. Currently available alternatives [14,25] remain rudimentary and/or experimental and thus fall short for professional applications. For organizations seeking to leverage process models for workflow automation or technical integration, this presents a substantial obstacle, as modern businesses often rely on these tools to efficiently manage and streamline their processes. Consequently, the lack of workflow engines for PASS likely deters organizations from adopting this otherwise promising approach.

Therefore, the goal of this work is to explore the possibilities and limitations of converting subject-oriented PASS models into more widely supported and executable BPMN models. Consequently, the investigated research question is which parts of PASS can be translated into BPMN while preserving as much of the execution semantics of PASS as possible during this conversion, and if not completely, how much can be transferred? To facilitate this, methodological wise a prototype tool was developed that is capable of automatically converting PASS models in the official PASS OWL exchange standard [2][1] into the official BPMN XML exchange standard (as defined in the BPMN specification [18])[2], allowing organizations to model their processes in PASS and deploy them to BPMN-based execution environments.

2 Related Work

The topic of converting PASS to BPMN is not a new one, but only a limited number of relevant works exist, which are all covered here. Notably, [24] explored

---

[1] Supported by the execution semantics of PASS from [6] since the original execution semantic specifications [3] is incomplete in regards to the current model standard.

[2] Note that there is no direct formal specification of the execution semantics of BPMN and this work is based on interpretation and experience with the interpreter behavior of the Signavio BPMN engine.

mapping possibilities in 2012 when BPMN's proliferation and its establishment as an industry standard became evident. The primary objective of his work was to mitigate vendor lock-in for PASS customers. A key focus of [24]'s study was to minimize information loss during language translation while preserving the descriptive content of process models. The translation of executable models was not within the scope of [24]'s work, though it was identified as a subject for future research. A further limitation of [24]'s approach is that it was based on the PASS implementation of the Metasonic Suite [15], which supports only a subset of the current PASS standard [2]. Consequently, [24]'s work is limited to converting only the most basic model elements. More advanced elements and concepts, including *Macro Behaviors*, *Guard Behaviors*, *State References*, *Return to Origin* links, *User Cancel Transitions*, *Time Transitions*, and *Sending Failed Transitions*, which are all part of the PASS standard, were not addressed. [24] also developed a prototype capable of performing the conversion, albeit with the aforementioned limitations. However, the program and its source code were not publicly available, preventing further evaluation. Furthermore, the conversion naturally relied on Metasonic's proprietary exchange format for PASS models, as the official OWL exchange standard had not yet been established.

More recently, [23] published a study building on the findings of [24]. [23] developed a more advanced conversion tool claimed to be capable of retaining the execution semantics of PASS models. Unfortunately, the details of the conversion process are not included in the publication; instead, they are part of an unpublished master's thesis. Furthermore, the developed tool and its source code are also not publicly available. However, based on the limited information provided in the paper, certain conversions, such as those related to Start States, do not appear to accurately replicate the expected execution semantics of PASS. Moreover, like [24]'s work, [23]'s approach is also based on the PASS implementation of the Metasonic Suite. Consequently, [23]'s research remains limited to the same subset of the PASS standard and to the same proprietary exchange format. Therefore, further research is still required to achieve a comprehensive conversion of the complete PASS standard into BPMN.

Additionally, more loosely related research provides insights into converting PASS to BPMN. [19] presents a holistic comparison of the structure and concepts of PASS and BPMN through a production use case. The study highlights several advantages of PASS, including its ability to improve the comprehension of complex models and enable simpler, faster modeling. [4] explores the feasibility of converting PASS to Petri nets, demonstrating that PASS semantics cannot be fully translated into simple Place/Transition Petri nets, leaving only indirect and assumptive statements about the feasibility of precisely converting execution semantics from PASS to BPMN.

In the other direction of trying to convert BPMN diagrams to PASS, there have also been efforts, especially recently [26]. However, those are not of direct relevance here.

3 Notes on PASS and BPMN

Due to the limitations of this work, fundamental knowledge about the structure and elements of PASS [2,6] (SIDs, SBDs, Subjects, Messages, Do/Send/Receive States and their corresponding Transitions) as well as BPMN [18] (general constituency of BPMN activity diagrams, Activities, Gates, Events etc.) is in general necessary to understand this work.

However, there are a few aspects that should explicitly be discussed:

Multiple Behaviors in PASS: One of those aspects that has a large impact on its execution semantics is that a subject may have *more than one behavior*:

Macro Behaviors represent recurring patterns that can be *"called"* from any state in any SBD - theoretically even recursively. When such a *Macro Calling State* is reached, execution of the Macro Behavior takes precedence before the activity of the Macro State.

The second specialized behavior, the *Guard Behavior*, is designed to model the handling of interrupts. This mechanism is useful for handling urgent events that require immediate attention. When an incoming message specified in a Guard Behavior arrives, the execution of the currently active state is suspended, and the Guard Behavior is started.

Asynchronous Communication and Loose Coupling In PASS: PASS execution always is done under the assumption of an independent *Input Pool* that each subject instance possesses, where messages can be buffered and stored. All communication is therefore assumed to be asynchronous, in turn considering subjects as only *loosely coupled* as the default case. Synchronous communication, where the receiver must be in a corresponding receive state, can be enforced via input pool restrictions, but that is a specific case.

BPMN does not natively define an equivalent and, in general, assumes synchronous communication as the default case. Whether and how messages are buffered in an asynchronous case is an implementation detail left to the BPMN engine. While some BPMN engines support this mechanism, the BPMN specification does not define this as a standardized concept.

Flow and Tokens in BPMN: While there are multiple diagram types in BPMN, what is being executed in BPMN are the *process diagrams* that have an internal *sequence flow*. Sequence Flows establish connections between *Flow Nodes*. Each Sequence Flow has a single source and target, indicating the traversal of *tokens*. A token is a theoretical execution concept used throughout the BPMN specification to aid the definition of execution semantics and process behavior. It is not a model element but serves as an indicator of the current point(s) of execution, similar to tokens in Petri-Nets.

Diagrams vs. Models. The general structure of the PASS process model always has a clear separation between communication (SID) and internal execution of Subjects (SBD) that together represent the overall process model and are never considered to be separate.

Within the BPMN standard [18], there are three different primary types of diagrams: *Collaboration Diagrams*, *Choreography Diagrams*, and the actual core of BPMN, the *Process or Activity Diagrams*.

BPMN models CAN—but are not required to—assume a similar structure as PASS. A BPMN model CAN BE considered to *"contain"* Collaboration Diagrams, which in turn *contain Process Diagrams*. Unlike PASS, BPMN Collaboration Diagrams and Process Diagrams can exist independently. Note, however, that there is never a formal link between diagrams required by the language itself. It is up to the modeler to keep consistency between the two diagrams if they are concerned with the same process system.

A process diagram that models an organization's workflow does not need to be explicitly associated with a Participant in a Collaboration Diagram. This distinction highlights BPMN's activity- or control-flow-oriented approach, where execution is rooted *in Process Diagrams* rather than the overarching BPMN model. Consequently, collaboration diagrams and participants are also not part of BPMN execution semantics. Instead, communication between different "processes"[3] is managed using correlation information within the messaging system.

Although Collaboration Diagrams are not strictly necessary for converting executable PASS models to BPMN, as they do not influence execution semantics, they still provide significant structural and visual value. They consolidate individual Process Diagrams into a unified model, enabling a more faithful conversion of a PASS model into a single BPMN model. Without this consolidation, each PASS Subject would require a separate BPMN model, fragmenting the representation. By incorporating Collaboration Diagrams, the conversion process maintains coherence, covering both the transformation of SID into Collaboration Diagrams and SBD into Process Diagrams within a single BPMN model.

4 Considering Conversion

As explained in Sect. 1, the goal is not merely to transform a PASS process model into BPMN for descriptive or illustrative purposes, but to faithfully replicate its execution semantics.

Ensuring this level of accuracy may lead to conversion rules that appear overly complex, potentially reducing the readability and information transmission capabilities of the resulting BPMN model. However, such complexity is often necessary to preserve the precise execution semantics. Despite this, efforts are made to balance execution accuracy with clear and practical model representation wherever possible.

---

[3] Note that usually this formulation is also BPMN specific, where "a process" is considered to be something active that can communicate...which is not the logic of PASS/SO.

4.1 Subject Interaction Diagram

The conversion of SID is relatively straightforward, as BPMN provides similar concepts and elements. Each *Subject* is converted to a *Participant* - A *Fully Specified Subject* into a standard Participant that "includes a process", while an *Interface Subject* is transformed into a black box Participant without an internal process. If a Subject is classified as a *Multi-Subject*, its corresponding Participant is denoted as a *Multi-Instance Participant*, and the Maximum Subject Instance Restriction property is mapped to the Participant Multiplicity property. *Message Exchanges*, which define communication between Subjects, are converted into *Message Flows*.

Note that BPMN typically combines the Collaboration and Process views into a unified diagram, where *Message Flows* can also directly attach to specific process flow elements, such as tasks or events responsible for sending or receiving messages. This could be possible for standard Participants (Fully Specified Subjects) with an internal process. However, such a direct connection can only be generated if, for each message defined in the SID, there are singular send and receive states in the SBDs of the sender and receiver. Otherwise, if there are multiple states where the same message could be sent or received (which is perfectly normal in PASS, especially across multiple behaviors), a correct matching can not be guaranteed (Fig. 1).

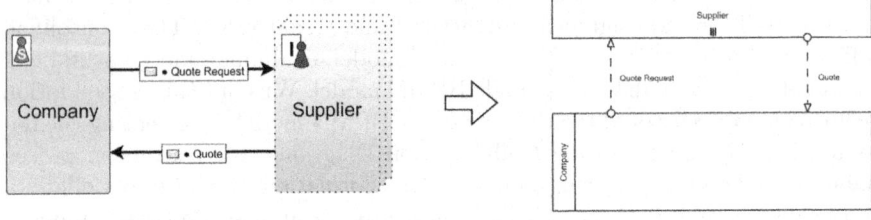

Fig. 1. Conversion of a Subject Interaction Diagram to a Collaboration Diagram.

4.2 Subject Behavior Diagram Conversion

Differences Between State and Task: SBDs consist of two primary elements requiring conversion: *States* and *Transitions*. Initially, mapping *States* to *Tasks* and *Transitions* to *Sequence Flows* seems intuitive. Both *States* and *Tasks* represent the execution of work, while *Transitions* and *Sequence Flows* define the flow or traversal of the process. This straightforward but naive approach works well for simple *Base Behaviors* containing only the three standard state types, provided each state has at most one outgoing standard transition. However, this approach breaks down as soon as states have multiple outgoing transitions, due to subtle yet significant semantic differences between *States* and *Tasks*, as well as between *Transitions* and Sequence Flows.

In PASS, a transition defines an exit condition for the *State* it originates from. The transition can be followed if its condition evaluates to true. In BPMN, *Sequence Flows* may also contain conditions, but when attached to *Tasks* (or Activities in general), these conditions are evaluated *after* the preceding *Activity* has already finished. Thus, while *Transitions* in PASS define when a *State* is left and what happens next, Sequence Flows in BPMN only determine the flow after an *Activity* has finished executing. Furthermore, PASS differentiates between multiple types of *Transitions*, whereas BPMN uses a single generic Sequence Flow type.

These challenges that arise from these differences become evident, for example, when converting a Receive State to a Receive Task. While *being in a* Receive State, a subject is assumed to be continuously checking its message inbox. The Receive State itself is not tied to one specific message; rather, each outgoing Receive Transition defines a particular message that should be looked for and serves as the leave condition for the state (e.g., Message X is available). Once the condition is met, the transition is followed. In BPMN, however, a Receive Task behaves slightly differently. It defines a specific message that would be waited for and is only considered to be traversable if that message has arrived and is chosen to be taken out of the input pool. The outgoing Sequence Flow(s) are evaluated only after the Receive Task has already finished execution and thus are dissociated from the receipt of the message itself. As a result, a Receive State with multiple outgoing Receive Transitions requires multiple Receive Tasks to replicate the same behavior, whereas a Receive State with a single outgoing Receive Transition can be mapped directly to a single Receive Task.

This example highlights one of the many challenges in converting PASS elements to their BPMN counterparts. It also illustrates the interconnectedness of *States* and *Transitions* in PASS and the conceptual differences to BPMN. Since no universal conversion rule applies to all state-transition combinations, each must be addressed individually.

Do State and Do Transition: Do States can be loosely mapped to one of the non-message-related *Tasks* in BPMN. However, unlike BPMN, PASS does not explicitly distinguish between different types of work performed within a Do State. Thus, it is not possible to automatically determine the appropriate *Task* type for the conversion to BPMN. To reflect this unspecified nature, Do States are mapped to the *Generic Abstract Task*, which could be manually specified afterwards to ensure semantic and executional conformance.

The condition of a Do Transition typically represents the completion or outcome of the associated Do State. Conceptually, this corresponds to evaluating transitions after the state has completed execution, a behavior that, as previously discussed, aligns with that of Sequence Flows. Consequently, Do Transitions, along with their conditions, are directly converted to Sequence Flows. If a Do State has only one outgoing Do Transition, its leave condition generally denotes the completion of the state, allowing the corresponding Sequence Flow to be directly attached to the Abstract Task. When a Do State has multiple outgoing Do Transitions, the path taken depends on the outcome of the state.

This behavior resembles an *XOR* decision and can be effectively represented in BPMN using an *Exclusive Gateway* as a decision point, with each Do Transition mapped to a distinct outgoing Sequence Flow from the *Exclusive Gateway* (Fig. 2).

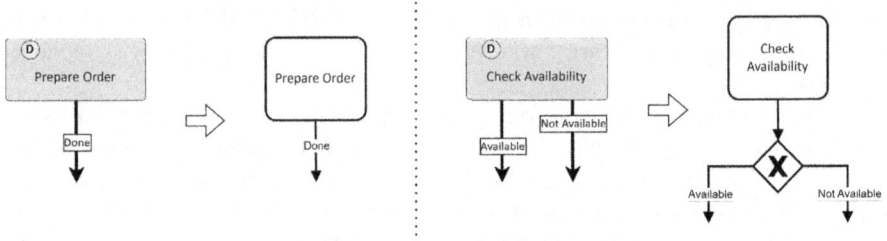

Fig. 2. Conversion of Do State with one (left) and multiple (right) outgoing transitions.

Send State and Send Transition: Send States and Send Transitions facilitate message transmission between Subjects. The Send State itself primarily handles message preparation, while the actual sending occurs in the moment that the Send Transition is taken (e.g., the condition message has been sent turns true). Because a Send Task in BPMN inherently includes both message preparation and sending – and only completes once the message has been dispatched – it serves as a natural counterpart for a Send State. A single Send Task is sufficient to represent the expected behavior without the need for gateways.

Note that the conversion of Send States/Transitions with a sending type other than *"Send Type Standard"* (e.g., multi-send to a new subject instance) could not be covered within this but could be explored in future research.

Receive State and Receive Transition: Analogous to the conversion of a Send State with one Send Transition, a Receive State with a single Receive Transition can simply be converted into a single Receive Task.

As mentioned in the introduction to this section, the challenge arises when a Receive State has multiple outgoing Receive Transitions, each corresponding to a different message. Since a Receive Task in BPMN can only wait for a single, pre-defined message, each Receive Transition must be mapped to a separate Receive Task. To replicate the race condition between these Transitions, an (exclusive) *Event-Based Gateway* is placed *before* the multiple Receive Tasks, allowing the process flow to proceed based on whichever message arrives first.

Again, conversion of different *Receive Types* other than *"Receive Type Standard"* is to be addressed by future research.

User Cancel Transition: A *User Cancel Transition* provides a mechanism to exit an active *State* arbitrarily, redirecting the process flow accordingly. In BPMN, *Conditional Events* can replicate the same behavior by using a condition to trigger the cancellation (Fig. 3).

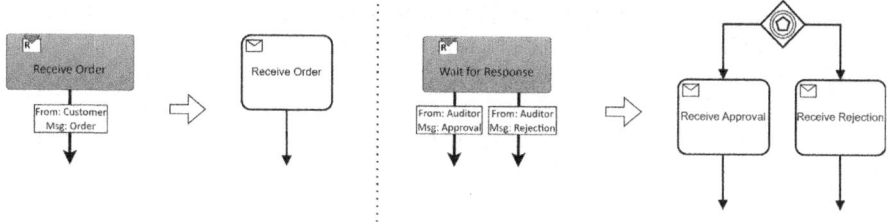

Fig. 3. Conversion of Receive State with one (left) and multiple (right) transitions.

For a User Cancel Transition originating from a Do State or Send State, a *Conditional Boundary Event* is attached to the corresponding BPMN Task – either an Abstract Task or a Send Task. As long as the Task remains active (e.g., the work is not yet completed or the message has not been sent), the Conditional Boundary Event can be triggered by the cancellation condition, redirecting the execution flow. To accurately reflect the behavior of User Cancel Transitions in PASS, the Boundary Event must be interrupting, ensuring the Task is canceled and preventing any other Sequence Flows from being taken.

A similar approach can be applied to Receive States, but with one key difference. Since a Receive State with multiple outgoing Receive Transitions is converted into multiple Receive Tasks, each corresponding to a specific message, there is no single task to which a Conditional Event can be attached. However, because the conversion of Receive States and Transitions already employs an Event-Based Gateway to handle different incoming messages, the Conditional Event can be seamlessly integrated as an additional option at the gateway. Since the exclusive Event-Based Gateway functions as an event-driven XOR, triggering the Conditional Event prevents any other paths from being taken, ensuring the expected PASS behavior is accurately preserved (Fig. 4).

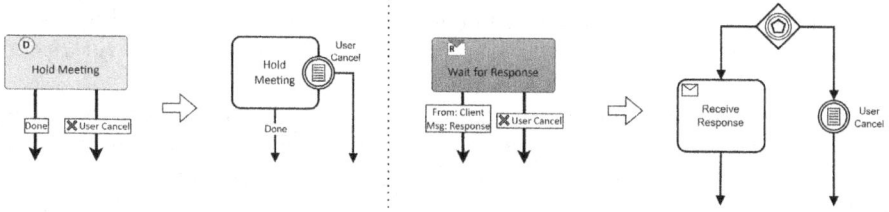

Fig. 4. Conversion of User Cancel Transition originating from Do/Send and Receive

Time Transitions: The conversion of *TimeOut Transitions* follows a similar approach to that of User Cancel Transitions. However, instead of a conditional event, a *Timer Event* is used, as the transition's condition is based on a time-constraint rather than an arbitrary user decision. A *Timer Event* can be configured to activate after a specific duration, at a fixed date-time, or at recurring points in time, making it well-suited to handle both types of Time Transitions – Timer Transitions and Reminder Transitions.

According to the PASS standard, TimeOut Transitions should not be attached to Send States, as timeout considerations are handled with the Sending Failed transition. While converting them would be technically feasible, it is unnecessary and therefore omitted (Fig. 5).

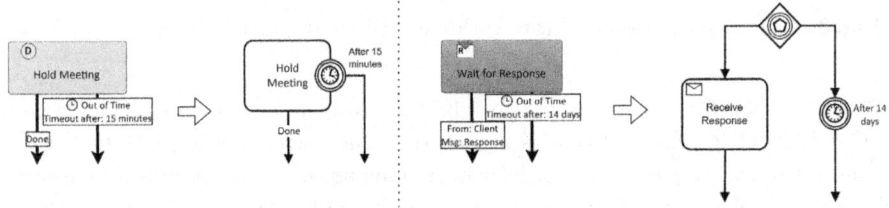

Fig. 5. Conversion of a Time Transition originating from a Do (or Send) State (left) and from a Receive State (right).

Note that the consideration of *Reminder Transition* is left to future research

Sending Failed Transitions. A Sending Failed Transition defines how the process should respond when a message cannot be successfully sent (within a defined timeout time). This situation resembles an error or exception that may be handled appropriately. BPMN provides two types of events suited for such cases: *Error Events* and *Escalation Events*. Both propagate upward from the (Sub-) Process in which they are thrown and can be handled using corresponding catching events.

Semantically, *Error Events* are designed for handling critical failures and always interrupt the process, whereas *Escalation Events* (by default) are non-interrupting and typically indicate non-critical concerns, including regular communication. Since message sending failures are unexpected and should not occur frequently, treating them as critical errors is appropriate, making *Error Events* the preferred choice.

Following the same approach as User Cancel Transitions and TimeOut Transitions, the *Error Event* is attached to the corresponding Send Task as a *Boundary Event*. If a message fails to be sent, a *Error Event* is expected to be thrown within the Send Task, propagating upward and triggering the Boundary Event. Since Sending Failed Transitions can only originate from Send States, alternative configurations with other States do not need to be considered.

Start States: In PASS, a State can be defined as a *Start State*, marking the entry point of an SBD. Each SBD should have exactly one Start State. The activation of a Start State depends on its type. Subjects with a Do Start States and Send Start States are automatically activated when the process is initialized. A Receive Start State, on the other hand, implies that a Subject is only instantiated when the first relevant message is received (Fig. 6).

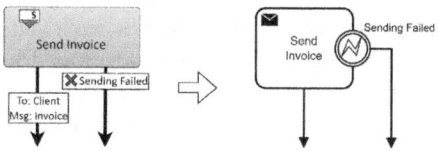

Fig. 6. Conversion of a Sending Failed Transition originating from a Send State.

In BPMN, Start Events generally initiate processes[4]. When a Start Event occurs, a new process instance is created, and execution begins at the Start Event. The trigger for the Start Event depends on the type of Start Event. BPMN also provides a *None Start Event*, which is triggered when the process is instantiated externally.

Since Do Start States and Send Start States in PASS activate automatically upon initialization of their SBD, a BPMN *None Start Event* might seem like a natural equivalent, as it automatically occurs once the process is instantiated. This is also the approach suggested by [24], who refers to it as an active start. However, this conversion does not fully capture PASS's initialization behavior. In PASS, when a model is instantiated, all Start States across all relevant Subjects are initialized at once. In BPMN, however, Processes exist independently and must be instantiated separately. To simulate the behavior of PASS, a user or the BPMN engine would need to manually instantiate all relevant Processes simultaneously, which is impractical. To address this, *Signal Start Events* are proposed as a replacement for None Start Events. All relevant Processes listen for the same signal, ensuring that when that signal is published, they are instantiated and started simultaneously. The Do State or Send State is converted as usual and placed directly after the Signal Start Event. This approach embeds the responsibility of joint initialization into the BPMN model itself, improving transparency and ensuring that execution aligns with that of PASS.

For Receive Start States, on the other hand, a Message Start Event initially appears to be an appropriate replacement since both cause their behavior or process to be initialized upon receipt of a relevant message. This is also the conversion suggested by [24], who calls it a passive start. However, this approach introduces several issues: In PASS, a Receive Start State only initializes the Subject upon receiving the first message. For subsequent messages, it functions as a normal Receive State. In BPMN, however, a Message Start Event typically instantiates a new process instance for every received message or creates a new token in the existing instance[5]. Another issue is that this approach

---

[4] Start Events are the primary mechanism for initiating Processes, but alternative elements and methods exist.

[5] In BPMN, the handling of a Message Start Event receiving multiple messages with identical correlation information is ambiguous and not explicitly defined in the BPMN specification. Depending on the BPMN engine and version, different behaviors have been observed, including ignoring the Event, instantiating a new process instance, or generating a new token within an existing instance.

does not support the conversion of Start States with outgoing special Transitions since there is no Task or Event-Based Gateway to that the Event(s) of the special transition conversion can be attached. (Message) Start Events themselves cannot have incoming Sequence Flows, making it impossible to convert Receive Start States with incoming Transitions. To overcome these limitations, Receive Start States are converted similarly to Do Start States and Send Start States – by using a Signal Start Event. Instead of waiting for the arrival of the first message to initialize the process, it was instantiated and started from the beginning alongside all other process instances, using a Signal Start Event. The Receive Task is converted as usual and placed directly after the signal start event to handle incoming messages. While this approach separates process initialization from message reception and does not precisely mirror PASS behavior on a conceptual level, it accurately replicates its execution semantics. This approach ensures that subsequent messages are handled correctly, and it supports conversion of Receive Start States with incoming Sequence Flow as well as outgoing special Transitions, making it a more accurate and comprehensive solution.

As previously mentioned, this thesis focuses solely on the standard send and receive types. Other types that may lead to the instantiation of additional Multi-Subject instances are not covered here.

End States: When a Subject reaches an End State, it becomes eligible for termination. However, termination should only occur once all (Fully Specified) Subjects are in an End State and thus eligible for termination. Notably, an End State can be exited again if the Subject has not yet been terminated, continuing its execution and making it ineligible for termination again.

In BPMN, Processes typically conclude with End Events, which consume tokens upon their arrival. A process instance is terminated once all its tokens have been consumed. Unlike PASS, BPMN does not have a concept of eligibility for termination. Moreover, there is no overarching execution context that coordinates the joint termination of multiple process instances. Each process instance operates and terminates independently. Additionally, since End Events consume tokens immediately, they do not allow execution to continue again[6].

One possible solution is to prohibit End States from having outgoing Transitions. This would ensure that once a Subject reaches an End State, it remains there, effectively rendering it dead while awaiting termination. Semantically, this is equivalent to terminating the Subject immediately. With this restriction, End States in PASS would behave similarly to End Events in BPMN, even without explicit coordination of joint termination. However, this approach fails in the presence of Guard Behaviors, which can interrupt execution unexpectedly and redirect it to continue within their own behavior. Since End Events in BPMN immediately consume tokens, they can prematurely terminate the process, preventing any future interruptions that might have otherwise occurred. Because the timing and occurrence of such interruptions are unpredictable, accurately converting PASS's End State and termination logic using standard BPMN is not feasible. While non-standardized workarounds using Script Tasks could achieve

---

[6] Note that this does not affect the continued execution of any remaining tokens.

the desired behavior, they introduce significant complexity and, more importantly, necessitate BPMN engine-specific implementations.

The approach implemented by the converter tool simply appends an End Event to the converted End State and designate its Sequence Flow as the default, establishing it as the primary execution path. As explained, this does not faithfully capture the execution semantics of PASS, as it does not actually coordinate the joint termination of all Participants' Processes or account for future interrupts (Fig. 7).

Fig. 7. Simple Conversion of a Start State (left) and an End State (right).

4.3 Macro Behavior

Macro Behaviors are essentially reusable pieces of behavior. When a *Macro Calling State* is reached, the referenced *Macro Behavior* is invoked. Macro Behaviors should always conclude with a *Return to Origin state*, ensuring the continuation of execution at the Macro Calling State. Multiple approaches exist for converting Macro Behaviors to BPMN.

The most straightforward approach is to convert the Macro Behavior into an *Embedded Sub-Process* and insert it at every location in the base *process* where a macro call occurs. The elements within the Macro Behavior are converted as usual and placed inside the Sub-Process. A *Return to Origin state* is translated into a Sequence Flow connecting the Sub-Process to the Macro Calling State (or rather its BPMN conversion). From an execution perspective, this approach accurately replicates PASS's behavior. However, it defeats the fundamental purpose of consolidating recurring behavior into something reusable. Any modifications to the Macro Behavior would require updating every inserted Sub-Process.

Alternatively, BPMN offers an element that serves a similar purpose to PASS macros, allowing for the consolidation of reusable behavior: Call Activities. A Call Activity functions similarly to a normal Task, but instead of executing an atomic unit of work, it invokes and transfers control to a referenced process. Once the called process finishes, the calling process resumes execution. This approach closely replicates macro invocations of PASS with one key distinction: the process referenced by a Call Activity must be a global process, existing independently of the calling process and its participant. Consequently, the referenced process can be called from any process and is not confined to a particular Participant. However, this is only feasible for *Global Macros* and not **subject-specific Macros**.

A third approach, utilizing Event Sub-Processes, combines the advantages of the previous two methods. By converting a Macro Behavior into an Event Sub-Process, the embedded nature of the macro is preserved, maintaining access to the scope of the process while ensuring the reusability of a unified macro definition. The Event Sub-Process is triggered by an Escalation Event at the macro call location. The Escalation Event is caught by an Escalation Start Event within the Event Sub-Process, initiating its execution. The Start State inside the Macro Behavior is therefore converted as a normal, non-start State. Upon completion of the Event Sub-Process, execution must resume at the original call location. However, unlike Embedded Sub-Processes, Event Sub-Processes cannot have outgoing Sequence Flows, nor can Sequence Flows (or Link Events) cross process boundaries. The next most obvious alternative for continuing execution outside the Event Sub-Process is the use of Escalation Events. However, (Escalation) Boundary Events cannot be attached to Event Sub-Processes, also rendering this option unfeasible. Instead, throwing a Signal Event can be used to notify the parent process of the Event Sub-Process's completion. The signal is then caught by a catching Signal Event in the parent process, which resumes execution at the appropriate location. Importantly, the intermediate Signal Event must be active to catch the trigger. Therefore, the Escalation Start Event of the Event Sub-Process must be non-interruptible to prevent the cancellation of the catching Signal Event (Fig. 8).

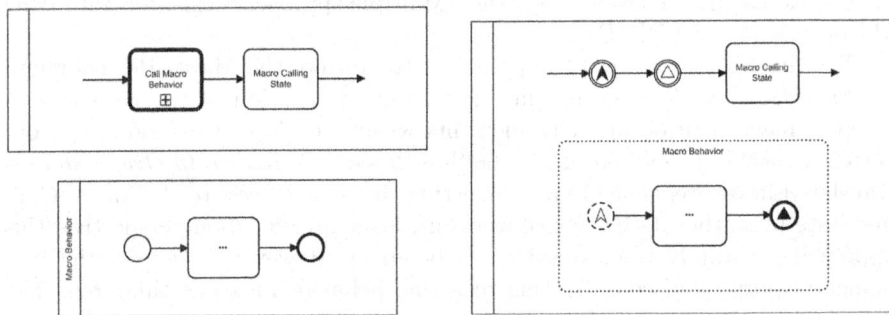

Fig. 8. Conversion of a Macro Behavior to a global process invoked via a Call Activity (left) and to an Event Sub-Process (right).

All proposed solutions present their own advantages, disadvantages, and intricate nuances that cannot be exhaustively discussed here. An inherent characteristic of all conversion approaches is separating the macro call from the Macro Calling State. While this distinction is generally correct for Send and Receive States, where a macro call introduces additional logic, it is often unnecessary for Do States, where the macro call typically serves as a replacement for the internal activity of the Do State. In such cases, converting the Do State itself becomes redundant, leading to an additional Abstract Task without a distinct purpose. However, since it cannot be determined whether the macro call fully replaces the Do State or merely supplements its functionality, this redundancy remains unavoidable.

The prototype tool implements the third approach, as it ensures the highest correctness in terms of execution semantics while retaining macro reusability.

4.4 Guard Behavior

Guard Behaviors allow Subjects to react to critical messages by interrupting their current execution to prioritize some other (more important) work. When a Guard Receive State (or more precisely, its outgoing Receive Transitions) in a Guard Behavior receives a relevant message, the Subject's ongoing execution is interrupted, and the Guard Behavior starts. A Guard Behavior can guard either a specific state or an entire behavior. As long as the guarded state or behavior remains active, an interrupt may occur.

Guarding of a Behavior. BPMN provides two mechanisms similar to Guard Behaviors: Boundary Events and Event Sub-Processes. For Guard Behaviors that guard an entire behavior, Event Sub-Processes serve as a suitable BPMN counterpart. For its conversion, a Guard Behavior is mapped to an Event Sub-Process placed inside the process it guards. The elements within the Guard Behavior are converted as usual and placed inside the Event Sub-Process. The Guard Receive State, however, requires a special conversion. Unlike a standard Receive State, receiving a message (denoted by the outgoing Receive Transitions) should trigger an interrupt and start the Event Sub-Process. Therefore, the outgoing Receive Transitions of the Guard Receive State must be converted into interrupting Message Start Events. When a relevant message arrives and triggers the corresponding Message Start Event, the parent process is interrupted, and the Event Sub-Process starts.

This conversion of the Guard Receive State aligns with the initial approach for converting Receive Start States. However, for normal Receive Start States, the approach was ultimately abandoned because it could not support states with incoming transition or special outgoing transitions[7]. This limitation is equally problematic for Guard Receive States. However, an alternative approach to the ultimately proposed conversion of normal Receive Start States is required, as interrupting Message Start Events must be used in this scenario to initiate the Event Sub-Process.

A different workaround is possible, considering the actual behavior of a Guard Receive State with incoming Transitions. When execution returns to the Guard

---

[7] Arguably, special transitions are not intended to be attached to Guard Receive States and generally serve no practical purpose, as Guard Receive States are typically not active in the conventional sense. However, in cases where a Guard Receive State is "reentered" and activated through an incoming transition – though this practice is itself questionable – the outgoing special transitions can still be executed.

Receive State through an incoming transition, the state becomes active and functions like a normal Receive State, meaning it can only be exited through an outgoing transition or another, higher-priority interrupt. To replicate this, the Guard Receive State is converted twice: Once, as already exaplained, as an interrupting Message Start Event, ensuring that the receipt of a relevant message triggers the Event Sub-Process and interrupts the parent process, and once as a standard Receive Task, which represents the Guard Receive State as a normal Receive State in case it is reentered. This dual conversion accounts for scenarios where the Guard Receive State is activated not by an external message but through an incoming transition. In such cases, the Proxy Receive State ensures that the execution can proceed as if the Guard Receive State were a standard Receive State, allowing Transitions to be followed as expected. All incoming Transitions of the Guard Receive State are converted as usual, but the corresponding Sequence Flows now target the Proxy Receive State rather than the Message Start Event. The outgoing Sequence Flows of the Proxy Receive State merge with the outgoing Sequence Flows of the corresponding Message Start Events. Special Transitions, which could not be handled in the original approach, are now supported through the Proxy Receive State. This approach preserves execution semantics by allowing reactivation of the Guard Receive State without interfering with the interrupt-driven behavior of the Event Sub-Process (Fig. 9).

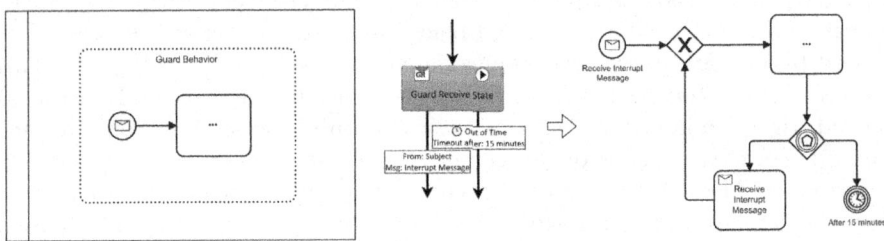

Fig. 9. Conversion of a Guard Behavior that guards a behavior to an Event Sub-Process (left) and conversion of a Guard Receive State with an incoming transition and outgoing Timer Transition (right).

Guard Behaviors, like Macro Behaviors, may also end in a *Return to Origin State*. However, the conversion of a *Return to Origin State* within a Guard Behavior necessitates a different approach. Macro calls occur at predefined, explicit locations, allowing for clear anticipation of where execution should resume after the Macro completes. As detailed in Sect. 4.3, various approaches can model this behavior, with the third approach even showing how execution can return to the parent process after completing an Event Sub-Process. This works because the return is predictable, allowing it to be handled via a catching Signal Intermediate Event.

In contrast, Guard Behaviors can be triggered at any point during the execution, making it impossible to know where execution should return to once the interrupt occurs, at model time. When the interrupt occurs, all active elements in the parent process are canceled, leaving no straightforward mechanism to resume execution at the same point. Most other apparent workarounds will be proven impossible as part of the State Reference conversion. The conversion of a Return to Origin state inside a Guard Behavior to native BPMN is therefore not considered possible.

To still achieve this conversion in a non-standardized way, the active element(s) of the parent process would have to be manually stored when an interrupt message arrives, but before the parent process is interrupted. Otherwise, the elements to be stored will have already been canceled by the interrupt. Once the Event Sub-Process (e.g., the Guard Behavior) finishes, the BPMN engine must be manually instructed to return to the previously active element(s) and continue execution from there. Figure 10 shows how this can be implemented using Script Tasks. It should be stressed that this is a non-standardized solution, as custom scripts are still required for the Script Tasks. The actual code and feasibility of this implementation depend on the specific BPMN engine. In the prototype implementation, the step of storing the currently active elements is omitted for simplicity, as the conversion is non-functional regardless.

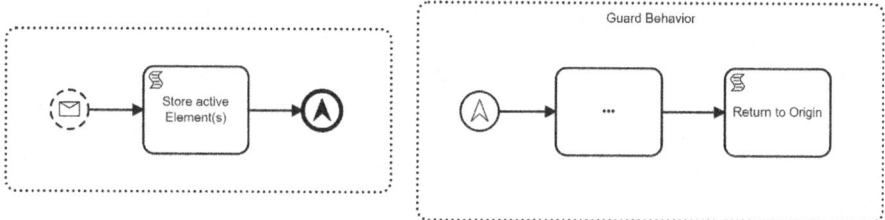

Fig. 10. Conversion of a Return to Origin State inside of a Guard Behavior.

In addition to the already discussed behavior-composing elements, Guard Behaviors may contain an additional type of State: State References. Conceptually, a State Reference functions as a pointer to another State - usually in the Base Behavior. In BPMN, this could typically be replicated by connecting the Sequence Flows corresponding to the incoming Transitions of the State Reference directly to the referenced State (or, more specifically, its equivalent conversion) or by using Link Events. However, if the referenced State is not part of the same Guard Behavior), the Sequence Flow or Link Events would have to cross the boundaries of the Event Sub-Process. Unfortunately, BPMN does not allow this type of cross-boundary sequence flow. Other potential solutions also fail for various reasons. For example, throwing and catching an event at the boundary of the Event Sub-Process to escape the Event Sub-Process is also not possible, as Event Sub-Processes cannot have Boundary Events. Another apparent solution is to use a Signal Event, as demonstrated in the third conversion approach for a Macro Behavior's Return to Origin. However, this also fails because the catching Signal Event is canceled when the interrupt occurs, preventing it from actually catching the signal. Other possible workarounds either fail due to similar limitations or introduce critical side effects, such as preventing process termination.

Escaping the Event Sub-Process upon completion of its work and continuing execution at a specific place within the same process instance is, not considered natively possible in standard BPMN. As a result, non-standardized scripts must be used to achieve the desired behavior. By converting the State Reference to a Script Task, the BPMN engine can be manually instructed to jump to a specific place, effectively replicating the State Reference from PASS (Fig. 11).

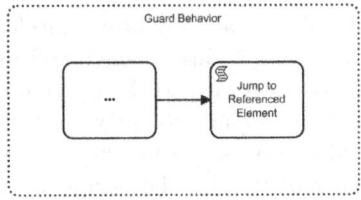

Fig. 11. Conversion of a State Reference.

Although the conversion of State References is not possible for Guard Behaviors converted into Event Sub-Processes, a potential workaround exists that avoids the use of Event Sub-Processes altogether. This is achieved by separately guarding each State of the guarded behavior, following the conversion rules for Guard Behaviors that guard a specific State, as detailed below. It should be noted that, while this approach preserves the execution semantics of PASS, it results in a highly convoluted model due to the need for duplicating the Guard Behavior conversion for every State in the guarded behavior. This significantly increases complexity and limits its usefulness beyond execution purposes. Due to time constraints, this conversion has not yet been verified or implemented in the prototype tool.

One key challenge between PASS's Guard Behaviors and the BPMN conversion remains: In PASS, behaviors are assigned a priority number, and an interrupt only occurs if the Guard Behavior has a higher priority than the currently active behavior. However, BPMN lacks a native mechanism for prioritizing interrupts in Event Sub-Processes or Boundary Events. As a result, when a Start Message Event occurs, it always triggers and interrupt and starts the Event Sub-Process, irrespective of its intended priority[8]. Unfortunately, there is no solution to this discrepancy that can be implemented within standard BPMN.

---

[8] For this reason, the outgoing Receive Transitions of the Guard Receive State can actually be ignored during the conversion to the Proxy Receive State. This is because the resulting Receive Tasks (and their Sequence Flows) are irrelevant, as they are waiting for the same message as the Message Start Events. When a relevant message is received, the Event Sub-Process will interrupt its existing instance, if one exists, deeming the Receive Tasks unnecessary. In the prototype implementation, the Receive Tasks are retained for clarity and comprehensibility, though their presence is not strictly necessary for the execution behavior.

Guarding of a State. As previously explained, Guard Behaviors may also guard a specific state rather than an entire behavior. This conversion follows a similar structure to that of Guard Behaviors that guard entire behaviors, with a few key differences. Instead of converting the Guard Behavior into an Event Sub-Process that guards its parent process, it is converted into an Embedded Sub-Process. Furthermore, rather than transforming the Guard Receive State and its outgoing Receive Transitions into Message Start Events for triggering the Event Sub-Process, they are converted into interrupting Message Boundary Events and attached to state conversion they are meant to guard (e g., to the corresponding Abstract Task for Do States or Send Task for Send States). If the guarded State is a Receive State, a Message Intermediate Catch Event is added after the Event-Based Gateway instead. The Message Boundary Event or Message Intermediate Event is then connected to the Embedded Sub-Process, initiating it upon receipt of an interrupt message. Again, like for the conversion of Guard Behaviors guarding entire behaviors, an additional Proxy Receive State is necessary to address the shortcomings resulting from this conversion. The implementation of the Proxy Receive State follows the method already described. One advantage of this conversion, which transforms the Guard Behavior into an Embedded Sub-Process instead of converting it into an Event Sub-Process (as done for guarding entire behaviors), is that State References can be converted to native BPMN. This eliminates the need for Script Tasks and is accomplished by using escalation events to direct the sequence flow to the referenced state (or its BPMN conversion, to be precise).

An alternative approach involves wrapping the guarded element(s) within an Embedded Sub-Process and applying the same conversion method used for guarding entire behaviors. This standardizes the conversion for both types of Guard Behaviors, ensuring consistency. However, this comes at the cost of once again losing native support for State References (Fig. 12).

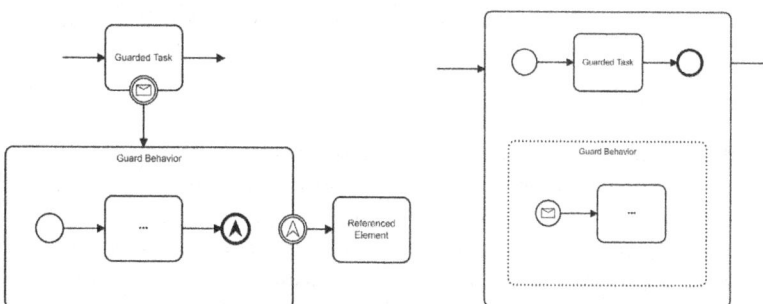

Fig. 12. Conversion of a Guard Behavior that guards a specific State and ends in a State Reference to an Embedded Sub-Process (left) and alternative conversion to an Event Sub-Process (right).

5 Validation/Proof of Concept

A prototype was developed to validate the theoretical conversion framework, demonstrating the practical feasibility of automatically transforming PASS models to BPMN, considering the aforementioned limitations. The tool was created in C# that is able to generate a valid BPMN model in the official OMG-XML standard based on PASS models in the official PASS OWL standard [8] using the alps.net.api [7]. It is available at:

https://github.com/pass-bpmn-converter/pass-bpmn-converter

6 Conclusion

This work investigated the feasibility and limitations of converting subject-oriented PASS models into BPMN, with a focus on preserving execution semantics. The motivation for this research stemmed from the limited availability of workflow engines for PASS, which hampers its adoption despite its potential advantages, as well as the scientific need to gain a detailed understanding of the structural and semantic differences between the two languages.

Although a direct, one-to-one mapping is often unfeasible due to fundamental differences between PASS's subject-oriented paradigm and BPMN's activity-oriented approach, as well as conceptual disparities between their elements, a substantial portion of the PASS standard can still be effectively converted to BPMN. However, certain aspects of PASS remain challenging or impossible to reproduce in BPMN. Specifically, the precise execution semantics of End States and process termination cannot be faithfully represented in BPMN. Furthermore, BPMN lacks a direct counterpart for the *Input Pool* concept present in PASS. The conversion of *Guard Behaviors* also presents difficulties, as *Return to Origin states* and *State References* cannot always be implemented using standard BPMN constructs, requiring non-standardized workarounds such as Script Tasks. Additionally, BPMN does not support behavior prioritization.

6.1 Limitations

Despite the contributions of this research, several limitations must be acknowledged. First, the conversion rules and the prototype tool do not yet cover the entire PASS standard. Certain concepts and elements, including the *Choice Segment*, non-standard *Send and Receive Types*, and Data Objects, remain to be addressed by future research. Also, implementing adapters for specific BPMN engines would enable immediate execution capabilities for converting *State References* and *Return to Origin states* within *Guard Behaviors*. Third, while this work deliberately focused on standard PASS, more advanced extensions, such as Abstract Layered PASS [10], were not covered and offer further potential for future research.

References

1. Börger, E.: Approaches to modeling business processes: a critical analysis of BPMN, workflow patterns and yawl. Softw. Syst. Model. **11**(3), 305–318 (2012)
2. Börger, E., et al.: Pass standard book (2021). https://github.com/I2PM/PASS-Standard-Book-Tex-Project
3. Börger, E.: A subject-oriented interpreter model for S-BPM. In: Fleischmann, A., Schmidt, W., Stary, C., Obermeier, S., Börger, E. (eds.) Subjektorientiertes Prozessmanagement, chap. Appendix. Hanser-Verlag, München (2011)
4. Elstermann, M.: Mapping PASS graphs to petri-nets: possibilities and limits for converting PASS graphs to petri-nets. In: Fischer, H., Schneeberger, J. (eds.) S-BPM ONE 2013. CCIS, vol. 360, pp. 91–106. Springer, Heidelberg (2013). https://doi.org/10.1007/978-3-642-36754-0_6
5. Elstermann, M.: Executing Strategic Product Planning - A Subject-Oriented Analysis and New Referential Process Model for IT-Tool Support and Agile Execution of Strategic Product Planning. KIT Scientific Publishing, Karlsruhe (2020). https://doi.org/10.5445/KSP/1000097859
6. Elstermann, M.: Proposal for a recursive interpreter specification for PASS in PASS. In: Elstermann, M., Dittmar, A., Lederer, M. (eds.) S-BPM ONE 2023. CCIS, vol. 1867, pp. 187–201. Springer, Cham (2023). https://doi.org/10.1007/978-3-031-40213-5_14
7. Elstermann, M., Gnad, L.: An im- and export library for the subject-oriented exchange standard. In: Elstermann, M., Betz, S., Lederer, M. (eds.) S-BPM ONE 2022. CCIS, vol. 1632, pp. 23–40. Springer, Cham (2022)https://doi.org/10.1007/978-3-031-19704-8_2
8. Elstermann, M., Krenn, F.: The semantic exchange standard for subject-oriented process models. In: Proceedings of the 10th International Conference on Subject-Oriented Business Process Management, pp. 1–8. ACM, Linz (2018). https://doi.org/10.1145/3178248.3178257
9. Elstermann, M., Kuhn, S.: Subject-oriented modeling workflow control patterns with pass. In: Elstermann, M., Lederer, M. (eds) S-BPM ONE 2024. CCIS, vol. 2206. pp. 145–152. Springer, Cham (2025). https://doi.org/10.1007/978-3-031-72041-3_9
10. Elstermann, M., Ovtcharova, J.: Revisiting the ALPS - an investigation of abstract layered pass. In: Elstermann, M., Dittmar, A., Lederer, M. (eds.) S-BPM ONE 2023. CCIS, vol. 1867, pp. 263–283. Springer, Cham (2023). https://doi.org/10.1007/978-3-031-40213-5_19
11. Farshidi, S., Kwantes, I.B., Jansen, S.: Business process modeling language selection for research modelers. Softw. Syst. Model. **23**(1), 137–162 (2024)
12. Fleischmann, A.: Distributed Systems: Software Design and Implementation. Springer, Heidelberg (1994).https://doi.org/10.1007/978-3-642-78612-9
13. Fleischmann, A., Schmidt, W., Stary, C., Obermeier, S., Börger, E.: Subject-Oriented Business Process Management. Springer, Heidelberg (2012). https://doi.org/10.1007/978-3-642-32392-8
14. I2PM: Python-pass-workflow-engine (2024). https://github.com/I2PM/Python-PASS-Workflow-Engine. Accessed 28 Apr 2025
15. Metasonic: Metasonic suite (2016). https://web.archive.org/web/20160513231557/https://www.metasonic.de/metasonic-suite
16. Moattar, H., Bandara, W., Kannengiesser, U., Rosemann, M.: Control flow versus communication: comparing two approaches to process modelling. Bus. Process. Manag. J. **28**(2), 372–397 (2022)

17. Muehlen, M., Recker, J.: How much language is enough? Theoretical and practical use of the business process modeling notation. In: Bubenko, J., Krogstie, J., Pastor, O., Pernici, B., Rolland, C., Sølvberg, A. (eds.) Seminal Contributions to Information Systems Engineering, pp. 429–443. Springer, Heidelberg (2013). https://doi.org/10.1007/978-3-642-36926-1_35
18. Object Management Group: Business process model and notation (BPMN) – version 2.0.2 (2014). https://www.omg.org/spec/BPMN
19. Piller, C.: Comparing BPMN 2.0 and pass: a review and analysis of previous research. In: Elstermann, M., Dittmar, A., Lederer, M. (eds.) S-BPM ONE 2023. CCIS, pp. 163–179. Springer, Cham (2023). https://doi.org/10.1007/978-3-031-40213-5_12
20. Recker, J., Rosemann, M., Indulska, M., Green, P.: Business process modeling- a comparative analysis. J. Assoc. Inf. Syst. **10**(04), 333–363 (2009). https://doi.org/10.17705/1jais.00193
21. Roy, S., Sajeev, A., Bihary, S., Ranjan, A.: An empirical study of error patterns in industrial business process models. IEEE Trans. Serv. Comput. **7**(2), 140–153 (2014). https://doi.org/10.1109/TSC.2013.10
22. Russell, N., ter Hofstede, A., van der Aalst, W., Mulyar, N.: Workflow control-flow patterns: a revised view. BPM reports, BPMcenter. org (2006)
23. Schulz, C.: S-BPM as an alternative to BPMN in the context of low-code: applicability, user experience and transformation from S-BPM to BPMN. In: Elstermann, M., Lederer, M. (eds.) S-BPM ONE 2024. CCIS, vol. 2206, pp. 160–169. Springer, Cham (2025). https://doi.org/10.1007/978-3-031-72041-3_11
24. Sneed, S.: Mapping possibilities of S-BPM and BPMN 2.0. In: Oppl, S., Fleischmann, A. (eds.) S-BPM ONE 2012. CCIS, vol. 284, pp. 91–105. Springer, Heidelberg (2012). https://doi.org/10.1007/978-3-642-29294-1_7
25. Wolski, A., Borgert, S., Heuser, L.: A CoreASM based reference implementation for subject-oriented business process management execution semantics. In: Proceedings of the 11th International Conference on Subject-Oriented Business Process Management, S-BPM ONE 2019. Association for Computing Machinery, New York (2019). https://doi.org/10.1145/3329007.3329018
26. Zeisler, G., Braunauer, T., Fleischmann, A., Singer, R.: Pass as an intermediary for BPMN execution: a feasibility study. Int. J. Bus. Process Integr. Manage. **15**(2), 123–137 (2024). https://arxiv.org/html/2406.12302v1

Design Science Research Approach to Minimal Viable Product Validation Using PASS Diagrams

Sleiman El Bobbou[1(✉)], John Geiger[2], Jakob Bönsch[2], and Jivka Ovtcharova[1,2]

[1] Institut für Informationsmanagement im Ingenieurwesen (IMI), Karlsruhe Institute for Technology (KIT), Kaiserstraße 12, 76131 Karlsruhe, Germany
sleiman.bobbou@kit.edu
[2] GFT Software Solutions GmbH, Reichenaustraße 39a, 78467 Konstanz, Germany
https://www.imi.kit.edu/, https://www.gft.com/

Abstract. This paper presents a hybrid approach to requirements engineering for the development and validation of a Minimum Viable Product (MVP) within the IntWertL project. By combining the formal modeling capabilities of the Parallel Activity Specification Schema (PASS) with qualitative, expert-driven input, we establish a dual-source requirements specification methodology. The PASS model enables structured, scenario-based derivation of implementation-ready requirements, while expert contributions ensure incorporation of cross-domain concerns such as scalability and governance. These inputs are consolidated into a unified requirements document, which informs both MVP development and a structured stakeholder validation process. Results show that integrating formal modeling with qualitative expertise significantly improves clarity, traceability, and alignment across a complex, multi-partner development environment.

Keywords: PASS Modeling · Minimum Viable Product (MVP) · Design Science Research (DSR) · Agile Development

1 Introduction

The transformation of organizational collaboration and value co-creation by digital platforms has increasing the demand for tools that enable transparent, interdisciplinary innovation in the initial stages of development. This is especially critical in cross-organizational settings, where stakeholders from various domains must align on shared goals, processes, and technologies.

This paper presents the development and validation of a Minimum Viable Product (MVP) designed to facilitate early-stage innovation within this context. Developed as part of the "Intelligent Value Networks for Lightweight Vehicles in Small Quantities" (IntWertL) project, the MVP aims to provide a digital environment for small and medium-sized enterprises (SMEs) to collaboratively share ideas, evaluate innovation potential, and strategically align on product development.

The IntWertL ecosystem connects manufacturers and engineering service providers in dynamically evolving value creation networks. These networks enable SMEs to produce complex products in small quantities, enhancing competitiveness through cooperation and shared digital infrastructure. Hence the IntWertL project enhances the Coopetition between the companies. Coopetition refers to a bilateral relationship in which Stakeholders simultaneously engage in both cooperative and competitive interactions with the same partner. This complex relationship enables companies to jointly develop resources or technologies while competing in downstream markets, creating mutual advantages through a strategic separation of collaborative and rivalrous activities. Coopetition is particularly effective when cooperative efforts are focused on input activities distant from the customer, while competition is maintained in output activities closer to the market [2].

Creating an MVP is a foundational step in demonstrating the feasibility of such a platform. Well-known examples like Airbnb and Dropbox have shown how MVPs help test assumptions, minimize risk, and attract early interest. [5,11] In IntWertL, the MVP also serves as a means for stakeholder alignment and iterative development.

While techniques like user stories and business model canvases are commonly used in MVP development, they often lack the formal structure needed in interdisciplinary and multi-stakeholder environments. These approaches can lead to ambiguity or misinterpretation when requirements span organizational or technical boundaries. In contrast, the Parallel Activity Specification Scheme (PASS) modeling language enables scenario-based, formal specification of processes and interactions, improving clarity, consistency, and traceability across teams.

To ensure the MVP addresses user needs, we implement a structured validation process. Employees from project partners who have no prior exposure to the MVP are selected to provide unbiased feedback. These participants receive technical documentation, a validation plan, and undergo an onboarding process. Feedback is collected using standardized forms and interviews.

This paper details the combined use of Design Science Research (DSR) methodology and the utilization of PASS to specify, implement, and validate MVP requirements. We highlight the benefits and limitations of this hybrid methodology and provide practical insights for its application in complex, multi-stakeholder software initiatives.

This paper investigates the following research question: How can the utilization of PASS enhance the specification and validation of MVP requirements in complex, cross-organizational development settings?

2 Research Method

This section first introduces the modeling language PASS and then details the DSR approach applied in the design and evaluation of the MVP.

2.1 Introduction to PASS

PASS is the only fully executable, Turing-complete modeling language specifically designed to operationalize the principles of subject-orientation. Originally introduced for the description of distributed information systems by [7] and formalized in detail by [8], PASS positions communicating entities—referred to as subjects—at the conceptual center of every model. Each subject is regarded as an autonomous agent capable of performing internal tasks and exchanging typed messages with its counterparts; no actions occur outside the purview of a responsible subject, and all coordination is externalized as explicit information flow.

PASS separates these two concerns into a pair of complementary diagram types. A Subject Interaction Diagram (SID) captures the network of subjects and the messages they exchange. For each fully specified subject in the SID, a dedicated Subject Behavior Diagram (SBD) details the internal control flow through three state classes: send, receive, and function states. This minimal yet expressive state machine can encode any computable coordination pattern while maintaining intuitive alignment with the natural language triplet of subject, object, and predicate. Consult Elstermann [6] for further details on the PASS notation and its proposed advantages; a comprehensive description is also available on GitHub[1]. Nevertheless, the developers and validators involved in the MVP were provided with only a limited introduction to PASS, during which the fundamental concepts of the modeling language were explained.

2.2 Design Science Research Approach

This research is based on the principles of DSR for information systems, as presented by [10,12]. The primary objective is to create a purposeful, utility-driven artifact through iterative development and evaluation. This paper specifically discusses how findings from the third step, treatment validation, in the design cycle can be traced back to the design process as outlined in [15]. An in-depth description of the problem domain is omitted, as it has already been published in [3].

The development process utilizes an agile approach, characterized by iterative two-week sprints and continuous feedback loops from stakeholders to improve adaptability and responsiveness. Requirements are systematically documented in a product backlog using a hybrid strategy. Some requirements are based on expert-driven inputs, while others are derived from a comprehensive scenario. The corresponding scenario process is based on the Synthesis Model presented in [3] and is formally modeled in a subject-oriented manner, employing the Parallel Activity Specification Schema. The design artifact is deemed "satisficing" [13], i.e. good enough, when the MVP is capable of supporting the entire scenario process.

---

[1] PASS-Standard-Book-Project is available under https://github.com/I2PM/PASS-Standard-Book-Tex-Project.

Evaluation design follows the Framework for Evaluation in Design Science Research (FEDS) [14]. The MVP itself is formative for later stages of the IntWertL platform. Nevertheless, the primary focus of the evaluation is to perform a summative analysis of the artifact and its design process, as well as to investigate the implications of utilizing the PASS scenario model. Analytical software tests are conducted as part of the agile development process. However, the focus of an MVP is to establish the utility of the functionality with real users. Consequently, a predominantly naturalistic evaluation paradigm has been chosen. The resulting evaluation strategy is analogous to the "Human Risk & Effectiveness" strategy from [14]. The main evaluation episode discussed in this paper is a scenario analysis. Real users engage with the MVP to follow the scenario process and assess completeness, effectiveness, and usability.

3 MVP Development

The MVP was developed as part of the research project IntWertL. It is designed to support collaboration between different industrial partners and help align technical and organizational processes. The following section introduces the steps taken during the MVP development, highlighting how structured modeling and agile methods were applied to translate interdisciplinary requirements into a functional, scalable prototype.

3.1 Structural Conditions for MVP Development

The IntWertL project aims to enable collaborative innovation by connecting diverse stakeholders across all stages of the value chain. This value chain encompasses development through integration, facilitating the creation of Intelligent Value Networks. This approach scales the innovation potential proportionally with the number of cooperating partners and fosters the creation of tailored products, including both physical components and intangible services like simulations. The complexity of linking multiple stakeholders in intelligent value creation networks presents both opportunities and challenges. On one hand, collaboration unlocks synergies, accelerates innovation, and allows SMEs to expand their roles, fostering a more inclusive industrial ecosystem. On the other hand, it requires careful coordination to address misalignment, communication challenges, and intellectual property concerns. The success of such networks hinges on effective tools, clear role definitions, and trust-building mechanisms to balance the complexity and fully realize their transformative potential [1,4].

By combining PASS with conventional requirement documentation, both the structured capture of system functionality and the broader contextual framing of project goals were addressed. This hybrid approach provided flexibility while promoting clarity and alignment across diverse contributor groups.

3.2 MVP Implementation

The process of developing and evaluating the MVP was guided by the principles of the DSR. During the first year of the project, the DSR approach served as a systematic framework to guide the iterative development, evaluation, and refinement of the software artifact. We previously presented in [3] the so-called Synthesis Model, which served as a starting point for developing the formal scenario model. This scenario served as the foundation for the subsequent agile development cycles. To realize the software MVP, this research-driven approach was operationalized through a conventional agile development process characterized by iterative sprints and a modular software architecture. This combination ensured that scientific rigor was maintained through systematic evaluation, while agile development facilitated rapid prototyping, continuous stakeholder feedback, and flexible adaptation to emerging requirements.

In the initial project phase, interdisciplinary working groups, composed of partners from various domains, collaboratively gathered high-level requirements. These requirements were initially documented using informal tools such as whiteboards and text-based notes. The content focused on describing desired interactions, information flows, and overarching goals rather than technical specifications. However, due to the heterogeneous backgrounds of participants, the collected input was often fragmented and unstructured, making it difficult to directly derive actionable development tasks.

To overcome this, the project employed the PASS as a formal modeling language. The utilization of PASS played a crucial role in structuring and synthesizing the diverse inputs into a coherent, scenario-based process model. This scenario illustrated a realistic sequence of actions involving representative user personas and the key information exchanges between them. As a result, PASS provided a shared and formalized representation of stakeholder requirements that bridged the gap between informal ideas and implementable design.

This structured scenario became the cornerstone for the subsequent agile development process. The development team used the PASS model to populate the product backlog, translating its process elements into user stories and technical tasks. The MVP was implemented iteratively, following a microservice-based web architecture to support modularity and scalability. Throughout the sprints, functional and technical testing ensured that each module performed as expected, but the primary focus remained on realizing the interactions and data flows defined in the PASS model.

Figure 1 illustrates the overall process from initial requirements gathering to the implementation and validation of an MVP. At the beginning of the project, domain-specific requirements were collected and structured using PASS, which allowed for a precise and executable representation of the real-world use case. This formalized process model served as a foundation for deriving a structured software backlog, referred to as the MVP backlog. Once the backlog contained a sufficient set of well-defined requirements, the agile development phase commenced. Development was organized into sprints, each comprising sprint backlog definition, planning, implementation, testing, and deployment. Upon completion

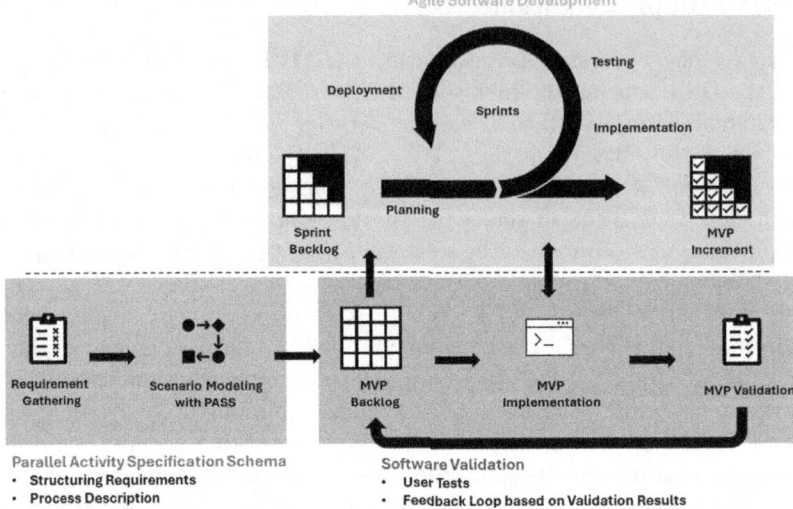

Fig. 1. From structured requirements via PASS modelling to MVP implementation, followed by agile sprints. User validation and feedback informed iterative improvements.

of the MVP implementation, the software was evaluated by participants from the IntWertL project who had not been involved in the development process. Their feedback informed subsequent refinements, and the validation activities were systematically documented to support traceability, quality assurance, and future development cycles.

4 MVP Validation

To ensure that the MVP fulfilled the preset requirements, a structured validation process was carried out. This process involved participants from the IntWertL project who had no prior involvement in the MVP's development. Their external perspective enabled unbiased feedback on functionality, usability, and completeness.

4.1 Requirement Specification for MVP Validation

In complex software development initiatives, particularly those involving an MVP, the requirement specification process is crucial for defining the core functionalities necessary to deliver initial value to users. Various documentation methods are typically employed to gather and articulate requirements, ranging from informal tools like whiteboards for brainstorming to more structured, text-based documents. [9] However, these methods often fall short in interdisciplinary projects that span multiple domains and stakeholder groups. Unstructured information can lead to misinterpretation, especially when contextual clarity is lacking.

Projects with diverse contributors often encounter challenges in aligning expectations and addressing the varying information needs of stakeholders from different fields. Communication gaps are common, particularly in large-scale initiatives with multiple working groups. Misalignment may occur when teams are unaware of decisions made in parallel tracks, and conflicting requirements often arise due to inconsistent documentation practices across organizational boundaries.

Another recurring challenge is assigning responsibility for requirement implementation. In collaborative environments composed of independent partners, each with their own objectives and areas of accountability, coordinating development tasks and enforcing specific requirements becomes difficult. When MVP development is distributed among specialized teams, integration complexity increases. Building a unified platform from modular components requires clearly defined interfaces and close coordination to prevent redundancy and miscommunication.

These structural and organizational challenges often result in a fragmented and inefficient validation process. This underscores the need for systematic methods to structure, communicate, and validate requirements throughout the development cycle.

To address these issues, our project adopted a structured approach using PASS for defining and managing key MVP requirements. Using PASS allowed a structured yet flexible framework for collaboratively identifying and refining requirements. It supports a stepwise process that begins with clear problem articulation, followed by joint analysis of the existing context and constraints, leading to solution design, and culminating in the formal specification of functionalities.

This approach was especially valuable in our multi-organizational environment, where stakeholders represented a broad range of organizations and disciplinary domains. The PASS model helped establish a shared language and reference structure, which facilitated cross-functional communication and ensured that all parties maintained a common understanding of project objectives.

By clearly separating problem identification from solution formulation, the application of PASS minimized premature convergence on technical solutions and encouraged thoughtful reflection on actual user needs and pain points. This distinction helped prevent the inclusion of unnecessary or misaligned features in the MVP. Furthermore, the structured transition from abstract problems to concrete requirements improved traceability, allowing design decisions to be linked back to their original motivations. This enhanced both transparency and accountability within the development process.

The complete set of requirements was compiled into a validation document shared with participants. This document consisted of two main sections: the first containing requirements derived from traditional text-based sources—such as stakeholder definitions, need statements, and project deliverables, and the second containing requirements modeled using the PASS, as described above.

4.2 MVP Validation Process

The final stage of one MVP development cycle is the validation phase, which assesses how effectively the system meets predefined requirements and aligns with stakeholder expectations. To ensure transparency, reproducibility, and depth in the evaluation, a structured validation process involving participants from IntWertL, was implemented. These individuals had no prior exposure to the MVP, ensuring unbiased and fresh perspectives.

Each participant received a validation plan that detailed the validation objectives, listed the individual requirements, and outlined the procedures to follow. Alongside this, they were provided with comprehensive platform documentation, explaining the MVP's features, intended use cases, and technical foundation. Before starting, all participants joined an onboarding session to walk them through the validation process, clarify the context of the MVP, and explain how to give structured feedback.

The validation plan categorized requirements into two main types. A portion of the functional requirements was derived from the formal PASS model, providing structured and scenario-based specifications. The remaining requirements originated from more traditional sources, as definitions, stakeholder needs, and deliverables.

The validators were asked to assess each requirement and to provide comments where necessary, using a standardized scale of: fulfilled, partially fulfilled, or not fulfilled.

Feedback was collected through a structured table, designed to capture quantitative evaluations. To support the development of the MVP, all findings were logged in GitLab in the form of issues, using a predefined template. This ensured consistency in reporting and enabled the development team to efficiently address bugs, usability problems, and improvement suggestions. In addition, follow-up interviews were conducted to explore the feedback in greater depth and resolve any ambiguities.

Overall, this combination of a formal validation framework, systematic feedback collection, and collaborative review enabled a thorough assessment of the MVP. It also facilitated iterative refinement, helping the platform evolve in line with both technical goals and user expectations.

5 Results

The validation phase of the MVP revealed clear differences in how effectively requirements could be interpreted and evaluated, depending on their origin. The validators reported that requirements derived from the PASS model, wehich were based on detailed, scenario-driven representations of user interactions, were significantly easier to understand and assess. The formal modeling approach offered structure and clarity, making the expectations behind each function explicit. As a result, the alidators were able to efficiently determine whether these requirements were fulfilled, and their feedback was more consistent and actionable.

In contrast, the validators noted that the text-based requirements, gathered through traditional methods such as workshops, interviews, and documentation were often more abstract. While these requirements captured important insights and high-level needs, they tended to lack specificity. This abstraction led to inconsistencies in interpretation during validation and often required further explanation or clarification. The validators reported also, that in several instances the vagueness of these traditional requirements made it challenging to directly translate them into technical specifications or objectively assess whether they had been met.

A key challenge early in the project was precisely this lack of concreteness in many of the initial requirements. For instance, a typical requirement might state that integrators should be able to assign tasks to production or engineering service providers. While such a statement outlines a general goal, it does not provide the procedural detail necessary for implementation or evaluation. This scenario defined a realistic flow of interactions between stakeholders and the software system, allowing the team to extract precise technical and procedural requirements.

The use of PASS modeling facilitated a common understanding among project partners, who possessed diverse technical backgrounds and areas of expertise. The visual and formal nature of the model helped align perspectives, reduce ambiguity, and guide development decisions throughout the process. Requirements derived from this shared scenario were not only easier to implement but were also consistently confirmed by validators as fully satisfied, highlighting their practical relevance and accuracy.

By translating high-level goals into structured user stories and epics grounded in real-world use, the formal modeling approach significantly contributed to the success of the MVP. It bridged the gap between abstract ideas and implementable features, supported efficient validation, and ensured that the final product met both functional expectations and user needs. In contrast, while the text-based inputs provided valuable domain context, their lower precision often limited their usefulness during the implementation and evaluation stages. Overall, the combination of formal modeling with domain expertise proved essential; however, the structured approach ultimately delivered a greater impact on the effectiveness and clarity of both development and validation. This finding reinforces the need for participatory requirement engineering approaches, particularly when targeting modular or platform-based systems intended for broad, heterogeneous user bases. Contextual grounding through domain-specific user stories, emerges as a best practice for increasing comprehensibility and reducing ambiguity in system validation.

Furthermore, the results suggest that successful validation is not solely a technical exercise but also a communicative one: clear articulation of validation expectations, accessible documentation (e.g., validation plans), and structured feedback mechanisms (e.g., GitLab issue templates) are essential for translating complex requirements into actionable validation tasks. As the project moves forward, these insights provide guidance for refining the requirements engineering and validation processes, ensuring future iterations better support validators in producing reliable and interpretable feedback.

6 Practical Implications

The structured approach using PASS diagrams provided clear benefits for this complex, interdisciplinary project. Translating unstructured requirements into a formal process model helped align diverse stakeholder perspectives and created a shared understanding of the system to be developed. The use of PASS enabled the identification of gaps, redundancies, and dependencies early in the process, which improved the quality of the derived MVP backlog. Based on the lessons learned, we plan to further formalize our validation process in future projects, using PASS not only as a modeling tool but also as a bridge between domain experts and technical teams. We do not see PASS as a one-size-fits-all solution but as a highly valuable method in settings where complexity and interdisciplinarity demand clarity and structure. In such cases, having dedicated PASS experts who can facilitate the translation from informal input to formal process models can significantly enhance project communication, traceability, and implementation quality.

7 Conclusion

This paper presents the requirements engineering and validation process for a digital engineering and production platform developed within the IntWertL research project. The project's goal—to enable SMEs to participate in low-volume, high-complexity vehicle production through a distributed digital platform—demands a close alignment between technical development and user needs.

The results demonstrate the effectiveness of using PASS to derive requirements. Requirements based on user stories from project partners were found to be both understandable and verifiable, and were successfully validated. In contrast, requirements developed independently by technical experts, without the context of user stories, resulted in confusion during validation and were not confirmed. This highlights the necessity of embedding domain context into requirements and involving end users early in the specification process.

The structured validation process, which includes detailed validation plans and a collaborative issue-tracking workflow in GitLab, has proven valuable for organizing and documenting feedback. Nonetheless, the clarity and specificity of requirements remain crucial determinants of successful validation outcomes.

Moving forward, the project will enhance its approach to requirement definition by placing a greater emphasis on participatory design practices. These practices will help ensure that the digital platform addresses real-world needs while remaining usable, effective, and scalable for SMEs aiming to compete in dynamic, value-driven mobility markets.

8 Outlook

The results of the validation process underline the effectiveness of user-centered modeling approaches, such as PASS, in specifying system requirements that are both understandable and verifiable by diverse stakeholders. Moving forward, the integration of such models into early stages of platform development will be further refined to enhance requirement clarity and stakeholder alignment. In particular, automated derivation of testable validation criteria from PASS models may streamline future validation efforts.

Furthermore, the observed challenges in validating expert-derived requirements highlight the necessity for improved communication formats and specification standards. Future work will explore hybrid approaches that combine formal modeling with explanatory narratives, examples, and interactive elements to better support non-expert stakeholders.

In the next project phases, the focus will shift toward expanding the MVP into a fully operational platform. This includes technical enhancements, further user interface improvements, and optionally the onboarding of additional SMEs to validate the scalability and generalizability of the approach. Ultimately, the IntWertL platform aspires to serve as a blueprint for decentralized, value-driven production ecosystems in mobility and beyond.

Acknowledgments. This work has been supported by the research project IntWertL under the reference 19S22003Q, that is funded by the Federal Ministry for Economic Affairs and Climate Action (BMWK). Some language editing and rephrasing assistance was provided using AI-based tools (e.g., OpenAI's ChatGPT) to improve clarity and readability. All content was authored and verified by the authors.

References

1. Audretsch, D.B., Belitski, M., Caiazza, R., Phan, P.: Collaboration strategies and SME innovation performance. J. Bus. Res. **164**, 114018 (2023). https://doi.org/10.1016/j.jbusres.2023.114018
2. Bengtsson, M., Kock, S.: "Coopetition" in business networks–to cooperate and compete simultaneously. Ind. Mark. Manage. **29**(5), 411–426 (2000). https://doi.org/10.1016/S0019-8501(99)00067-X, https://www.sciencedirect.com/science/article/pii/S001985019900067X
3. Bönsch, J., Hauck, S., Elstermann, M., Ovtcharova, J.: An approach to create a common frame of reference for digital platform design in SME value networks. Elstermann, M., Dittmar, A., Lederer, M. (eds) S-BPM ONE 2023. CCIS, vol. 1867, pp. 63–82. Springer, Cham (2023). https://doi.org/10.1007/978-3-031-40213-5_5

4. Bönsch, J., Jelschow, V., Haking, M., Bobbou, S., Deisser, O.: Intelligente Wertschöpfungsnetzwerke für individuelle Fahrzeugentwicklung. Zeitschrift für wirtschaftlichen Fabrikbetrieb **119**(12), 902–906 (2024). https://doi.org/10.1515/zwf-2024-1173, https://www.degruyter.com/document/doi/10.1515/zwf-2024-1173/html, publisher: De Gruyter
5. Eisenmann, T.R., Pao, M., Barley, L.: Dropbox: "it just works" (2011). Harvard Business School Case 811-065
6. Elstermann, M.: Executing Strategic Product Planning - A Subject-Oriented Analysis and New Referential Process Model for IT-Tool Support and Agile Execution of Strategic Product Planning. KIT Scientific Publishing, Karlsruhe (2020). https://doi.org/10.5445/KSP/1000097859, section: 334
7. Fleischmann, A.: Distributed Systems. Springer, Heidelberg (1994).https://doi.org/10.1007/978-3-642-78612-9
8. Fleischmann, A., Schmidt, W., Stary, C., Obermeier, S., Börger, E.: Subjektorientiertes Prozessmanagement: Mitarbeiter einbinden, Motivation und Prozessakzeptanz steigern, vol. 4. Hanser München (2011)
9. Glinz, M.: On non-functional requirements. In: 15th IEEE International Requirements Engineering Conference (RE 2007), pp. 1–10. IEEE (2007)
10. Hevner, A.R., March, S.T., Park, J., Ram, S.: Design science in information systems research. MIS Q. **28**(1), 75–105 (2004)
11. Negi, G., Tripathi, S.: Airbnb phenomenon: a review of literature and future research directions. J. Hospit. Tour. Insights **5**(4), 1–20 (2022). https://doi.org/10.1108/JHTI-04-2022-0133
12. Peffers, K., Tuunanen, T., Rothenberger, M.A., Chatterjee, S.: A design science research methodology for information systems research. J. Manag. Inf. Syst. **24**(3), 45–77 (2007)
13. Simon, H.A.: The Science of the Artificial, 3rd edn. MIT Press, Cambridge (1996)
14. Venable, J., Pries-Heje, J., Baskerville, R.: FEDS: a framework for evaluation in design science research. Eur. J. Inf. Syst. (2016). https://doi.org/10.1057/ejis.2014.36, https://www.tandfonline.com/doi/abs/10.1057/ejis.2014.36
15. Wieringa, R.J.: Treatment Validation. In: Wieringa, R.J. (ed.) Design Science Methodology for Information Systems and Software Engineering, pp. 59–69. Springer, Heidelberg (2014).https://doi.org/10.1007/978-3-662-43839-8_7

webPASS: A Lightweight Web-Native, Collaborative PASS Editor for Subject-Oriented Process Modeling

Jakob Bönsch[✉][iD], Timo Lizak[iD], Simon Heß[iD], and Leon Patrick Okello[iD]

Karlsruhe Institute of Technology, Karlsruhe, Germany
boensch@kit.edu
http://www.imi.kit.edu

Abstract. This paper introduces webPASS, a lightweight, web-native PASS modeling environment designed to democratize access and foster collaboration. webPASS integrates a metamodel-based validation engine to ensure semantic consistency, supports real-time multi-user editing with change tracking, and allows customization and integration with existing S-BPM toolchains. The frontend is based on TypeScript, Vue 3, and Pinia, providing an interactive user interface. The backend facilitates seamless data exchange between clients, enabling communication through WebSocket connections. The proposed model editor utilizes JSON-LD as the internal representation format for models, as it offers a standardized, flexible, and extensible approach to representing complex data structures. Our solution eliminates traditional barriers to entry, thus making advanced process modeling accessible to a wider audience. The integrated versioning capabilities allow users to track changes, revert to previous states, and branch models for experimental modifications. This functionality is critical for maintaining audit trails in regulated industries and academic research.

Keywords: PASS · S-BPM · Subject-Orientation

1 Introduction

In contemporary business environments, the increasing complexity and interdependence of organizational processes necessitate modeling paradigms that emphasize the autonomy of actors and the semantics of their interactions. Subject-oriented Business Process Management (S-BPM) addresses this by following the paradigm of subject-orientation, centering on "subjects" (i.e., autonomous agents) and the messages they exchange as the fundamental elements of process design. At the core of S-BPM lies the Parallel Activity Specification Schema (PASS), first articulated by [4]. PASS comprises two views: the Subject Interaction Diagram (SID) and the Subject Behavior Diagram (SBD) [5]. A comprehensive list of advantages of PASS over other process modeling languages, along with a complete introduction to the notation, is provided in [2].

Despite its theoretical appeal, PASS has seen limited adoption in both industrial and academic settings. Existing implementations are largely confined to proprietary environments—most notably the Metasonic Suite, whose PASS support was informed by practical experiences in large-scale deployments [3], and a set of Visio stencils[1] maintained by the I2PM community for creating standard and Abstract Layered PASS (ALPS) diagrams. These offerings, while functional, possess several critical shortcomings: they are neither freely available nor open for extension, and they lack support for collaborative, real-time co-authoring.

Such tooling limitations have tangible consequences. First, the absence of open, metamodel-driven editors hinders consistency checking, potentially leading to modeling errors. Second, modern process engineering is inherently collaborative, involving distributed teams of business analysts, software engineers, and domain experts [1,6]. However, current PASS tools do not provide features for version control, concurrent editing, or integrated discussion, forcing teams to rely on manual synchronization through document exchanges.

To address these gaps, this paper introduces webPASS, a web-native PASS modeling environment designed to democratize access and foster collaboration. Here, we present our current work in progress toward a Minimum Viable Product (MVP) to collect feedback and define a comprehensive set of requirements for further development. The current requirement specification is incomplete and derived from arbitrary experiences with online collaboration tools (e. g., Conceptboard, Miro, Mural) and findings from [1]. webPASS integrates a metamodel-based validation engine to ensure semantic consistency, supports real-time multi-user editing with change tracking, and is open for customization and integration with existing S-BPM toolchains. In the following sections, we present the architecture and user interface of webPASS and introduce the intention of modular development through three use cases.

2 Technical Architecture

webPASS is developed using a modern frontend architecture based on Vue 3, complemented by Vue Flow and Element Plus for interactive interfaces and Pinia for state management. JSON-LD enables efficient communication with the Node.js backend, where Express.js handles REST-API requests and WebSockets facilitate real-time updates. We plan to use Neo4J for persistent storage and deploy both frontend and backend in separate Docker containers. This technology stack was selected for its balance of development efficiency, scalability, and maintainability, allowing for a uniform development process using TypeScript while providing essential functionalities for interactive interfaces, state management, and data storage. The key technologies used in webPASS are summarized in Table 1.

---

[1] The Visio stencils are publicly available under https://subjective-me.jimdofree.com/.

Table 1. Technologies utilized in webPASS.

Technology	Description
Vue 3	Reactive frontend framework using the Composition API.
Vue Flow	Customizable Vue 3 component for interactive flowcharts.
Element Plus	UI component library for consistent interface elements.
Pinia	State management with persistent storage support.
JSON-LD	Structured data format for linking and describing data.
Neo4J	Graph database for efficient data storage and retrieval.
Express.js	Framework for building RESTful APIs with Node.js.
Node.js	JavaScript runtime environment for server-side execution.
WebSocket	Real-time, bi-directional client-server communication.
Docker	Containerization platform for consistent deployment environments.

Logically, webPASS consists of four components: Viewer, Editor, Shared Editing, and Backend. The principal architecture and its subcomponents are illustrated in Fig. 1.

Our primary requirements include viewing, editing, and collaborative editing of models. These requirements are reflected in our technical architecture. Viewing and editing functionalities are implemented through dedicated Viewer and Editor components. Shared editing is facilitated through message exchange between the Backend and the Editor component, in conjunction with the Shared Editing component.

This separation was chosen to enable the independent development of all components and to facilitate collaborative editing via standardized communication interfaces among each component.

From a user perspective, this approach simplifies access management for the created models. Subsystems, such as the Viewer component, can be accessed independently, integrated into external contexts, and made available to users who have been granted read privileges for the model.

2.1 Frontend

Both the Viewer and Editor are components of the frontend. The viewer includes all controls necessary for displaying and navigating PASS diagrams, with model information loaded directly from a Pinia *Model Store*. The Editor component updates the contents of this store either directly or through a WebSocket. This update logic is discussed in the backend section, while the focus here is on the Viewer component.

The Viewer comprises the SID-View and SBD-View components illustrated in Fig. 2. These components primarily serve as containers for the corresponding diagrams and are built using Vue Flow. Furthermore, several features unrelated

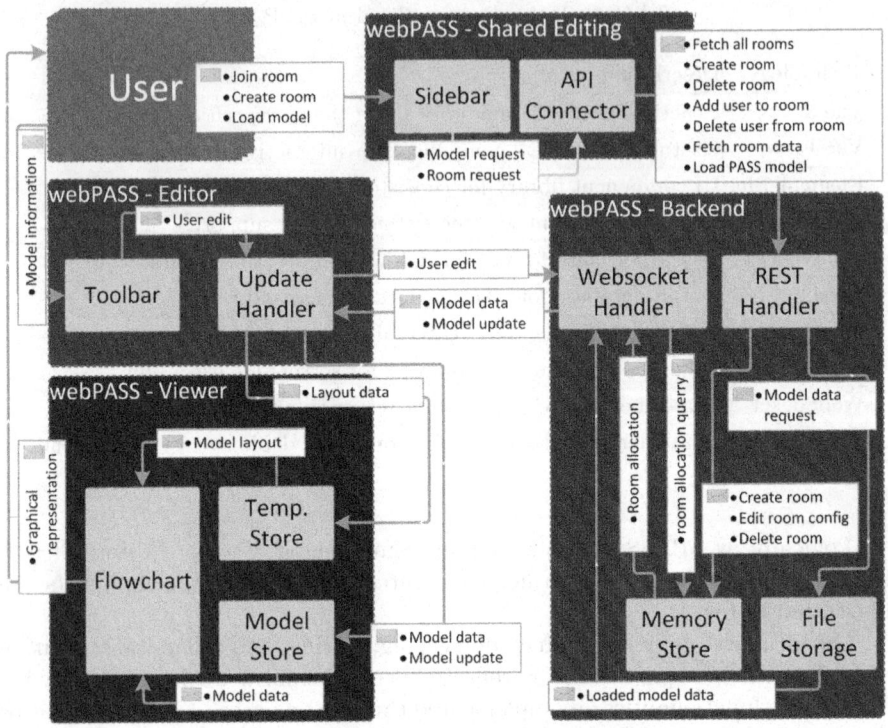

Fig. 1. SID of the webPASS architecture.

to Vue Flow, including *auto-arrange*, *clear local storage* and *zoom reset* are incorporated.

These views also synchronize and update a secondary *Temporary Information Store* that retains chart-relevant data, including the positions of elements, their sizes, the number of handles, and connector elements, among others.

Vue Flow includes built-in features such as zoom and pan controls, single and multi-selection capabilities, draggable elements, customizable nodes and edges, and various event handlers.

The SID- and SBD-View employ similar logic, consisting of:

The **Vue 3 template (1)** component is imported, receiving nodes, edges, and background as properties. In the future, we plan to implement a minimap component.

The **Vue Flow instance (2)** component includes several listeners, most notably the *onDragStop()* listener. In this listener, we update the position data for node elements within the *Temporary Information Store*, which is persisted in local storage to prevent the nodes from snapping back when the page is reloaded and to provide a smoother and more intuitive user experience. Other listeners include the *onViewPortChange()* listener, which retrieves the current scale and informs the user of the zoom level and extent of panning of the graph; and the

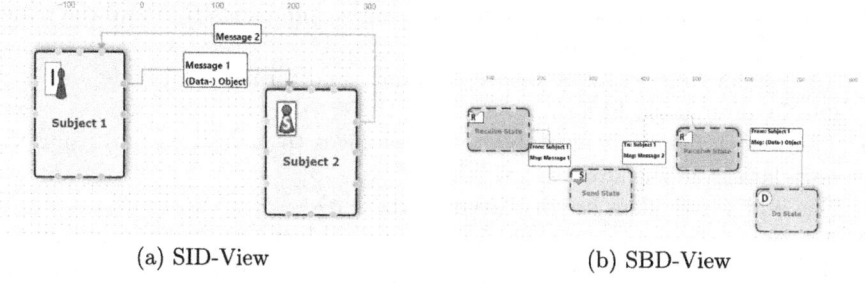

Fig. 2. Screenshots of the webPASS-viewer.

updateNode listener, which promptly updates node positions within the chart after being dragged, rather than waiting for a render due to changes in the store. It is also utilized in the *forceUpdatePosition()* function, which ensures that once the nodes are auto-arranged, they are placed quickly instead of waiting for the store to update.

Computed Refs (3) fetches data from the *Model Store*. This data is then employed in the render function to construct the node and edge objects, which are integrated into the node and edge references utilized by Vue Flow. This process creates a map, where the key is the ID of the PASS type and the value comprises the subject, state, connection, and transition.

A **render function (4)** utilizes data from the computed references (e. g., Subjects, Connection) and inputs it into the respective rendering functions (e. g., renderNodes, renderEdges) to format it into the appropriate structures for nodes and edges references.This process involves iterating over the Map returned by the computed references, passing the data element by element into the rendering functions to format it into the desired structure. It also ensures compatibility with custom Node and Edge templates. It is invoked in every watcher when the store is updated, ensuring that any changes are immediately rendered on the screen.

Emits (5) After arranging the nodes, the fitView function is used to focus on the nodes in their new positions. The changes are emitted to the SID or SBD view. The resetZoom emits utilizes the fitView function from the vueFlow instance to focus on all nodes on the screen, including those that are hidden or outside the user's field of view.

Watchers (6) watch for changes in the store and re-render the nodes and edges with the new data using the *render function*.

A summary of how the charts work can be derived from the flow of data as follows.

1. User model input via export or loaded from the backend
2. Data is stored in the model store of the application
3. The SID and SBD Views get the data from the model store, input, and format it into the Pinia store for chart data

4. The data is then computed by the flowchart components to fill up the nodes and edges needed by Vue Flow
5. The render functions iterate over the data and format each node and edge into he desired visual form.
6. The render functions also update any changes to nodes or edges using the new data from the store
7. The nodes and edges are displayed on the screen.
8. As the user interacts with the visual elements. Listeners and watchers in the chart - SID and SBD components, then update the data in the stores, and those changes are reflected in the backend

2.2 Backend

The proposed webPASS backend is designed to facilitate real-time collaboration and efficient data exchange between clients. It utilizes virtual collaboration spaces, referred to as 'rooms', leveraging WebSocket connections and RESTful APIs. The backend is designed to be scalable and efficient in handling real-time updates. At its core, the backend revolves around the concept of 'rooms', which serve as virtual spaces for users to collaborate on models, facilitating communication between clients through WebSocket connections. An overview of the architecture, including the frontend, is shown in Fig. 1.

A room is defined as a container that holds a specific model, identified by a unique namespace. Each room is associated with a channel ID, which facilitates communication between the frontend and backend through WebSocket messages. Additionally, the room is designed to contain the latest version of the model in JSON-LD format, enabling efficient processing and storage.

To facilitate seamless data exchange and synchronization, we utilize a combination of RESTful APIs and WebSocket protocols. When a user requests to load a model, the backend verifies whether a corresponding room already exists for that specific model. If no such room exists, it creates a new room with a unique channel ID and notifies the user to join the room. Upon entering the room, the backend provides the JSON-LD representation of the model and the channel ID to the frontend, which then initializes the model editor. Users are mapped to specific rooms to synchronize their editing actions. This configuration enables efficient routing of messages between clients within the same room.

Regarding the data exchange concept, webPASS utilizes a standardized format for the exchange of data between the frontend and backend. We have selected JSON-LD as our internal representation format for models, as it offers a standardized, flexible, and extensible approach to representing complex data structures. The adoption of JSON-LD also facilitates the conversion of model representations to and from OWL.

This data format facilitates the efficient processing and manipulation of the model graph within the frontend application. When a user modifies the model, these updates are transmitted to the backend through WebSocket messages. These messages include information regarding the type of action performed (create, update, or delete), along with the specific payload data relevant to that action and the sender ID for identifying the user making the change.

The backend processes incoming messages and broadcasts them to all connected clients within the same room, ensuring that each user's view of the model remains up-to-date and synchronized in real-time. The payload of each message contains the relevant data in JSON-LD format, allowing the backend to efficiently process and store the updates. In turn, the backend relays these updates to all other users within the same room, ensuring that every user has an up-to-date view of the model.

As part of our future plans, we intend to integrate Neo4j as a persistent datastore for the backend. This will enable efficient storage and management of large volumes of model data. The use of a graph database like Neo4j provides advanced querying capabilities, facilitating the analysis and understanding of complex models and their relationships.

3 Use Cases

webPASS provides significant advantages over existing solutions in modern process modeling. Our tool eliminates traditional barriers to entry, making advanced process modeling accessible to a broader audience.

- **Open-Source Roadmap**: Our project is intended to be open-source and therefore everybody can host and use it however they wish, free of charge. This also makes it ideal for educational institutions, small businesses, as well as other open-source projects.
- **Ease of Use**: Because the tool operates entirely in a browser-based environment, it eliminates the need for specialised software installations on the client side. This also ensures compatibility across operating systems and devices, enabling seamless access from desktops, tablets, or mobile devices.
- **Collaborative Modelling**: Multiple users can edit a single PASS model in real time, fostering teamwork across geographically dispersed teams.
- **Storage and Versioning**: The editor automatically stores models on the host server, ensuring data safety and reducing reliance on local storage. The integrated versioning capabilities allow users to track changes, revert to previous states, and branch models for experimental modifications. This is critical for maintaining audit trails in regulated industries or academic research.

We highlight several use cases of our software in the following subsections. In this context, we use the term "use case" as it is commonly understood in software development—that is, as examples or scenarios that illustrate different ways the software can be used in practice. It is important to note that the Viewer, Editor, and Shared Editing modules, although distinct, are built upon one another. The Viewer serves as the foundation, rendering models and offering import/export options. The Editor expands these capabilities, allowing users to modify the models rendered by the Viewer. At the uppermost layer, Shared Editing facilitates simultaneous collaboration among multiple users on the same model.

3.1 Viewer

Before Project Manager Matthes can view a PASS model, two preconditions must be met: a valid PASS model must exist in the database, and Matthes must possess the appropriate viewing rights for this model. Once these conditions are satisfied, Matthes receives a link to the model via email. He clicks on this link and is prompted to enter his credentials on the website to verify his identity. Upon successful authentication, the website loads the SID and all corresponding SBDs associated with the PASS model. Matthes can then navigate through the PASS model at his convenience or, if necessary, export the model in either JSON-LD or OWL format.

3.2 Editor

In the case of the Editor the process begins with two preconditions: Project Manager Simon must be logged into the service, and he must already have an existing, valid PASS model in OWL (or JSON-LD) format. With these requirements satisfied, Simon proceeds to import the existing model, which allows him to navigate through the SIDs and SBDs. He then adds two new SBDs, gaining immediate access to two new tabs for these additions. Simon continues by adding several messages to the model, which he edits to meet his specific requirements. After completing the desired modifications, Simon saves the updated model on the server for easier access in the future. Additionally, Simon exports the model, enabling him to continue working on it even without an internet connection, such as during a flight.

3.3 Shared Editing

For shared modeling, the process starts with both Jakob, the project manager from Company A, and Anne, the project manager from Company B, logging into the website. Once both are online, Jakob initiates the collaboration by creating a shared editing room. Anne reviews the list of existing rooms and joins the one Jakob has set up. She contributes by adding an SBD, a change that is immediately registered in the backend and broadcast to Jakob, allowing him to see the new SBD as well. Jakob then creates another SBD and populates it with several send and receive states, as well as transitions. To prevent editing conflicts, the SBD Jakob is working on is temporarily locked for Anne, though she remains occupied anyway while editing the SBD she previously created. Together, Jakob and Anne collaboratively develop a PASS model for an inter-company process, which they can subsequently share with all relevant stakeholders.

4 Conclusion and Outlook

webPASS reduces the barriers to subject-oriented process modeling by integrating a browser-based Vue 3 front-end with a metamodel-aware, real-time collaboration backend. By utilizing JSON-LD, open protocols, and an extensible validation engine, the platform merges semantic rigor with ease of adoption, making PASS accessible to distributed teams, regulated industries, and educational environments.

Future work will enhance this integration. Notably, we propose extending the PASS ontology with an *optional positioning module* that records diagram coordinates and layout hints as first-class semantic elements. Persisting such data—whether authored manually or generated by auto-layout—would enable editors to exchange not only the logical model but also its visual arrangement. This approach would yield consistent views across tools while maintaining full backward compatibility for repositories that choose to disregard layout information.

Beyond this, we envision several further enhancements. Integration of Neo4j as a persistent backend will enable advanced querying and analytics on process models. We also plan to expand support for import and export formats, facilitating interoperability with a wider range of S-BPM and BPM tools. In the long term, features such as role-based access control, as well as enhanced commenting and discussion tools, could further strengthen collaborative modeling and improve model quality.

With these extensions, webPASS advances the vision of a fully open, interoperable, and collaborative S-BPM ecosystem, supporting both practical applications and future research.

Acknowledgement. This work is associated with the research project IntWertL, 19S22003Q. Funded by the Federal Republic of Germany and the European Union. Funding bodies: Federal Ministry for Economic Affairs and Energy based on a resolution of the German Bundestag, and the European Union. The authors used artificial intelligence assistance to support the drafting and editing process. The authors are responsible for the final content and accuracy of the work.

References

1. Choudhury, A., Malavolta, I., Ciccozzi, F., Aslam, K., Lago, P.: The technological landscape of collaborative model-driven software engineering. Softw. Syst. Model. pp. 1–25 (2025)
2. Elstermann, M.: Executing Strategic Product Planning - A Subject-Oriented Analysis and New Referential Process Model for IT-Tool Support and Agile Execution of Strategic Product Planning. KIT Scientific Publishing, Karlsruhe (2020). https://doi.org/10.5445/KSP/1000097859, section: 334
3. Elstermann, M., Seese, D.: A proposal for modeling standards for subject-oriented modeling with PASS. In: Oppl, S., Fleischmann, A. (eds.) S-BPM ONE 2012. CCIS, vol. 284, pp. 16–32. Springer, Heidelberg (2012). https://doi.org/10.1007/978-3-642-29294-1_2
4. Fleischmann, A.: Distributed Systems. Springer, Berlin, Heidelberg (1994). https://doi.org/10.1007/978-3-642-78612-9

5. Fleischmann, A., Schmidt, W., Stary, C., Obermeier, S., Börger, E.: Subjektorientiertes Prozessmanagement: Mitarbeiter einbinden, Motivation und Prozessakzeptanz steigern, vol. 4. Hanser München (2011)
6. Young, S.: examining collaborative business process modeling techniques. J. Enterprise Bus. Intell **3**(2), 22–31 (2024)

Human or Artificial Intelligence in BPM?

Describing and Analyzing AI Agents with the Tools We Already Trust: A Comparative Study of PASS and BPMN

Christoph Piller[✉]

Am Berg 15a, 85095 Denkendorf, Germany
chpiller@live.com

Abstract. Recent advances in large-language-model tooling have propelled *AI agents*, autonomous, goal-driven software entities, into everyday business operations. While research proposals for new 'agent-aware' notations abound, industry still relies on the well-established standards BPMN and PASS to document and govern its processes. This paper, therefore, addresses a pragmatic question: *Are those existing notations already sufficient to model AI agents?*

We first extract four canonical agent capabilities—environment perception, autonomous action, goal orientation, and temporal persistence—and map them to BPM constructs: subjects in PASS and pools and lanes in BPMN. A conceptual analysis, a hands-on modeling study of an intelligent call-center scenario, and empirical validation through expert interviews show that (i) PASS offers an immediately natural fit, and (ii) BPMN attains functional parity when collaboration diagrams and disciplined message flows are applied. No structural limitations were identified, and perceived BPMN weaknesses can be mitigated by modeling guidelines.

The findings, supported by expert insights, reinforce the hypothesis that mainstream BPM notations already cover the descriptive and analytic needs of AI-agent integration. Rather than inventing new diagram types, practitioners can extend their current tool chains and governance routines. Future work should catalog domain-specific use cases, enhance conformance tooling, and explore oversight mechanisms for self-learning agents.

Keywords: AI agent · S-BPM · BPM · PASS · BPMN

1 Introduction

During the last eighteen months the term *AI agent* has traveled from technical blogs to productive shop floors. Frameworks such as AutoGPT [27] and enterprise deployments like Microsoft Copilot [18] already execute complete task chains—planning, calling APIs, even negotiating hand-offs—with only high-level human guidance. Business–Process Management (BPM) is therefore confronted with a central research question:

How can these non-human participants be described, analysed and governed within our existing process models?

A quick scan of recent literature shows two camps. One calls for entirely new notations tailored to 'agentic' behaviour [23]; the other (still rather quiet) suspects that the established arsenal may already suffice. This paper takes the pragmatic side and formulates the guiding hypothesis:

> With the established BPM notations, in particular BPMN [12] and the subject-oriented PASS language [9], it is already possible to describe, analyze and govern AI agents in a sufficiently precise and actionable way.

Two observations underpin this claim:

1. **Conceptual match.** Pools and lanes in BPMN as well as subjects in PASS are autonomous, message-exchanging entities. Generative AI agents, by definition, share the same characteristics: autonomy, communication, encapsulation and goal orientation.
2. **Operational continuity.** Organisations have invested years of modeling effort, tool customisation and staff training around BPMN or PASS. Re-using these assets is faster—and markedly less risky—than introducing yet another diagram type whose semantics are still in flux.

To evaluate the hypothesis the paper proceeds as follows. Section 2 distills a working definition of generative AI agents and isolates four core features: environment perception, autonomous action, goal orientation and temporal persistence. Section 3 revisits the notion of 'subjects' in BPM, contrasting BPMN's activity-oriented roots with the communication-first stance of PASS. Section 4 places agents and subjects side by side and shows that the conceptual gap is, in truth, a thin line. Section 5 grounds the discussion in practice, modeling an intelligent call-center scenario in both notations, and presents new empirical validation through expert interviews (Sect. 5.3), which confirm the sufficiency and practical relevance of these notations for AI agent modeling. Finally, Sect. 6 summarizes the findings, outlines open research issues (auditability, non-determinism, agent life-cycle metrics) and sketches next steps.

The aim is not to crown a single 'best' notation. Instead, we show that AI agents can be integrated into the modeling languages BPM practitioners already master today, without waiting for a new standard to emerge.

2 Definition of AI Agents: Understanding the Emerging Paradigm

The concept of AI agents has experienced a remarkable surge in attention and relevance in the past 18 months. Google Trends data reveal that search interest for the term "AI agent" increased by approximately 320% between January

2024 and April 2025, with particularly sharp increases following key industry announcements [11]. Similarly, LinkedIn data shows that mentions of "AI agent" in professional posts increased by more than 450% in the same period, reflecting the rapid integration of this concept into business and technology discussions [16].

This dramatic increase in interest coincides with several pivotal developments in the landscape of AI. The introduction of AutoGPT in April 2023 demonstrated the potential for goal-driven autonomous systems built on large language models [27]. Microsoft's integration of agent-based capabilities into their Copilot suite in late 2023 brought the concept into mainstream enterprise applications [18]. Most recently, Google's whitepaper on AI agents [29] has provided a structured perspective on this emerging field.

The timing of this surge is not coincidental. It represents the convergence of several technological capabilities that have reached sufficient maturity: large language models with reasoning capabilities, improved frameworks for tool integration, and advancements in planning algorithms. This convergence has transformed AI agents from a theoretical concept into a practical reality with immediate applications across industries.

2.1 Various Definitions of AI Agents in the Literature

The concept of AI agents has evolved significantly over time, with various scholars and industry leaders offering distinct perspectives.

Academic Definitions: Russell and Norvig [24] provide perhaps the most widely cited definition in their seminal textbook: "An agent is anything that can be viewed as perceiving its environment through sensors and acting upon that environment through actuators." This definition emphasizes the perception-action cycle that distinguishes agents from passive computational systems.

Wooldridge [30] offers a more constrained definition focused on autonomy: "An agent is a computer system that is situated in some environment, and that is capable of autonomous action in this environment in order to meet its delegated objectives." This definition highlights the self-directed nature of agents.

Franklin and Graesser [10] propose a definition emphasizing temporal continuity: "An autonomous agent is a system situated within a part of an environment that senses that environment and acts on it, over time, in pursuit of its own agenda and so as to effect what it senses in the future." Their emphasis on persistence and agenda-driven behavior distinguishes agents from simple reactive systems.

Industry Perspective: More recently, industry leaders have offered definitions that reflect the practical implementation of agents in commercial applications:

Sam Altman, CEO of OpenAI [2], described AI agents as "systems that can take actions in digital environments based on goals, learn from feedback, and improve over time without explicit programming for each scenario." This definition emphasizes adaptability and goal orientation.

Demis Hassabis of DeepMind [14] characterizes agents as "AI systems that can perceive, decide, and act with increasing levels of autonomy to achieve specific objectives." His definition highlights the spectrum of autonomy that agents can exhibit.

Google's recent framework [29] defines generative AI agents as "autonomous and able to act independently of human intervention, especially when provided with proper goals or objectives they are meant to achieve." This definition specifically incorporates the role of generative AI in modern agent architectures.

2.2 Synthesis of AI Agent Definitions

Analyzing these definitions reveals several common elements.

- Environment perception
- Autonomous action
- Goal orientation
- Temporal persistence

The key differences lie primarily in:

- The degree of autonomy required
- The emphasis on learning and adaptation

In this paper, we focus specifically on generative AI agents operating in digital environments. This focus allows us to narrow our scope to agents that leverage generative AI models (particularly large language models) to interact with digital systems, tools, and information sources.

Based on this analysis and our specific focus, we propose the following comprehensive definition.

A generative AI agent is a computational system that autonomously perceives its digital environment, maintains an internal state, reasons about its observations using generative AI capabilities, and takes actions to achieve specified goals or fulfill delegated tasks, with the capacity to adapt its behavior based on experience and feedback.

This definition encompasses the essential characteristics identified in the literature while acknowledging our specific focus on generative AI agents in digital contexts. This definition also serves as our anchor to explore our hypothesis throughout this paper.

2.3 Key Characteristics of Generative AI Agents

The definition we have established encompasses four fundamental characteristics that distinguish generative AI agents from other computational systems. While some of the following characteristics may be found individually in other computational systems, it is their unique combination that sets generative AI agents apart:

Environment Perception: Generative AI agents actively collect and process information from their digital environment through multiple channels, including knowledge bases, APIs, user inputs, and tool interactions. This multi-faceted perception enables them to construct a comprehensive understanding of their operational context and available options. For example, a customer service agent might simultaneously access a product database, review conversation history, and monitor user sentiment to inform its responses.

Autonomous Action: These agents can independently select and execute appropriate actions based on their perception and goals without requiring step-by-step human guidance. While operating within defined parameters, they make independent decisions about which specific actions to take in different situations. For instance, a scheduling agent might autonomously determine whether to propose alternative meeting times, request clarification, or directly book an appointment based on calendar availability and user preferences.

Goal Orientation: Generative AI agents work toward specific objectives, whether explicitly defined in their instructions or implicitly derived from context. This involves planning action sequences, prioritizing tasks, and adjusting strategies when initial approaches prove ineffective. A research agent, for example, might decompose a complex query into sub-questions, pursue multiple information sources, and synthesize findings to achieve its goal of providing comprehensive information.

Temporal Persistence: Unlike simple query-response systems, generative AI agents maintain continuity of operation over time, preserving relevant state information between interactions, learning from past experiences, and adapting behavior based on historical outcomes. This enables them to engage in extended task sequences while maintaining context. A personal assistant agent demonstrates this by remembering user preferences, referencing previous conversations, and improving its recommendations based on past feedback.

2.4 Distinction from Other Intelligent Systems

To further clarify the concept of generative AI agents, it is useful to distinguish them from related technologies:

Traditional Software Applications execute predefined instructions and follow explicit programming logic. In contrast, generative AI agents can reason about novel situations and generate appropriate responses without explicit programming for each scenario.

Expert Systems rely on predefined rules and knowledge bases to make decisions within narrow domains. While powerful for specific applications, they lack the adaptability and learning capabilities of generative AI agents, which can continuously improve their performance through experience.

Process Automation Tools follow rigid workflows or perform repetitive tasks according to fixed patterns and predefined decision points. However, Generative

AI agents can handle complex and dynamic situations that require judgment, reasoning, and adaptation to changing circumstances.

Large Language Models (LLMs) by themselves are not agents but rather components that can be incorporated into agent architectures. An LLM provides reasoning and generation capabilities, but lacks the complete perception-action cycle that defines a true agent unless integrated with additional components for environment interaction.

These distinctions highlight the unique position of generative AI agents in the spectrum of intelligent systems, combining the reasoning capabilities of advanced AI models with the action-oriented nature of autonomous systems. It is important to note that, given the wide range of computational systems, some may share individual features with generative AI agents. However, it is the integration of reasoning, learning, adaptability, and autonomous action within a single system that uniquely characterizes generative AI agents. This combination enables them to operate effectively in complex, dynamic environments, distinguishing them from other intelligent systems.

2.5 Conclusion of the Definition of AI Agents

The emergence of generative AI agents represents a significant evolution in artificial intelligence, moving beyond passive response systems to active, goal-oriented participants in digital environments. By integrating the perception-action cycle with the reasoning capabilities of large language models, these agents offer unprecedented potential for automating complex tasks, augmenting human capabilities, and transforming how we interact with digital systems.

As the field continues to evolve, the definition and characteristics we've established provide a foundation for understanding and evaluating generative AI agents. The four key characteristics—environment perception, autonomous action, goal orientation, and temporal persistence—offer a framework for assessing the capabilities and limitations of different agent implementations.

With a working definition of AI agents in place (see Subsect. 2.2), we next examine how BPM treats its own autonomous participants, known as subjects. We will explore how subjects respectively process participants are defined in the context of Business Process Management (BPM) and if this could support the description and analysis of deployed AI agents in specified processes.

3 Definition of Subjects in Business Process Management

In the realm of business process management (BPM), clearly defining process participants is crucial for effective modeling, analysis, and execution. These participants, often referred to as "subjects", play distinct roles and responsibilities within a process[1]. This chapter provides an overview of how subjects are defined

---

[1] In the context of PASS modeling, it is important to differentiate between the active entity or person (referred to as the "actor" or "subject carrier") and the "subject" as a model component within a Subject Interaction Diagram (SID), which represents a process-specific role rather than the active entity itself (see [9]).

and handled in different process management notations, with a focus on Business Process Model and Notation 2.0 (BPMN) and Parallel Activity Specification Schema (PASS).

3.1 Subject Orientation in Business Process Management (S-BPM)

Subject-Oriented Business Process Management (S-BPM) places the "subject" at the center of process design. According to Albert Fleischmann et al. [9], a subject is an autonomous entity that communicates with other subjects to achieve a common goal. In S-BPM, subjects are not merely passive executors of tasks but active participants that make decisions and control their interactions.

Core characteristics of subjects in S-BPM include:

- **Autonomy:** Subjects have the ability to make decisions and act independently within the boundaries of the process.
- **Communication:** Subjects interact with each other through message exchange, enabling coordination and collaboration.
- **Encapsulation:** Subjects encapsulate their internal behavior and data, exposing only necessary interfaces to other subjects.

The Parallel Activity Specification Schema (PASS) serves as the modeling notation for S-BPM, providing a graphical language to represent subjects, their interactions, and the overall process flow [9].

Roles and Responsibilities of Subjects in Processes. In general process management literature, roles and responsibilities are essential for defining who does what within a process. Roles define the expected behavior of a process participant, while responsibilities specify the tasks and decisions they are accountable for [6].

PASS formalizes these concepts through the subject construct, where each subject embodies specific roles and responsibilities. The subject's behavior is defined by the messages it sends and receives, as well as the internal logic that governs its actions. While PASS emphasizes the autonomy and communication of subjects, BPMN offers a complementary approach to representing process participants, which we discuss next.

3.2 Process Participants and Swim Lanes in BPMN

BPMN is a widely adopted standard for modeling business processes. In BPMN, process participants are represented through pools and lanes. Pools are used to define the boundaries and participants of a process, and a BPMN diagram may contain multiple pools to represent different participants or organizations. Each pool typically encapsulates the process flow for a specific participant, while lanes within a pool represent organizational units or roles within that participant's process [12].

BPMN uses swim lanes to visually represent the responsibilities of different process participants. Each lane is assigned to a specific role or organizational unit, and activities within that lane are performed by the corresponding participant. To provide a broader context, the following section briefly compares BPMN and PASS with other modeling approaches that also address process participants.

3.3 Brief Comparison with Other Modeling Approaches

Other process modeling approaches, such as Event-driven Process Chains (EPC) and UML Activity Diagrams, also provide mechanisms for representing process participants. EPC uses functions to represent activities and organizational units to assign responsibilities [26]. UML Activity Diagrams use swim lanes and actors to model process participants [13] and are similar to BPMN.

However, this chapter focuses on BPMN and PASS due to their widespread adoption and specific emphasis on subjects and their interactions. BPMN is the most widely accepted modeling language, while PASS is specifically designed to capture the subject-oriented nature of processes.

3.4 Conclusion of the Definition of Subjects in Business Process Management

Defining process participants is essential for effective process management. PASS, the process notation of S-BPM, places the "subject" at the center of process design, emphasizing autonomy, communication, and encapsulation. BPMN, a widely adopted standard, uses pools and lanes to represent process participants and their responsibilities. While other modeling approaches exist, this chapter focuses on BPMN and PASS due to their relevance and focus on subjects.

It is noteworthy that the definition of a "subject" in process management, especially as described in S-BPM for PASS, shares remarkable similarities with the emerging concept of AI agents. Both are characterized by autonomy, the ability to communicate, and encapsulated behavior. This conceptual overlap raises interesting questions about the relationship between subjects and AI agents in modern process management. In the following chapter, we will explore this connection in greater detail and examine how the subject concept can inform the understanding and modeling of AI agents in business processes.

4 Comparison of Subjects and AI Agents

4.1 Research Overview: AI Agents in Business Process Management

Before contrasting subjects with agents, we summarize recent research that frames this comparison. The intersection of AI agents and Business Process Management (BPM) has become a vibrant area of research, especially with the rise of generative AI and autonomous systems. Recent scientific literature highlights several key trends and challenges in this domain.

A 2024 editorial in Information Systems and e-Business Management outlines how BPM is being transformed by AI, noting a shift from traditional automation to "autonomization," where AI agents are not only automating tasks but also making decisions and adapting processes dynamically. The authors emphasize the emergence of conversational BPM, where both humans and AI agents engage in process-related dialogues, and the need for BPM to integrate both transactional and conversational logic. This work also points out that the next generation of BPM will require new conceptualizations of process participants, including non-human agency such as AI agents [23].

Another recent open-access paper, "Responsible AI-Based Business Process Management and Improvement" (2024), discusses the integration of AI agents into BPM from a governance and ethics perspective. The authors propose that responsible and trustworthy BPM systems must include well-defined control points and audit mechanisms, especially as AI agents become more involved in process execution and decision-making. They highlight the importance of explainability, transparency, and compliance with regulations such as GDPR when deploying AI agents in business processes [21].

A systematic review published in July 2024 provides a comprehensive analysis of how AI and machine learning are being integrated into BPM. The review categorizes the literature according to the BPM lifecycle and finds that AI agents are increasingly used for both process enhancement (analyzing and describing process information) and process improvement (redesigning processes based on AI-driven insights). The authors note that while AI agents offer significant potential for optimizing processes, there remain open research questions regarding their integration, governance, and the modeling of their behavior within established BPM frameworks [1].

Related Modeling Approaches. The integration of AI agents into business process management builds on a rich landscape of related modeling approaches, each contributing valuable concepts and techniques. Three particularly relevant streams are agent-oriented software engineering (AOSE), the broader field of BPM+AI, and the integration of Decision Model and Notation (DMN) with AI.

AOSE provides a methodological foundation for designing complex systems as collections of interacting autonomous agents. AOSE methodologies such as ADELFE, ASPECS, INGENIAS, MaSE, PASSI, Prometheus, SODA, and Tropos have been developed to address the challenges of autonomy, communication, and collaboration in distributed systems. Recent reviews highlight that while AOSE offers robust frameworks for modeling agent behavior and interaction, its application to business process modeling remains limited, often lacking a direct focus on the specific requirements and context of business processes (see [5]).

The integration of artificial intelligence into business process management (BPM+AI) has gained significant momentum in recent years. As discussed in [7], Chap. 4.4 "Einbeziehung von Künstlicher Intelligenz" ("Inclusion of Artificial Intelligence"), AI is increasingly used to enhance process execution, enable predictive analytics, and support intelligent automation. Notably, several findings and conceptual frameworks from this chapter are highly relevant to our work. The approaches described in the book typically position AI as an enabler for process optimization, decision support, and automation, but often treat AI as a supplementary tool rather than as an integral, generative component of the process model itself.

Decision Model and Notation (DMN) has emerged as a standard for modeling and automating business decision logic. Recent work demonstrates how DMN, when integrated with AI, enables the automation of complex, data-driven decision-making within business processes (see [3] and [19]). DMN provides a formal, transparent, and auditable framework for decision automation, and its integration with BPMN and AI technologies allows for the creation of flexible, adaptive process solutions. However, DMN-based approaches typically focus on the formalization and automation of decision logic, rather than on the dynamic, generative capabilities of AI agents.

In summary, while AOSE, BPM+AI, and DMN integration each offer valuable perspectives and tools for modeling intelligent, automated processes, our work focuses specifically on AI agents created with generative AI and automation. These agents are conceived as integral, adaptive components of business processes, capable of autonomous learning and innovation. This focus distinguishes our approach from existing methodologies, which either emphasize agent interaction in general software systems, the supportive role of AI in BPM, or the formalization of decision logic without generative intelligence.

These recent studies collectively indicate that the research community is actively exploring the role of AI agents in BPM, with a particular focus on their autonomy, interaction modalities, and the challenges of responsible integration. Although the challenges for integrating such AI agents are known, no prior work examines how traditional BPM tools, especially subject-oriented approaches, can support the modeling and analysis of AI agents and overcome those challenges.

4.2 Properties and Capabilities: A Comparative Analysis

Both subjects and AI agents are defined as autonomous entities capable of perceiving their environment, making decisions, and interacting with other participants. In PASS, subjects are process participants that encapsulate their own behavior and data, communicate via message exchange, and act independently within the boundaries of the process [9]. Similarly, generative AI agents are computational systems that autonomously perceive their digital environment, maintain internal state, reason about observations, and take actions to achieve specified goals (see Subsect. 2.2).

A closer look at their core characteristics reveals the following parallels:

- **Autonomy:** Both subjects and AI agents act independently, making decisions based on their internal logic or learned models. Importantly, both are constrained by the boundaries of the process in which they operate. For AI agents, this means that their generative capabilities and adaptive behaviors are only exercised within the scope defined by the process model—just as

human subjects are autonomous only within the limits of their assigned process roles. The degree of autonomy is thus not a function of being human or artificial, but of the granularity and openness of the process description itself.
- **Communication and Interaction:** Subjects interact through explicit message exchanges, coordinating process execution. AI agents, especially in multi-agent systems, also communicate—either with other agents, users, or digital systems—using structured protocols or natural language. While it may appear that AI agents have more freedom in their interaction modalities, in a well-modeled process, the communication of AI agents should also be described, at least to some degree, ensuring consistency and predictability.
- **Encapsulation:** Subjects encapsulate their internal state and expose only necessary interfaces. AI agents similarly maintain an internal state, often including memory, goals, and learned knowledge, and interact with their environment through defined APIs or interfaces.
- **Goal Orientation:** Both are driven by objectives—subjects by process goals, AI agents by delegated tasks or user-defined goals, which can themselves be process or sub-process goals.
- **Temporal Persistence:** Subjects and AI agents both exhibit continuity over time, maintaining context across multiple interactions or process steps.

4.3 Autonomy, Decision-Making, and Interaction: Nuances and Boundaries

While the similarities are substantial, it is important to address the nuances in autonomy, decision-making, and interaction:

- **Degree of Autonomy:** Both human subjects and AI agents can only act autonomously within the boundaries defined by the process or their behavioral models. The apparent difference in autonomy is often a reflection of the level of detail in the process description. If a process is described at a high level, both human and AI subjects have greater freedom to interpret and act; if the process is highly detailed, both are more constrained. Thus, the modeling approach, not the nature of the participant, determines the scope of autonomy.
- **Decision Making:** Similarly, the decision-making capacity of both subjects and AI agents is bounded by the process model. Human subjects may exercise judgment and discretion when the process is under-specified, just as AI agents may use probablistic or heuristic reasoning or learning algorithms within their allowed scope. The key point is that both are ultimately governed by the process boundaries and the granularity of the behavioral specification.
- **Interaction Modalities:** Although AI agents may technically be capable of a wide range of interaction modalities (e.g., APIs, natural language, multimodal interfaces), in a process management context, their communication should be modeled and constrained as part of the process design, just as is done for human subjects. This ensures that interactions remain predictable and aligned with process objectives.

4.4 Synthesis: PASS Sufficiency for AI Agent Modeling

The conceptual and functional overlap between subjects and AI agents suggests that established BPM methods are fully sufficient for modeling and analyzing AI agents. The subject construct in PASS (and BPMN when applied) already encapsulates the essential properties of autonomy, communication, and encapsulation. By extending the behavioral models of subjects to incorporate learning and adaptive capabilities, AI agents can be seamlessly integrated into existing BPM modeling frameworks like PASS and BPMN.

This perspective supports the hypothesis that the established BPM notations, particularly PASS, provide a robust foundation for the analysis and modeling of AI agents in business processes. Rather than inventing new modeling paradigms, practitioners and researchers can leverage the proven tools and methodologies of subject-oriented BPM to address the challenges and opportunities presented by AI agents.

The comparison of subjects and AI agents reveals a high degree of conceptual alignment, with both serving as autonomous, communicative, and goal-oriented participants in business processes. While AI agents introduce new capabilities in terms of learning and adaptability, their core characteristics are already well-represented in the subject-oriented BPM paradigms. This finding underscores the continued relevance of established BPM methods for the analysis and integration of AI-driven process participants.

5 Modeling of AI Agents in Process Models

The emergence of AI agents—capable of autonomous action, learning, and dynamic adaptation—poses new challenges for process modeling, but also reveals the flexibility of established notations.

The modeling approaches for AI agents presented in Elstermann et al. [7] have been particularly influential for this work, providing valuable conceptual frameworks and practical guidance that have shaped both the analysis and the modeling strategies discussed in this chapter. Also other research has begun to address the question of how agents can be effectively represented within business process models. For example, studies have explored the extension of BPMN to include intelligent service tasks or agent-like participants (e.g. [6]), while subject-oriented approaches such as S-BPM and PASS naturally align with the concept of autonomous, communicative entities. Despite these advances, there remains a lack of consensus on best practices for modeling AI agents, particularly regarding their roles, interactions, and boundaries within organizational processes.

5.1 Conceptual Integration of AI Agents

Integrating AI agents into process models requires a clear conceptualization of their function and status within the process. Two main approaches can be identified:

1. AI agents can be modeled as special process participants, similar to human actors or organizational roles. In this approach, the AI agent is assigned specific tasks or responsibilities within the process, and its interactions with other participants are explicitly defined. This method is compatible with both BPMN (using pools or lanes) and PASS, where each subject represents an autonomous entity.
2. AI agents can be represented as dedicated subjects, fully equivalent to human or organizational subjects. This approach leverages the inherent strengths of subject-oriented modeling, which emphasizes communication and autonomy. Here, the AI agent is not merely a tool or service, but an active participant capable of initiating and responding to process events.

The key challenge for both approaches lies in accurately capturing the AI agent's capabilities, decision logic, and interaction patterns. Unlike traditional automated tasks, AI agents may exhibit non-deterministic behavior, learn from experience, and adapt their actions over time. This necessitates a modeling paradigm that supports dynamic, context-sensitive behavior and clear interfaces for human-AI collaboration.

5.2 Modeling AI Agents: BPMN vs. PASS

To illustrate the integration of AI agents in process models, we compare two widely used notations: BPMN and PASS. Both notations offer mechanisms for representing autonomous entities, but differ in their conceptual foundations and modeling constructs.

In BPMN, AI agents can be modeled as separate pools or lanes, interacting with human participants via message flows (see Fig. 1). Tasks performed by the AI agent, such as analyzing customer sentiment or routing inquiries, are represented as service tasks or subprocesses. However, BPMN's focus on control flow and its limited support for explicit communication patterns can make it challenging to capture the full range of AI agent behaviors, especially when the AI agent interacts with multiple process participants. The different message flows and independent interactions are challenging to display in such cases with BPMN [20]. It is important to note that BPMN supports the concept of "black box" pools, where a participant's internal process is intentionally left unspecified and only its interactions with other participants are modeled (see [12]). This approach is particularly useful when the internal logic of an AI agent (or any external system) is either unknown, proprietary, or irrelevant to the current modeling scope. Nevertheless, modeling complex communication flows remains challenging.

In contrast, PASS is inherently subject-oriented, making it well-suited for modeling AI agents as autonomous subjects (see Fig. 2). Each subject in PASS encapsulates its own behavior and communicates with other subjects via message exchanges. Goals, required data, utilized software, and tools can be specified within the subject. This aligns closely with the AI agent paradigm, enabling a natural representation of both human and AI participants as peers within the process.

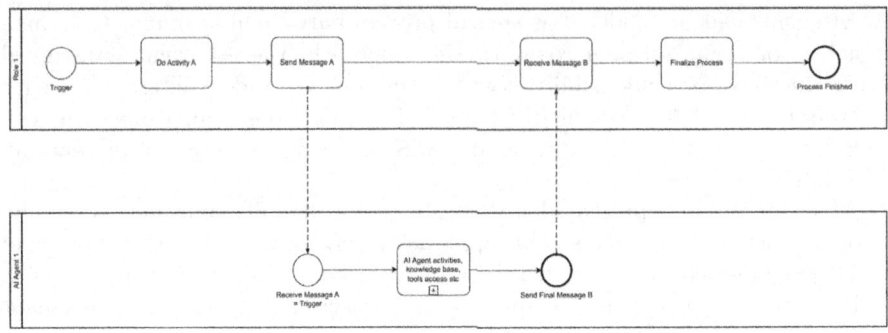

Fig. 1. Schematic representation of an AI agent with BPMN

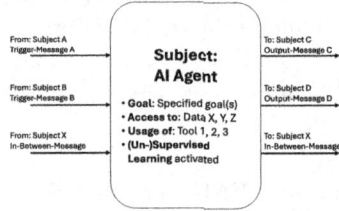

Fig. 2. Schematic representation of an AI agent as subject with PASS (Subject Interaction Diagram)

Application Example: Intelligent Call Center Agents. A practical example of AI agent integration can be found in modern customer service environments (see [22]), where intelligent call center agents orchestrate the handling of customer inquiries. In this scenario, AI agents analyze customer sentiment in real time, access relevant customer data, and propose solutions. They are capable of autonomously resolving simple requests and escalating more complex cases to human employees, providing all necessary context and information.

The process begins when a customer inquiry is received. The AI agent evaluates the request, determines its complexity, and either resolves the issue directly or forwards it to a human agent. Throughout the process, the AI agent maintains communication with both the customer and human staff, ensuring seamless information flow and efficient resolution.

In Fig. 3 we modeled the AI Agents behaviour with PASS and in Fig. 4 with BPMN and thus could define the requirements for this Customer Service AI Agent. Due to these complexities, we have refrained from modeling customer queries and more intensive communication with 2nd level support in BPMN. Albert Fleischmann has described the challenges of modeling choreographies (or message flows) with BPMN in detail in his paper "Limitations of Choreography Specifications with BPMN" [8].

The interaction between the AI agent and other process participants is characterized by clear handover points, transparent decision criteria, and continuous

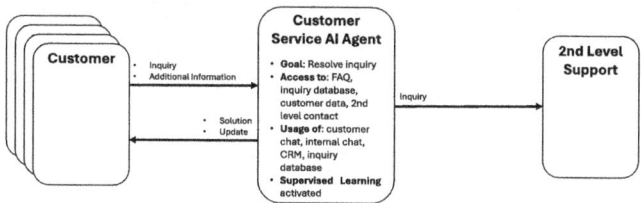

Fig. 3. Intelligent Call Center Agent described as subject within PASS (Subject Interaction Diagram)

feedback. The AI agent's ability to learn from past cases and adapt its behavior further enhances process efficiency and customer satisfaction. With PASS this interaction can be modeled without the need of new modeling rules, or complex models as the definition of an AI agent and a subject is very similar. On the other hand, with BPMN there are some challenges, as the representation of a complex process choreography faces some challenges. This is one of the reasons to extend the BPMN.

5.3 Empirical Validation: Insights from Expert Interviews

To empirically ground the central hypothesis of this work—that established process modeling notations, specifically PASS and BPMN, are sufficient to describe, analyze, and govern AI agents in business processes—a series of structured expert interviews was conducted. Six leading practitioners and researchers, each with substantial experience in designing and deploying AI agents, were invited to critically assess both the conceptual framework and the practical modeling approaches presented in this study [4, 15, 17, 25, 28, 31].

Validation of the Generative AI Agent Definition. Across all interviews, the synthesized definition of a generative AI agent—as an autonomous computational system capable of perceiving its digital environment, maintaining internal state, reasoning with generative AI capabilities, and adapting its behavior based on experience and feedback—was consistently validated [4, 15, 17, 25, 28, 31]. Experts highlighted the clarity and completeness of this definition, noting its alignment with both academic literature and current industry practice [17, 25, 28]. However, several interviewees emphasized that adaptive learning and behavioral change, while desirable, are not inherent to all agent implementations [4, 15, 31]. Instead, such capabilities typically require explicit design and, in most real-world scenarios, are realized through supervised or externally managed learning pipelines [4, 15]. This distinction is particularly salient in sensitive domains such as healthcare, where explainability, auditability, and robust feedback validation are paramount [15].

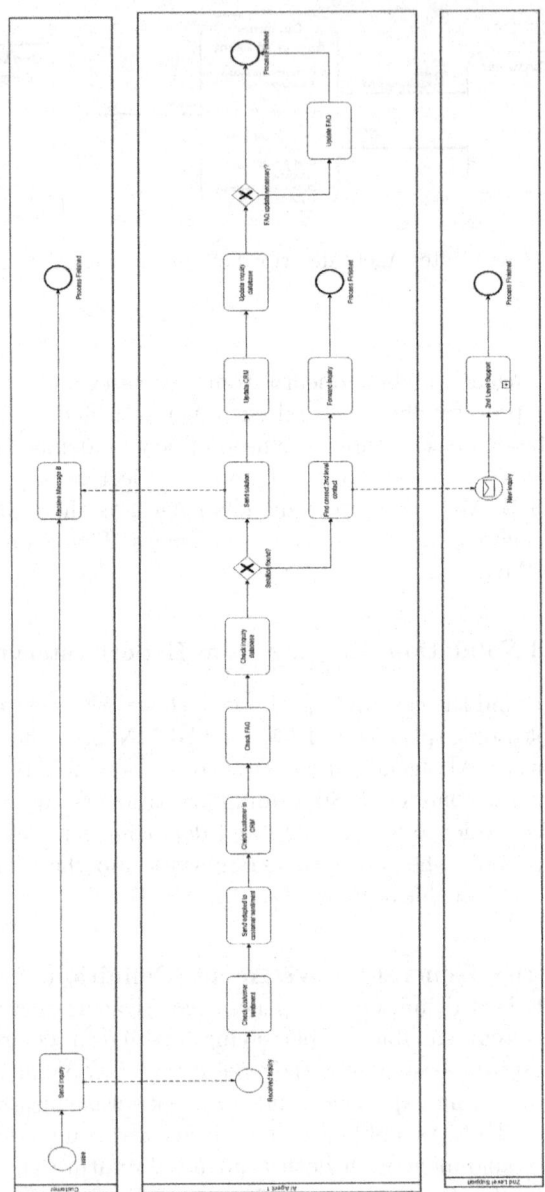

Fig. 4. Intelligent Call Center Agent described with BPMN

Modeling AI Agents with PASS and BPMN. The modeling of AI agents as subjects within PASS Subject Interaction Diagrams (SID) was universally regarded as both intuitive and effective [4,17,25,28]. Experts agreed that this approach naturally encapsulates the agent's goals, data access, tool usage, and learning mechanisms, providing a clear and actionable specification for development [17,25]. The use of BPMN, particularly through pools, lanes, and explicit message flows, was also seen as viable—especially in organizations with established BPMN toolchains and compliance routines [4,17]. Nevertheless, several experts noted that BPMN models can quickly become unwieldy when representing highly dynamic, agent-driven processes with complex communication patterns [25,28]. In such cases, the abstraction and communication-centric focus of PASS was seen as advantageous [28]. A recurring scenario throughout the interviews was the modeling of a customer service AI agent. Here, the agent's responsibilities—ranging from resolving inquiries using knowledge bases and CRM systems to escalating complex cases and integrating feedback for continuous improvement—were mapped in detail [4,17,25]. Experts stressed the importance of explicitly modeling agent autonomy, tool selection, and the boundaries between agent-driven and human-driven process steps [4,17,25]. The distinction between static automation and dynamic, tool-selecting agents was repeatedly highlighted as a critical modeling consideration [17,28].

Challenges and Recommendations. Several practical challenges emerged from the interviews. Chief among them were the assurance of explainability and traceability in agent decision-making, the validation and governance of feedback used for learning, and the integration of multi-agent architectures [4,15,25]. Experts recommended the implementation of robust logging and internal reasoning traceability, particularly in high-stakes or regulated environments [4,15]. The iterative, layered modeling of agent roles and interactions—starting from high-level communication flows and refining as needed—was identified as a pragmatic approach, balancing clarity with necessary detail [4,28]. Importantly, all experts concurred that existing BPM methods—PASS and BPMN—are fundamentally sufficient for modeling AI agents [4,15,17,25,28,31]. There was no perceived need for entirely new modeling languages. Instead, the combination of established notations with visual agent frameworks and disciplined modeling guidelines was seen as the most effective path forward [4,25].

Synthesis and Implications. The empirical findings from these expert interviews strongly support the central hypothesis of this work. The definition of generative AI agents was validated as both comprehensive and practically relevant, with the caveat that learning and adaptation must be explicitly designed and governed [4,15]. PASS and BPMN were both confirmed as suitable modeling languages for capturing the roles, interactions, and requirements of AI agents, though each presents distinct strengths depending on the complexity and dynamism of the process in question [17,25,28]. In summary, the interviews reinforce the argument that practitioners can—and should—leverage the modeling tools and process knowledge already embedded in their organizations to integrate AI agents into business processes [4,25]. Rather than awaiting new notations or paradigms, the focus should be on refining modeling discipline, ensuring traceability, and iteratively cataloguing domain-specific use cases. This empirical validation not only strengthens the theoretical foundation of this study but also provides actionable guidance for organizations seeking to operationalize AI agents within established BPM frameworks.

5.4 Discussion: Advantages and Challenges

The preceding analysis confirms that AI agents can be successfully embedded in both PASS and BPMN models, yet the two notations offer different strengths and expose different pain-points.

Conceptual Leverage in PASS. PASS reveals a near one-to-one mapping between the agent abstraction and its native subject construct. The strict separation of Subject Interaction Diagrams (communication) and Subject Behaviour Diagrams (internal logic) mirrors the separation between an agent's public API and its private reasoning cycle. This alignment keeps models compact and allows selective deep-dives into only those subjects that require inspection.

Breadth of Ecosystem in BPMN. BPMN wins on tooling maturity: almost every BPMS, simulation engine and governance dashboard understands its XML serialization. Integrated conformance checkers can flag missing agent references, while instance-level monitoring is widely supported. The price is diagram verbosity: complex agent conversations can result in numerous message-flow arcs, and BPMN's one-to-one send/receive rule demands work-arounds for broadcast or multi-cast events.

Research Outlook. This paper constitutes an initial probe; the real exploration begins now. Concrete next steps include:

- **Domain catalogs.** Curate reference models for customer service, supply-chain resilience, engineering change, etc., and test notation sufficiency case by case.
- **Dynamic conformance.** Extend process-mining and monitoring tools to recognize agent learning curves and detect policy drift.
- **Hybrid governance patterns.** Define escalation, roll-back and audit hooks that bind self-optimizing agents to human oversight without throttling their autonomy.

Despite these strengths, modeling AI agents presents ongoing challenges. Capturing non-deterministic behavior, learning, and adaptation requires annotation schemas or meta-models that can record adaptive logic without sacrificing model clarity. Governance of self-adaptation and runtime drift must be addressed, potentially through declarative overlays or enhanced monitoring tools. These challenges transcend notation boundaries and represent important areas for future research.

In summary, both BPMN and PASS provide robust mechanisms for integrating AI agents into process models. PASS offers a near one-to-one mapping between the agent abstraction and its subject construct, while BPMN benefits from a mature ecosystem and broad tool support. The choice of notation should be guided by the specific requirements of the modeling context, the desired level of abstraction, and the need for clarity in representing agent autonomy and interaction.

These avenues will deepen our understanding of where PASS and BPMN shine, where extensions are warranted, and how organizations can harvest the full value of AI agents while staying firmly in control. The insights pave the way for the synthesis presented in Sect. 6.

6 Summary and Conclusion

This study set out with a deliberately conservative hypothesis: established BPM notations, BPMN and PASS, are already fit to model AI agents. The investigation unfolded in four stages and produced four corresponding insights.

1. **A shared vocabulary.** Section 2 distilled generative AI agents into four essential capabilities: environment perception, autonomous action, goal orientation and temporal persistence. These capabilities form a checklist that any process notation must capture if it claims to support agent-centric scenarios.
2. **Conceptual alignment.** Section 3 revisited BPM's subject construct and showed that PASS subjects already embody the very same four capabilities and BPMN pools and lanes to some extent. No new symbol set is required, the semantics are in place.
3. **Pragmatic modeling.** In Section 4 the conceptual overlap was validated by a side-by-side comparison. PASS offers an immediately natural mapping: every agent becomes just another subject. BPMN, while more verbose, reaches functional parity when pools, lanes and explicit message flows are used consistently.
4. **Empirical evidence.** Section 5 not only translated an intelligent call-center scenario into both notations, but also incorporated new empirical validation through structured expert interviews (Sect. 5.3). These interviews confirmed the practical sufficiency of PASS and BPMN for modeling AI agents, highlighted the importance of modeling agent autonomy and learning explicitly, and identified best practices and challenges for real-world adoption.

Key Findings.

- The four agent capabilities map directly to PASS's design principles and can be rendered, with more diagrammatic effort, in BPMN.
- PASS excels in communication-centric and adaptive scenarios; BPMN remains advantageous in organizations with established tool-chains and compliance routines.
- No blocking syntax limitations were encountered; even perceived weaknesses in BPMN (e.g. one-to-one message bindings) can be mitigated through modeling discipline.

– Empirical validation from expert interviews strongly supports the central hypothesis, while also emphasizing the need for explicit modeling of learning, explainability, and governance in agent-driven processes.

Conclusion. The evidence supports the working hypothesis: **AI agents can be described, analyzed and governed today with mainstream BPM notations.** Practitioners therefore do not need to await a new modeling fad before they bring agentic automation under process governance; they can build on the diagrams, repositories and skill sets already in place.

Outlook. This paper should be read as a starting point, not a closing statement. Different application domains will pose distinct demands on agent autonomy, learning, and auditability. Future work should conduct controlled empirical comparisons of PASS and BPMN, catalog domain-specific use cases, extend tool support for conformance and monitoring, refine modeling guidelines for non-deterministic logic, and investigate governance mechanisms for self-improving agents.

By grounding these next steps in BPMN and PASS, the community can move directly from exploratory prototypes to auditable, enterprise-grade deployments, leveraging what it already knows while embracing the capabilities of AI agents.

References

1. Abbasi, M., Nishat, R.I., Bond, C., Graham-Knight, J.B., Lasserre, P., Lucet, Y., Najjaran, H.: A review of AI and machine learning contribution in predictive business process management (process enhancement and process improvement approaches). arXiv preprint arXiv:2407.11043 (2024). https://arxiv.org/abs/2407.11043
2. Altman, S.: The future of AI (6 2024). https://www.youtube.com/live/U9mJuUkhUzk?si=abY_2COiQDQVqrN. Keynote address at OpenAI DevDay, San Francisco, CA
3. Bonham, A.: The power of decision model and notation (DMN). https://medium.com/capital-one-tech/the-power-of-decision-model-and-notation-dmn-976de4f9d35e (2024). Accessed: 2025-06-04
4. Claus-Ahrens, M.: Expert interview on generative AI agents and process modeling (2025), expert in AI and AI Agents, Personal communication, 4 June 2025
5. Cossentino, M., Gleizes, M.P., Molesini, A., Omicini, A.: Processes engineering and aose. In: International Workshop on Agent-Oriented Software Engineering, pp. 191–212. Springer (2009)
6. Dumas, M., La Rosa, M., Mendling, J., Reijers, H.A.: Fundamentals of Business Process Management. Springer, 2 edn. (2018). https://doi.org/10.1007/978-3-662-56509-4
7. Elstermann, M., Fleischmann, A., Moser, C., Oppl, S., Schmidt, W., Stary, C.: Ganzheitliche Digitalisierung von Prozessen. Springer (2023)
8. Fleischmann, A.: Limitations of choreography specifications with BPMN. In: Subject-Oriented Business Process Management. The Digital Workplace–Nucleus of Transformation: 12th International Conference, S-BPM ONE 2020, Bremen, Germany, December 2-3, 2020, Proceedings 12. pp. 203–216. Springer (2020)

9. Fleischmann, A., Schmidt, W., Stary, C., Obermeier, S., Börger, E.: Subject-oriented business process management. Springer Nature (2012)
10. Franklin, S., Graesser, A.: Is it an agent, or just a program?: A taxonomy for autonomous agents. In: International Workshop on Agent Theories, Architectures, and Languages, pp. 21–35. Springer (1996)
11. Google Trends: Search term: "AI agent" (2025), retrieved April 20, (2025). from https://trends.google.com/trends/
12. Group, O.M.: Business process model and notation (BPMN), version 2.0.2. Tech. rep., Object Management Group (2013). https://www.omg.org/spec/BPMN/2.0.2/. OMG Document Number: formal/2013-12-09
13. Group, O.M.: Unified modeling language (UML), version 2.5.1. Tech. rep., Object Management Group (2017). https://www.omg.org/spec/UML/2.5.1/. OMG Document Number: formal/2017-12-05
14. Hassabis, D.: AI and the future of scientific discovery. Nature **617**(7960), 456–458 (5 2024)
15. Hölzle, C.: Expert interview on generative AI agents and process modeling (2025), master's programs in Medical Informatics at Harvard Medical School, specialized in AI, Personal communication, 5 June 2025
16. LinkedIn Economic Graph: Mentions of "AI agent" in professional posts (2025). retrieved April 18, 2025, from https://economicgraph.linkedin.com/
17. Mattiello, A.: Expert interview on generative AI agents and process modeling (2025), AI Academy Course Coordinator and Coaching Manager, Personal communication, 5 June 2025
18. Microsoft: Microsoft Copilot: Your everyday AI companion (2023). https://blogs.microsoft.com/blog/2023/09/21/introducing-microsoft-copilot-your-everyday-ai-companion/. Accessed: 2025-04-18
19. Nell, P.: From data to decisions: a more detailed look into decision automation with DMN. https://www.sulzer.de/en/news/from-data-to-decisions-a-more-detailed-look-into-decision-automation-with-dmn (2024). Accessed: 2025-06-04
20. Piller, C.: Comparing BPMN 2.0 and pass: a review and analysis of previous research. In: International Conference on Subject-Oriented Business Process Management, pp. 163–179. Springer (2023)
21. Pisoni, G., Moloney, M.: Responsible AI-based business process management and improvement. Digit. Soc. **3**(23) (2024). https://doi.org/10.1007/s44206-024-00105-2
22. Pratt, M.K.: 10 real-world agentic AI examples and use cases (2025). https://www.techtarget.com/searchenterpriseai/feature/Real-world-agentic-AI-examples-and-use-cases. Accessed: 2025-04-28
23. Rosemann, M., vom Brocke, J., Van Looy, A., Santoro, F.: Business process management in the age of AI - three essential drifts. IseB **22**, 415–429 (2024). https://doi.org/10.1007/s10257-024-00689-9
24. Russell, S., Norvig, P.: Artificial Intelligence: A Modern Approach. Pearson, 4 edn. (2020)
25. Salve, A.D.: Expert interview on generative AI agents and process modeling (2025), freelance Consultant and Coach in Generative AI and No-Code Automation, Personal communication, 5 June 2025
26. Scheer, A.W.: ARIS—Business Process Modeling. Springer (2000)
27. Significant Gravitas: AutoGPT (2023). https://github.com/Significant-Gravitas/AutoGPT

28. Wengel, J.: Expert interview on generative AI agents and process modeling (2025), sole Proprietor in the field of IT Training and Consulting, Personal communication, 5 June 2025
29. Wiesinger, J., Patrick, M., Vladimir, V.: Agents (2024). https://github.com/daiwk/collections/blob/master/assets/google-ai-agents-whitepaper.pdf
30. Wooldridge, M.: An Introduction to MultiAgent Systems. John Wiley & Sons, 2 edn. (2009)
31. Yu, J.: Expert interview on generative AI agents and process modeling (2025), AI Automation Development Consultant, Personal communication, 4 June 2025

From Process Designers to AI Facilitators: The Transformative Impact of Agentic AI on Business Process Managers

Saskia Schmid[✉] and Christian Schieder

Technical University of Applied Sciences Amberg-Weiden, Hetzenrichter Weg 15, 92637 Weiden, Germany
saskia.schmid95@gmail.com

Abstract. The increasing integration of agentic Artificial Intelligence (AI) – autonomous, adaptive AI systems – is fundamentally changing the role of business process managers (BPMs) in organizations. While BPMs have traditionally been responsible for modelling and standardizing processes, they are increasingly becoming facilitators of hybrid human-AI interactions. This paper analyses the impact on BPMs' tasks and competency requirements using a framework of five archetypes of human-AI hybrids. Our findings suggest that future BPMs will not only need to develop technical and methodological knowledge, but also skills in human-AI collaboration and ethical AI management. We provide a first conceptual classification of the changing role of BPMs in the context of the use of agentic AI and thus lay a foundation for empirical research to further deepen our understanding of the emerging human-AI hybrid reality of the future enterprise.

Keywords: Business Process Management · Human-AI Hybrid · Role Transformation

1 Introduction

Agentic Artificial Intelligence (AAI) describes autonomous systems capable of pursuing complex goals with minimal human intervention. Unlike conventional Artificial Intelligence (AI), which relies heavily on structured instructions and supervision, AAI is characterized by adaptability, autonomous decision-making and independence. Traditional AI systems are usually rule-based or use supervised learning for clearly defined tasks and work well in stable environments. However, they quickly reach their limits when sudden changes occur. AAI tends to operate in an autonomous and adaptable manner. Such systems react flexibly to real-time data, historical developments and unexpected changes, which makes them more resilient (Acharya et al. 2025).

The increasing integration of AAI systems is fundamentally changing traditional role models in organizations. Research shows that conversational agents (CAs) are no longer perceived merely as tools, but as digital employees (Wang et al. 2025). As a result, tasks, responsibilities and the self-image of employees are shifting. At the same time, new hybrid roles are emerging, for example in the monitoring or training of CAs. AAI has a profound impact not only on processes, but also on organizational roles and identity structures.

The traditional business process manager role (BPMr) was strongly characterized by the modelling and standardization of processes to efficiently designing structured workflows. According to van der Aalst (2021), many of these approaches failed due to the complexity of real processes, the inability to map human behaviour and the lack of evidence of real improvements. With the emergence of data-driven technologies such as process mining and robotic process automation (RPA), the BPMr is changing fundamentally: instead of modelling processes, it now analyses real processes based on event data and makes data-based decisions on where automation makes sense. In an increasingly hybrid working world, it coordinates the interaction between human and machine intelligence and thus becomes the designer of hybrid intelligence.

Given these developments, our short paper addresses the following research question: **What is the impact of AAI on the role of Business Process Managers (BPMs) in organizations?** The taxonomy of Fabri et al. (2023) is used as a conceptual basis to understand when human-AI hybrids can be used appropriately in the field of business process management. According to the authors human-AI hybrids are dynamic combinations of human and AI-based skills that complement each other in a symbiotic collaboration to solve tasks more efficiently.

2 Theoretical Background

As the integration of AI into organizational contexts continues, questions about human-AI interaction are becoming increasingly important. In their comprehensive, multi-level literature review, Bankins et al. (2024) provide a theoretical framework that analyses the impact of AI at the individual, group and organizational levels. Of relevance to the BPMr is the topic of "human-AI collaboration", which examines the conditions under which effective collaboration between human actors and AI systems succeeds. The authors emphasize that factors such as trust in technology, technological fit with the task and organizational cultural conditions are decisive for whether AI is perceived as a supportive resource or a threat.

2.1 BPM and the Traditional Role of Process Managers

Before analysing AAI's impact on BPMr, the traditional role definition must be specified. BPMr manages business processes for reliable results and improvements (Meierhöfer and Dorner 2023). The BPMr involves more than just modelling processes. As Schönig and Jablonski (2024) show, the BPM is the central interface between specialist departments, IT and management. It is responsible for designing processes that are both technically correct and professionally comprehensible and practicable. The focus is on process modelling, which not only requires formal correctness, but above all pragmatic appropriateness: models must be understandable and verifiable for domain experts. This is where BPMr comes into its own as a mediator – especially when standard notations such as BPMN reach their limits, for example in the representation of complex organizational structures. In addition, a BPMr must integrate multiple perspectives: functional, organizational, data-related, operational and behaviour-related views of a process. This complexity requires not only methodological but also communicative competence. Finally, the paper emphasizes that BPM professionals are also a driving force between research and practice. They identify gaps in existing systems and drive the development of practical solutions. In summary, the role requires a technical understanding, conceptual strength, practical relevance and a communicative bridging function – qualities that go beyond classic modelling skills. Across the BPM life cycle, roles such as analyst, modeler, optimizer, and monitor are typically involved (Dumas et al. 2018). In practice, however, these roles increasingly converge as BPM professionals take on broader responsibilities. AAI reinforces this trend by automating routine tasks and enabling the BPMr to act as integrators across technical and organizational boundaries. The archetypes discussed later illustrate how these traditional roles evolve and merge in different human-AI constellations.

2.2 Agentic Artificial Intelligence (AAI)

AAI describes a new generation of AI that is not limited to specific tasks, but is characterized by autonomy, decision-making ability and adaptability in complex, dynamic environments. In contrast to traditional AI, which usually operates in stable, controlled scenarios and is focused on automation, AAI goes far beyond this: it can pursue goals independently, adapt strategies flexibly and react to new situations in real time (autonomy & goal complexity, environmental & operational complexity, decision-making ability & adaptability) (Acharya et al. 2025; Ågerfalk 2020). This development is also reflected in the paradigm shift from automation to augmentation. Instead of replacing humans, AAI is used to support and augment them in a targeted manner – especially where human skills such as judgment, creativity or social intelligence are required (Fabri et al. 2023).

2.3 Human-AI Hybrids

With the emergence of diverse AI technologies such as ChatGPT, humans and AI agents are increasingly working together to solve complex tasks. In the scientific literature, this form of collaboration is referred to as human-AI hybrid (Fabri et al. 2023; Jarrahi et al. 2022; Mayer et al. 2024). According to Rai et al. (2019), this is a dynamic interplay between the capabilities of humans and AI. Ideally, this combination creates a hybrid intelligence in which the respective strengths of humans and AI complement each other. Fabri et al. (2023) define five human-AI hybrids as dynamic combinations of human and AI capabilities working together to perform tasks. These hybrids involve a symbiotic collaboration, where humans and AI each take on specific cognitive functions to complement one another, aiming to achieve better outcomes together than either could alone. They present a framework for systematically describing the cooperation between human actors and AI systems. Their taxonomy is based on the concept of "weak sociomateriality" and divides the interaction into three central levels: the human as a social actor, the AI as a material actor and the sociomaterial practices that result from their collaboration. On the human side, cognitive abilities such as perception, decision-making, explanation, creativity and empathy are considered. It also describes how humans interact with AI – for example, by supporting it, checking its results or supplementing them with their own actions. The focus of humans is often on tasks such as creating meaning, creative design, compassionate action or flexible problem solving. AI, on the other hand, contributes its own cognitive functions such as predicting, planning or making decisions. Its interactions with humans include supporting, complementing or even controlling activities. The focus of AI systems is either on automation or on the targeted support of human capabilities. Finally, the joint practices that arise from the collaboration are described: These can be either parallel, sequential or flexible. The interaction can also be singular or continuous. Emphasis is placed on learning behaviour: Here, either the human can learn, the AI, both separately - or there is a co-evolutionary further development in which humans and AI improve each other. This taxonomy provides a structured lens to examine human-AI collaboration.

3 Role Transformation of BPMs in Human-AI Hybrids

3.1 Archetypal Role Patterns

Fabri et al. (2023) discuss functional archetypes of human-AI hybrids that present different forms of division of work and interaction between humans and AI. These range from sequential automation to flexible co-evolution. Other research approaches focus on the perception of AI from a psychological perspective. For example, Karimova and Goby (2021) argue that the attribution of human characteristics (anthropomorphism) and the conscious staging of specific Jungian archetypes – such as the sage, the hero or the creator – can help to strengthen trust in AI systems and build an emotional bond. The presented archetypes of Fabri et al. (2023) will be used in this short paper to categorize the changing role of BPMs. The five archetypes range from AI assisting humans sequentially or in parallel, to increasingly collaborative and adaptive models. While the first two archetypes involve AI supporting routine tasks or preparing information, the latter three emphasize transformation through close human-AI collaboration, where AI acts as a decision supporter, orchestrator, or facilitator. Based on Sturm et al. (2021) Machine learning can help organizations learn faster and more efficiently by complementing employees' creative exploration – provided it is well adjusted and aligned with human learning. This requires initial investment, which is particularly worthwhile in a rapidly changing environment.

3.2 BPMs as Human-AI Hybrids

There are differentiated requirements for BPMs when designing processes with AI-based agents (Table 1). The AI pre-worker archetype focuses on the complete automation of clearly defined tasks. The AI pre-works processes sequentially and once. BPMs are required to identify suitable tasks, evaluate automation potential and systematically prepare for the integration of AI. Referring to the Outsourcing AI archetype, BPMs must define task packages that can be autonomously taken over by AI systems and define clear interfaces and responsibilities between human and artificial actors. Whereas the Superpower-Giving AI archetype focuses on selective, occasional support of human actors by AI. BPMs must shape the targeted use of AI to strengthen decision-making and problem-solving, whereby the final responsibility remains with the human. In the Assembly Line AI archetype, processes evolve iteratively as humans and AI adapt to each other. BPMs must orchestrate continuous learning and adaptation processes and establish dynamic governance structures to ensure efficiency and flexibility at the same time. The Collaborator AI archetype describes a highly adaptive collaboration between humans and AI. Tasks are distributed depending on the situation and context. BPMs are required to establish agile process structures, manage role allocations flexibly and actively control the mutual development of humans and AI. These archetypes do not replace traditional BPMr but rather illustrate how such roles are increasingly reshaped in hybrid human-AI constellation.

Table 1. BPMs as Human-AI Hybrids

Human-AI Hybrid Archetypes (Fabri et al., 2023)	Focus, Description, Example for Application (Fabri et al., 2023)	Way of Interaction (Fabri et al., 2023)	BPMs as "Human-AI Hybrids"
Sequential Automation ("AI Pre-Worker")	**Focus:** Automation **Description:** >Purpose of AI systems: To support (not replace) human agents >Cognitive AI Functions: Perceiving to Creating >Cognitive Human Functions: Reasoning, Decision-Making, Sensemaking **Example for Application:** In radiology, AI systems analyze images and make predictions. Human doctors then review the results, make decisions, and take further action	Sequential & Singular (one-time transfer of results)	>BPM needs to recognize and evaluate the potential of the use of AI for standardized tasks (Meierhöfer & Dorner, 2023) >Process mining helps to identify repetitive tasks and prepare them for automation (Van Der Aalst, 2021)

(*continued*)

Table 1. (*continued*)

Human-AI Hybrid Archetypes (Fabri et al., 2023)	Focus, Description, Example for Application (Fabri et al., 2023)	Way of Interaction (Fabri et al., 2023)	BPMs as "Human-AI Hybrids"
Parallel Automation ("Outsourcing AI")	**Focus:** Automation **Description:** >Parallel execution of tasks between humans and AI >Learning happens mostly separately. **Example for Application:** AI-enabled call center system; AI handles simple service requests (e.g., FAQs); Humans focus on complex cases that require sensemaking	Parallel & Continuous (simultaneous, ongoing collaboration)	>BPM needs to outsource suitable tasks, allow AI to act independently (Meierhöfer & Dorner, 2023) >BPM must design workflows in which humans and AI work in parallel, e.g. through Robotic Process Automation: RPA builds upon existing systems by taking over repetitive tasks from humans (Van Der Aalst, 2021)
Sequential Augmentation ("Superpower-Giving AI")	**Focus:** Augmentation **Description:** >Paradigm shift: AI facilitates human work as much as it supplements it >Learning: Mainly occurs on the human side >Cognitive Human Functions: Decision-making and interacting >Cognitive AI Functions: Reasoning and predicting **Example for Application:** Risk assessment in courts; AI predicts and reasons about risk; Judge interprets AI output for decision-making	Sequential & Singular (selective support)	>BPM needs to use AI in a focused way to enhance human capabilities, e.g. better decision-making (Meierhöfer & Dorner, 2023) >Hybrid intelligence promotes human strengths such as creativity through AI-supported information (Van Der Aalst, 2021)

(*continued*)

Table 1. (*continued*)

Human-AI Hybrid Archetypes (Fabri et al., 2023)	Focus, Description, Example for Application (Fabri et al., 2023)	Way of Interaction (Fabri et al., 2023)	BPMs as "Human-AI Hybrids"
Sequential Co-Evolution ("Assembly Line AI")	**Focus:** Augmentation **Description:** >Risk assessment in courts >AI performs reasoning and prediction to support judges >Helps reduce bias and enables judges to focus on interpreting results **Example for Application:** Hybrid ramp-up process in production	Sequential & Continuous (iterative interaction)	>BPM must adapt processes dynamically as humans and AI evolve together (Meierhöfer & Dorner, 2023) >BPM must control dynamic adaptations of humans and AI (high variability of real processes) (Van Der Aalst, 2021)
Flexible Co-Evolution ("Collaborator AI")	**Focus:** Augmentation **Description:** Continuous interaction & Co-evolution: both human and AI learn from each other **Example for Application:** Smart Augmented Instruction System for mechanical assembly	Flexible & Continuous (mutual adaptation)	>BPM must create flexible, adaptive working models in which AI and humans work collaboratively depending on the situation (Meierhöfer & Dorner, 2023) >BPM must organize hybrid teams where tasks switch dynamically between humans and AI (Van Der Aalst, 2021)

Overall, BPMs must take on different roles based on the hybrid model: from simple automation decisions to the orchestration of parallel division of work to the design of adaptive, cooperative systems. Managing hybrid processes requires both AI literacy and a human-centered process design perspective.

4 Implications and Discussion

4.1 Implications for Practice

The integration of AAI into business process design is leading to far-reaching changes in organizational structures and role profiles. The role of the BPM is experiencing a significant transformation: BPMs are increasingly developing into AI facilitators who not only design processes, but also actively coordinate the interaction between human and artificial actors. This requires new skills, particularly in human-AI interaction, the ethical management of AI systems and the design of adaptive, hybrid process landscapes. Organizations must recognize these new role profiles and create appropriate training opportunities and supporting framework conditions to ensure the successful integration of AAI. Berente et al. (2021) explain that the management of AI marks the beginning of a new era of technology, in which it is important to shape the handling of self-learning systems that are difficult to understand. Research and information systems play a central role in guiding these developments in a meaningful way. In addition, new requirements for governance structures are emerging existing process management approaches must be supplemented by mechanisms that enable the continuous co-evolution of human and AI. This is not just about the technical integration of AI systems, but also about creating a corporate culture that promotes openness for dynamic role allocations and continuous learning.

These developments align with findings by Hughes et al. (2025), who emphasize that generative agentic AI systems are likely to fundamentally alter business processes and organizational structures. Their analysis suggests a shift toward flatter hierarchies, reduced managerial oversight, and more decentralized, AI-supported decision-making. In this context, BPMs may find their role evolving into process orchestrators and ethical gatekeepers, coordinating distributed agents and ensuring responsible AI use across dynamic teams.

4.2 Implications for Research

From a theoretical perspective, the merging of BPM and AAI opens new, promising fields of research. There is a particularly urgent call for empirical studies that investigate the actual dynamics of collaboration between BPMs and AI systems. There is a need for further research into the development of integrated competence frameworks that systematically map the new requirements for BPMs. These frameworks should integrate both traditional BPM competencies and new skills such as understanding AI, ethical awareness and hybrid process design. In addition, a comparison of the archetypes of Fabri et al. (2023) with other existing taxonomies is recommended to capture the hybridization of the BPMr in different application contexts in a more differentiated way. Hemmer et al. (2021) suggest that effective human-AI team performance requires more than explainability. It also hinges on factors such as mutual trust, aligned mental models, and cognitive load – all of which demand targeted behavioral research.

5 Conclusion and Outlook

This short paper develops an initial conceptual understanding of the transformation of the role of BPMs in the context of AAI. It shows that BPMs are no longer just process designers but are increasingly developing into AI-collaborators and facilitators. The taxonomy offers a differentiated perspective on how human and artificial actors can interact and evolve together in different hybrid forms. Given the conceptual nature of this contribution, empirical validation remains a crucial next step. Future research should empirically examine the relevance and applicability of the proposed archetypes – for example through case studies, expert interviews, or surveys among BPM practitioners. This would strengthen the practical significance of the presented role transformations and test the robustness of the theoretical framework in real organizational settings. An

in-depth comparison of the human-AI hybrid archetypes with other theoretical models could also help to create a more comprehensive understanding of hybrid role development in BPM. Overall, AAI fundamentally challenges existing understandings of BPMs and opens new perspectives in the digital age.

References

Acharya, D.B., Kuppan, K., Divya, B.: Agentic AI: autonomous intelligence for complex goals – a comprehensive survey. IEEE Access **13**, 18912–18936 (2025). https://doi.org/10.1109/ACCESS.2025.3532853

Ågerfalk, P.J.: Artificial intelligence as digital agency. Eur. J. Inf. Syst. **29**(1), 1–8 (2020). https://doi.org/10.1080/0960085X.2020.1721947

Bankins, S., Oçampo, A.C., Marrone, M., Restubog, S.L.D., Woo, S.E.: A multilevel review of artificial intelligence in organizations: implications for organizational behavior research and practice. J. Organ. Behav. **45**(2), 159–182 (2024). https://doi.org/10.1002/job.2735

Berente, N., Gu, B., Recker, J., Santhanam, R.: Special issue editor's comments: managing artificial intelligence. MIS Q. **45**(3) 1433–1450 (2021)

Dumas, M., La Rosa, M., Mendling, J., Reijers, H.A.: Fundamentals of Business Process Management. Springer, Heidelberg (2018). https://doi.org/10.1007/978-3-662-56509-4

Fabri, L., Häckel, B., Oberländer, A.M., Rieg, M., Stohr, A.: Disentangling human-AI hybrids: conceptualizing the interworking of humans and AI-enabled systems. Bus. Inf. Syst. Eng. **65**(6), 623–641 (2023). https://doi.org/10.1007/s12599-023-00810-1

Hemmer, P., Schemmer, M., Vössing, M., Kühl, N.: Human-AI complementarity in hybrid intelligence systems: a structured literature review.In: PACIS 2021 Proceedings (2021). https://aisel.aisnet.org/pacis2021/78

Hughes, L., et al.: AI agents and agentic systems: a multi-expert analysis. J. Comput. Inf. Syst. **65**, 489–517 (2025). https://doi.org/10.1080/08874417.2025.2483832

Jarrahi, M.H., Lutz, C., Newlands, G.: Artificial intelligence, human intelligence and hybrid intelligence based on mutual augmentation. Big Data Soc. **9**(2), 20539517221142824 (2022). https://doi.org/10.1177/20539517221142824

Karimova, G.Z., Goby, V.P.: The adaptation of anthropomorphism and archetypes for marketing artificial intelligence. J. Consum. Mark. **38**(2), 229–238 (2021). https://doi.org/10.1108/JCM-04-2020-3785

Mayer, V., Schüll, M., Aktürk, O., Guggenberger, T.: Designing human-AI hybrids: challenges and good practices from a multiple case study. In: ICIS 2024 Proceedings (2024). https://aisel.aisnet.org/icis2024/aiinbus/aiinbus/3

Meierhöfer, S., Dorner, C.-M.: Through the Lens of cognitive functions and contextual factors – a study of the action potentials of artificial intelligence in business process management. In: Wirtschaftsinformatik 2023 Proceedings (2023). https://aisel.aisnet.org/wi2023/66

Rai, A.: Next-Generation Digital Platforms: Toward Human–AI Hybrids (2019)

Schönig, S., Jablonski, S.: Digitales Prozessmanagement: Eine Reflexion aus praktischer Sicht zur Förderung des Austauschs zwischen Forschung und Praxis. HMD Praxis der Wirtschaftsinformatik **61**(5), 1348–1365 (2024). https://doi.org/10.1365/s40702-024-01057-4

Sturm, T., et al.: Coordinating human and machine learning for effective organization learning. MIS Q. **45**(3), 1581–1602 (2021). https://doi.org/10.25300/MISQ/2021/16543

Van Der Aalst, W.M.P.: Hybrid Intelligence: to automate or not to automate, that is the question. Int. J. Inf. Syst. Proj. Manag. **9**(2), 5–20 (2021). https://doi.org/10.12821/ijispm090201

Wang, W., Hackett, R.D., Archer, N., Xu, Z., Yuan, Y.: Will AI-enabled conversational agents acting as digital employees enhance employee job identity? Inf. Manag. **62**(2), 104099 (2025). https://doi.org/10.1016/j.im.2025.104099

Narrative Identities for Contextualized, Human-Centric Process Knowledge Acquisition

Christian Stary

Johannes Kepler University, 4040 Linz, Austria
Christian.Stary@JKU.AT

Abstract. Articulating and representing work knowledge in models in a contextual and traceable form is an essential part of Business Process Management (BPM) activities in ecosystems of the platform economy. These ecosystems have significantly changed the way what motivates people to participate, how work is organized and how the networked stakeholders communicate. Such issues have in turn led to methodological challenges in acquiring process-relevant knowledge and mapping it to executable representations. This paper targets the perception of tasks of individual role carriers in the platform economy, and offers a corresponding elicitation and documentation scheme that finally supports the specification of business process models. Contextual process knowledge acquisition and representation is suggested applying Ricœur's concept of Narrative Identity. Self-knowledge is captured by individual stories on task-relevant information and interaction. The stories are analyzed by means of Rhetorical Structure Theory to identify information on business processes. The resulting representation facilitates business process modeling and validation. A first case study utilizing subject-orientation confirms the approach's potential and helps identifying topics for further research.

Keywords: Narrative Identity · Narrative Storytelling · Rhetorical Structure Theory · Subject-oriented Business Process Management

1 Introduction

Digital transformation has been established not only as continuous and highly dynamic process, but also has led to novel business models and stakeholder relations on the markets. In particular, the rise of the so-called platform economy has led to the application of Big Data, AI (Artificial Intelligence) agents, and Cloud Computing that changed the nature of work and the structure of the economy [1]. Termed 'platform capitalism', a dynamic set of new work modalities mediated by platforms enforces digital adjustments how work is conceived and organized [2].

Recognizing the purpose of a platform-oriented business model, namely to reach a monopoly position, and to set and control standards of supply, disruptions are likely to occur. Once regulations do not ensure fair treatment of suppliers and vendors (selling their products and services on the digital platforms), platform participants experience precariousness, insecurity, loneliness, miserable pay and a lack of safety net (cf. [3]) rather than entrepreneurship and self-realization (cf. [4]). Hence, they need mechanisms to participate and adapt on the operational level. Investigating people who work independently of location and maintain a mobile lifestyle, Thiel [5] took a closer look to how this group actually organizes their everyday life and work. Her multi-sited ethnographic fieldwork in global hotspots such as large cities, reveals the strive of younger, well-educated knowledge workers for a life beyond traditional permanent employment, focusing on self-realization and autonomy. These central values motivate them to run small organizations, e.g., one-person-companies, and to form particular identities in their business community. Such communities rely on communication and digital media.

The resulting ecosystem is not only driven by actors bringing in their individual identity but also by socio-technical developments - major components are social media (cf. [6]). They impact work behavior, learning (capabilities), as well as stress appraisal [7] and societal changes (cf. [8]). Business Process Management can serve as mediator between social and technological aspects when developing business operation to digital ecosystems (cf. [9]). This work addresses research to that respect:

Given the current development of socio-technical ecosystems, how can individual work practice and perception of business operation and development be captured for accurate modeling of business processes?

Once the self-knowledge of identity-driven actors can be acquired and represented in a model-based way, the ecosystem partners can share their individual role and network understanding in a transparent way, and adapt it for common operation. Hence, the goal of this work is to emphasize the stakeholder perspective when articulating business process-relevant knowledge concerning individual work behavior and collaborative interaction. The result should be some methodological guidance for authentic and transparent knowledge acquisition including its transfer capability.

In order to achieve that the presented work suggests to enrich storytelling as primary method of knowledge acquisition from both ends, when starting the process by guiding the elicitation to focus on experiential self-knowledge by means of individualized narratives, and when completing the process by structuring stories by rhetoric meta data.

The paper is organized as follows: Sect. 2 elaborates on Narrative Identities as introduced by Ricœur [10]. Due to their focus on reflected self-enactment, individual experiences can be the starting point of knowledge acquisition activities. Section 3 provides the methodological bridge to articulating experiential knowledge on business operation, and to structuring this knowledge by means of Rhetorical Structure Theory [11], before it discusses its transfer to business process models. The exemplification concerns an Industry5.0 [12] case. Section 4 concludes the paper with a discussion.

2 Narrative Identities

In this section we give an overview of the concept and its application. When developing the field of hermeneutic phenomenology Ricœur combined the interpretation of meaning with the study of lived experience [13]. Understanding human experience always involves interpretation, especially through language. Since language is inherently ambiguous and open to multiple meanings, interpretation is necessary to make sense of human experiences.

Humans construct their identities through the stories they tell about themsselves. There is *idem* identity, i.e. sameness over time, and *ipse* identity, i.e selfhood through change and development. Narratives help humans reconcile both aspects, as they are key for humans making sense of time and history, weaving together events into meaningful stories that help humans understand both themselves and the world.

The resulting selfhood of individuals is not a static substance, but rather a dynamic process that is shaped by the narratives humans construct and inhabit [13]. This shift from a focus on individuation and taxonomization of individuals means identity is fundamentally an existential and hermeneutical problem of sense-making [14].

Ricœur's nuanced understanding of how individuals make sense of themselves and their world through language is characterized by a willingness to embrace dualities and tensions, e.g., between freedom and necessity [13]. Accepting both helps resisting to reduce language and meaning, and to build on the openness and surplus of meaning in texts and actions. As such, Ricœur's philosophy centers on the interpretation of meaning in human life, built upon the narrative construction of identity.

Ricœur relies on an ontology of act and potentiality when considering the grasping of human behavior. A system of interpretation or a hermeneutic justification of facts helps 'backing then a framed use of the "analogy of agency" with language as one of the modes of action and with a philosophy of action as the condition of a relationship to being' ([15], p.171f.). Hence, an ontology of action is a precondition for the hermeneutics of the self ([15], p.173). Ricœur accounts 'for multiple meanings of being' in his conception of a hermeneutics of the self (ibid,) and distinguishes 'sameness', i.e. 'what does not change in personal identity' ([15], p. 174) from 'ipseity' i.e. 'what evolves while still linked to this "personal core" ' ([15], p. 174). The concept of Narrative identity encompasses both these two modes of identity [10].

Ricœur acknowledges the relation of action to language, as 'language may have triggered the widespread appearance of modern human behavior approximately 100 thousand years ago' [16]. Language enable narratives as constitutive role of selfhood, serving as the primary means through which individuals construct and understand their identity. Narratives bridge *idem* and *ipse* identity as a mediator, connecting continuity over time (sameness) and dynamic agency (selfhood). Both constructs become part of a coherent story through lived experiences.

A story is structured through emplotment, i.e. organizing events into a plot. In this way, individuals reconcile stability with change, creating a narrative unity [17]. It enables them to provide presence in situations, even during crises, and thus maintain continuity despite life's disruptions [18], and 'discover' themselves [19]. This self-discovery is an interpretative process, since selfhood is not pre-given but emerges through interpreting one's life as a narrative. The process of interpretation is termed by Ricœur 'hermeneutic labor'. Self-understanding through discovery means to reflect on actions, relationships, and moral choices rather than inventing the individual identity [17]. This process is dialogical, requiring engagement with others' perspectives and societal norms [20, 21]. By situating oneself within stories, individuals take responsibility for their actions and recognize their accountability to others. Ricœur considers selfhood as a social claim with narratives as embodiment of individuals in a network of mutual recognition and obligations [22]. However, Narrative Identity allows for fragility and vulnerability. Narratives help confront life's discordances – suffering, failure, or existential crises 'break the narrative thread'– by reframing them as part of a larger plot. Storytelling becomes a tool for reweaving meaning and restoring agency (*ibid.*) – reflecting Ricœur's view of selfhood as 'fragile freedom', where identity persists even amid vulnerability [13].

Narrative also links personal identity to historical and cultural contexts. By situating individual stories within broader collective narratives referring to communities, organizations or networks, Ricœur shows how selfhood is both unique and relational. Time becomes intelligible through storytelling, as past, present, and future are integrated into a meaningful whole [21, 23]. The future is related to imagination and creativity, with 'productive imagination' allowing individuals to envision alternative stories, enabling growth and ethical transformation. Ricœur's work intends to create a space to explore possibilities for selfhood, testing identities beyond immediate circumstances [17, 22]. Hence, narrative for Ricœur is the existential medium through which selfhood is articulated, sustained, and enacted. It transforms fragmented experiences into a coherent life story while maintaining openness to reinterpretation and dialogue with others.

3 Narrative Identities for Contextual Business Process Design

This section starts with narrative storytelling as means of eliciting and codifying individual experiences through natural language. The resulting textual information can be processed by means of Rhetorical Structure Theory as input for process modeling.

Developing Narratives. The value of telling experiential stories has been recognized in many disciplines, such as psychology [24], and across disciplines, e.g., philosophy and psychology [25]. There is consensus that personal narratives are a central component of one's identity. The embodied and experiential dimension of the self-forming identity needs to be touched in the course of explicating knowledge, as proposed for inner-speech episodes [25]. These narratives require self-reflection and autobiographical reasoning for extracting Narrative Identities [25, 26]. Self-reflection and the generation of ideas for change or improvement should be accompanied by verbal documentation [27, 28]. Then, stories create meaning and identity, making sense of complex realities and fostering community building [29].

Structuring Narratives. While storytelling leads to documented text, process representations require modeling constructs that capture the semantics of the articulated (process) knowledge. As intermediate schemes, meta-stories and action maps [28] have already been proposed to further process explicated knowledge. Rhetorical Structure Theory (RST) [11, 30, 31] provides a more fine-grained and systematic way for analyzing text using decomposition and relational annotations. The analysis according to RST leads to constructing a diagram through screening text and aiming to make explicit the storyteller's purpose perceived by the analyst in a structured form.

The unit of concern is a story as a single text document written in well-formed natural language, following the writer's style of language use [32]. The text's abstract structure is represented as Rhetorical Structure Tree (RSTree). Its leaves represent so-called elementary discourse units (EDUs). Further nodes represent contiguous text spans.

Text spans are text constituents and can be clauses, sentences, paragraphs, or larger spans. They are evaluated for their coherence. Coherence is given when two text spans have communicative roles with each other in a text.

A text span is labeled by a rhetorical relation. Rhetorical relations exist between two neighboring (non-overlapping) textual units. They specify how spans of text can co-occur when an analyst aims to capture the outcome of a text, i.e. what effect(s) the writer wants to have and what readers can recognize from the writers' intentions. Each field specifies particular judgements that the text analyst must make in building the RSTree. The text analyzer checks plausibility in the sense whether a described effect correspond to desired conditions. The structuring of spans in a RSTree is arranged from the left to the right side, so that reading of the leave node entries (EDUs) of an RSTree corresponds to reading the analyzed text unit in the same order.

For setting rhetorical relations along the order of the text input, Mann et al. provided 24 universal relations [30]. For Narrative Identities the *elaboration* relation is a promising candidate. It refers to the intention or effect of handling a work situation, detailing the so-called nucleus (which is about an activity) with the locus of the effect as nucleus *and* the satellite (with the latter being a situation that is unrealized, but is to be realized through the activity in the nucleus) (cf. [32]). Consider the following sample text entitled *Setting Up/Provision of Short-Range Wireless Communication:*

1. There are high expectations when wireless communication technologies are used.
2. Although each application case may require special preparation,
3. all interaction modalities can be supported when eliciting the proper context.

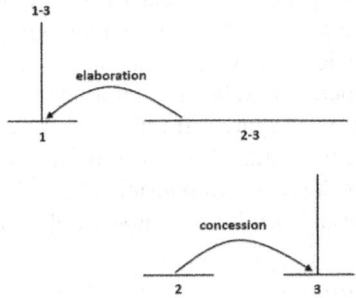

Fig. 1. RSTree for *Setting Up/Provision of Short-Range Wireless Communication.*

In Fig. 1 the curves represent relation holdings, and the straight lines refer to the 'nuclear span'. Multinuclear relations, like *sequence*, structure a text with patterns beyond a nuclear span. The numbers used indicate the text units that have been identified for the RST-based structuring. The lines indicate whether more than a single unit is concerned on the lower level. The *elaboration* relation is used, since unit 2 and 3 contain details on the concern or potential addressed in unit 1 – the *elaboration* relation captures the effect that a reader 'recognizes the situation presented in [the satellite] S as providing additional detail for [the nucleus] N' ([30], p. 278). The *concession* relation indicates that the reader appreciates how the concern or potential is handled - the 'reader's positive regard for the situation presented in N is increased' ([30], p. 255). Setting up an RSTree, a text analyst elaborates the effect of a text, i.e. which 'message' the text delivers. It is expressed by explicitly relating identified text units [33].

Application. In the following we demonstrate a Narrative Identity approach based on a reflection of 2 stories of a project manager in setting up and managing short-range wireless communication for CPS applications. Each of the stories has been scripted by the author and analyzed according to the order of their occurrence and its narrative reflection. One story concerns a healthcare case, the other one supply chain management. Both cases have a focus on experiences in the preparation of good delivery controlled with short-range wireless communication chips. For reconciling time and history from RSTrees to process models subject-oriented concepts [34] are applied.

(Story 1) Healthcare Resource Optimization. The first business case shows the Narrative Identity acquisition and subsequent application of RST components for optimizing hospital bed utilization with short-range wireless communication chips: Each bed keeps track and can report status, location, and availability for logistic operation.

The first part of the case lists the text spans as part of the textual description of the provision process. The second part contains the corresponding instance of a story ontology developed for RST applications [35]. It frames the RSTree through decomposing stories into scenes, e.g., preparing a good for transportation: Each *Scene* can be characterized by applying a certain *Concept*, e.g., Industry5.0 [12], an acting component (*Agent*) in a certain *Role*, e.g., a robot in the role of a transport system, and an *Act* that is refined in terms of situated activity (nucleus and satellite). The situated activity is linked to events and relations to capture the actual plot of the *Act* (for successful task accomplishment) – see also Fig. 2. The RST relations provide the relevant context for the subsequent process specification [36].

Handling a Healthcare Resource Optimization request addresses the preparation for reliable transportation until a bed can be moved from one location to another one:

1. The process of equipping hospital beds with short-range wireless communication devices and running their disposition is crucial, since all available resources of this type needs to be included for effective optimization. However, there is limited insight into the business logic the various stakeholders that could be involved in the healthcare facility's resource planning and optimization process.
2. Delivering beds requires some preparation. When a bed is to be moved from one location to another, its status needs to be checked before transportation and the requirements for its later use should be made available, if not stored on the chip.
3. The information on the utilization requirements has to be transmitted from the Enterprise Resource Planning (ERP) system of the healthcare facility and should be attached to the transportation request. It could also influence the conditions of transport that need to be checked for successful delivery.
4. In order to monitor transportation conditions and progress or disruption, the chip needs to connect to other sensors and information systems. In this way, the transport can be checked regularly and corresponding information can be transmitted. Reliability problems may occur when the short-range wireless communication chip has to rely on other communication systems of the healthcare facility.

5. As soon as the control chain for transportation could be tested successfully and has been established, the transport device can move to the new location of the bed, and transmit a respective message ('ready to deliver') to the monitoring ERP system.
6. Once the monitoring chain has sent its commitment, the transport can start.
7. From this point on, the status of the bed and the transport device are continuously transmitted and checked for deviations.

The transportation process itself can then be executed. Once the bed arrives at its destination location, the transport process is completed. Then, the monitoring process also ends. Figure 2 shows the result of applying the ontology introduced in to the business case text 1–7. Scene 1 is the arrival of the transport request. It is based on the *Concept* of Enterprise Resource Planning in the Industry5.0 [12] context and involves the *Agent* BedMover in the *Role* Transport System. The Delivery *Act* is based on the *Event* of Preparing the transportation according to the Requirements to be checked.

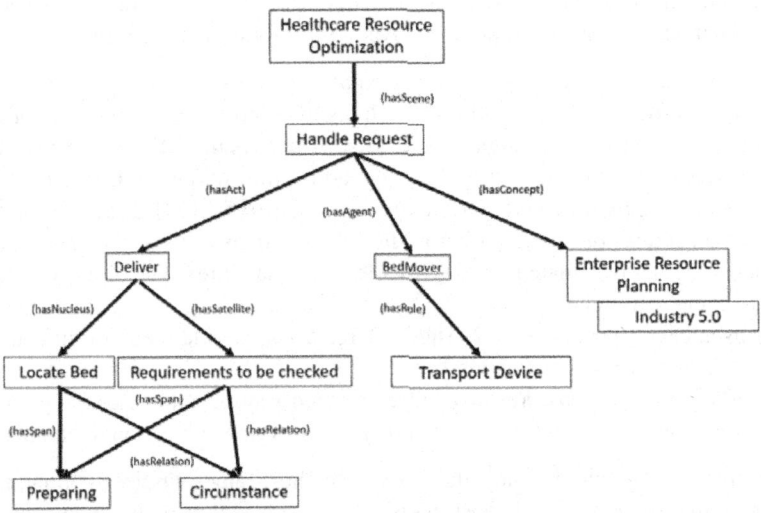

Fig. 2. Utilizing the RST ontology [35]: *Handling Request* in healthcare resource optimization

Figure 3 and 4 provides for each part of the story meta data, revealing the integrative nature of RST representations, with Fig. 3 showing the context specified in a declarative form, while Fig. 4 showing the procedural part of the business operation.

(Story 2) Resilient Supply Chain Management. The second case that followed the first one concerns the resilience of supply chains, i.e. preparing and finally optimizing a supply chain with respect to currently available resources. Again, the first part lists the text spans as part of a textual description of the process, the second part contains the instance of the *Story* ontology developed for RST representations [35]. The case is also detailed for the *Story*'s *Scene* Handle Request.

The numbers denote the sequential decomposition of the *Story* as required for RST applications, and refer to the relevant text parts of the diagrammatic structure of the *Story* in the subsequent figures.

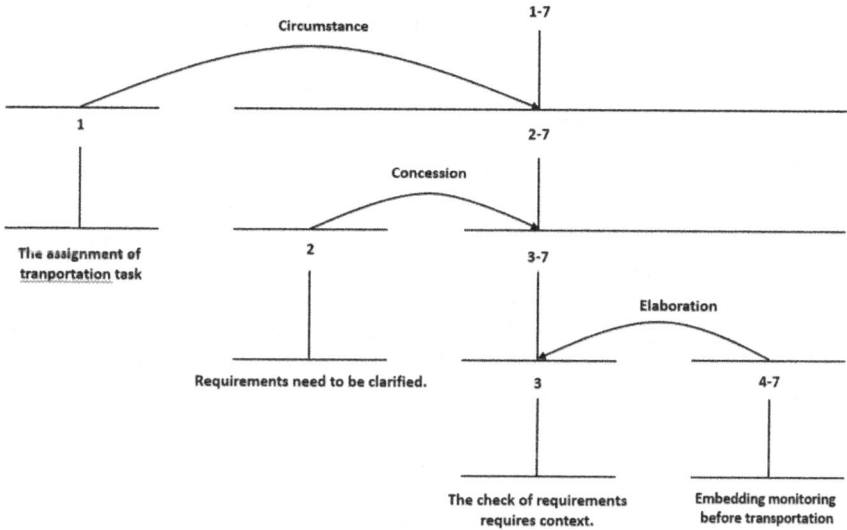

Fig. 3. The *Act* of Delivery in detail utilizing RST relations (part one).

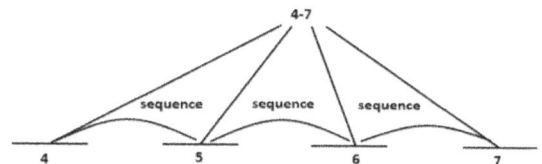

Fig. 4. The *Act* of Delivery in detail utilizing RST relation *sequence* (part two).

Handling a Resilient Supply Chain Management request captures the situation in a logistic process from initiation until the delivery of a chipped transport good can start:

1. What a challenge, that needs to be met when supply chains must be managed in a dynamic way successfully.
2. The enabler is a cyber-physical system that is a heterogeneous network of autonomous components.
3. When a logistic task is assigned to the autonomous network of goods, containers, and transport devices, the lack of a central control component to handle this task is quite different to a centralized logistic setting, e.g., controlled by an Enterprise Resource Planning system (like in the healthcare case). Only peer components also equipped with short-range communication chips can be used for monitoring in a decentralized setting. So-called monitoring tokens need to be passed to the next available network node along the transport process.
4. However, the process of preparing transport goods for delivery is crucial to ensure a reliable logistic operation. When applying concepts like Digital Twins for Cyber-Physical systems to manage preparation, special attention is required to control the process involving autonomous components. The conditions for the transportation of

goods need to be defined. This leads to storage and handling requirements according to the particularities of the transport good at hand.
5. The information on the storage and handling requirements comes attached to the good. It contains all requirements for transportation including the conditions for storing and transporting it.
6. The storage and transportation are done with containers (transport devices) that need to be equipped with sensors that monitor the conditions, and thus, can be controlled. The monitoring and mobility require context information. For instance, if a container is not available, and the good cannot be delivered, this information needs to be distributed for further decision making.
7. Monitoring needs to be set up before the drone flies to the place where the good to be delivered has been dropped off, and it scans the attached information for sensor equipment and container requirements.
8. According to the requirements, the drone moves to a rack with the relevant transportation equipment, i.e. the containers including the required sensors for transportation and delivery.
9. The drone picks up the logistic equipment and moves to a packing station.
10. At the packing station the good is put into the proper container, and the delivery process to the good's destination can start (Fig. 5).

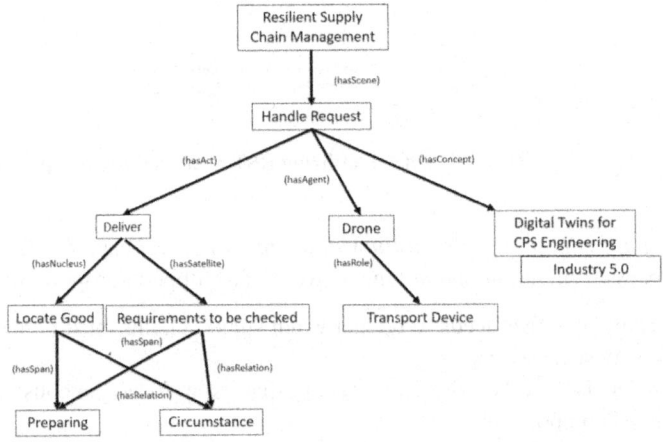

Fig. 5. Utilizing the RST ontology [35]: The first *Scene* of the supply chain management story.

Figure 6 provides the *Story*'s meta data for the upper part of the RSTree. The lower part contains the sequence of activities 6–10 in analogy to the previous case (cf. Fig. 4), and therefore has been omitted here.

Narrative Identity Insights. Following Ricœur's principles to recognize Narrative Identities [10] the interpretation of the text captures the language-based articulation with lived experience as follows:

1. The stories reveal how the project manager of the short-range wireless communication provider takes responsibility for his actions. Given the story and requests for context

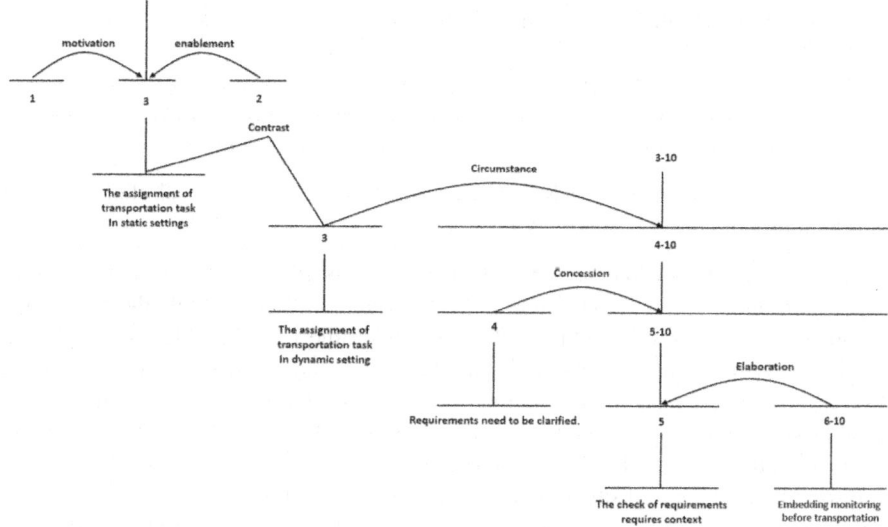

Fig. 6. The *Act* of Delivery in detail utilizing RST relations (upper part of the RSTree).

in some of the relations, he feels obliged to remind the customer on providing context information for successful delivery (*Act of Taking Responsibility*).
2. The task-specific plots reconcile stability with change for the project manager. All information perceived relevant concerning the situation has been be captured and interpreted in terms of statements referring to successfully complete the preparation tasks in the course of handling a request. Each plot reveals how actions, relationships, and choices promote self-understanding and self-discovery of the project manager's identity (*Plotting for Self-Discovery*).
3. Both, the *idem* identity (sameness over time) and the ipse identity (selfhood through change and development) have been revealed through the Narrative Identities' stories. 2 cases could be integrated into a meaningful whole, particularly facilitated by the means of RST. We could add future business cases based on the structured results (*Reconciling Time and History*).
4. The presented stories represent interpretations of the situation the project manager experienced. The meaning of the parts how they make sense can be identified by the RST meta data (*Interpretation Key to Sensemaking*).
5. Although specific meanings can never be explained by cognitive reflection, emotional statements like recognizing the challenge of decentralized coordination of logistic processes can be captured in their uniqueness and context (*Unique and Relational Selfhood*).
6. Rhetorical Structure Theory facilitates the use of language as one of the modes of action and potentiality that is interpreted. The presented narratives can be used for further dialogical engagement of others stakeholders, e.g., other project managers of the company (*Interweaving of Language and (Social) Action*).
7. Tensions referring to the fragility and vulnerability of the process, when the monitoring has to rely on other means than the company's chips, have been verbalized, thereby

indicating the willingness to complete delivery processes successfully (*Tensions and Dualities*).
8. The presented stories carry the selfhood of the project manager as a dynamic process - the recognized challenge in case 2 is decentralized monitoring (expressed by applying the *contrast* relation in the RSTree of case 2) (*Dynamics Matters*).

This reflection reveals the RSTree capability to support contextual elicitation and representation of coherent process knowledge.

From RST-Structured Narrative Identities to Process Models. The RST-based structuring is an intermediate step to modeling of business processes. While the declarative RST-relations frame role- and task-specific behavior, the *sequence* relations detail it in terms of activities to be set. Due to the similarity to behavior-centered process design, RST constructs and their representation (in form of RSTrees) facilitate the generation of subject-oriented business process models [36]. A RSTree provides the text of a *Story* and meta data. In particular, the scope of the model and granularity of modeling are addressed by the captured situation(s) (represented by satellites) and the activities realizing the situation (represented by nuclei). In Subject Behavior Diagrams (SBDs) the business logic can be detailed in terms of activities as given in the nucleus, with the satellite providing the situational context. In Subject Interaction Diagrams (SIDs) high-level specifications of role behaviors or task bundles of situations are represented as addressed by the satellites, with the nuclei representing the required refinements (in the corresponding SBD). Hence, the primary function of the RST for subject-oriented modeling is to identify all operational situations and role/task-specific refinements, i.e. subject-specific satellite-nucleus pairs.

When the text spans contain sequences of sentences relevant for role/task-specific behavior, they facilitate structuring a situation as SID and detailing it in terms of SBDs. The following RST relations detail the behavior to be captured in SBDs (cf. [36]):

- *Motivation*, as it provides specific reasons to follow a specific procedure for task accomplishment, i.e. a behavior sequence.
- *Circumstance*, as it details the condition(s) when an activity or a function (addressed by the nucleus) is executed.
- *Sequence* proposing successive set of actions given a certain situation.
- *Enablement*, as it considers the effectiveness of a specific set of actions as part of task/role accomplishment.
- *Elaboration* providing additional details for a specific activity.
- *Concession* expressing appreciation how a specific situation is handled.

The following RST relations refer to variants of behavior:

- *Contrast*, in case there are behavior differences to be recognized, e.g., through situation-specific information, or various ways of task accomplishment.
- *Joint* linking thematically adjunct activities, pointing to different ways of task accomplishment.

A *Story* title like Resilient Supply Chain Management refers to process-relevant knowledge and can be used to label a SID. A *Scene* as part of a *Story* denotes a refinement which allows to identify respective subjects. The concept behind the *Story* is to reveal a business case in terms of a network of *Actors*, e.g., a drone, that exchange messages or business objects. They contain data to control the flow of messages or business objects to be handled by the receiving subject. *Agents* can be considered role carriers that perform a task- or process-specific role.

We use the previously introduced use cases to exemplify derived process models for the Handle Request *Scene* addressing the preparation of delivery procedures.

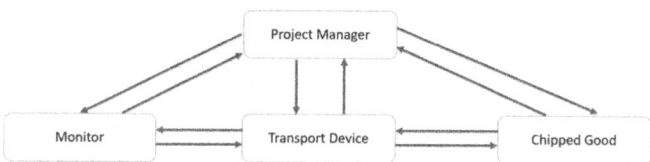

Fig. 7. Consolidated subject specifications and interaction relations as part of a SID Handling Requests in Healthcare Resource Optimization and Resilient Supply Chain Management.

Figure 7 shows the subjects involved in both business cases. The subject Project Manager requires interaction with the subject Chipped Good, the subject Transport Device, and the subject Monitor Although the exchanged messages and business objects are not included in the figure, the pattern of interaction can be recognized. The Project Manager and the Transport Device need to interact with all other subjects, since the preparation and operation of deliveries require their involvement in coordination.

Figure 8 shows the SBD for the Project Manager when setting up a transport. Preparing for delivery includes requirements capturing for transport, Transport Device positioning, and monitoring set up. In the diagram the positioning of the Transport Device is performed directly by the Project Manager, whereas the other activities require interaction with the subject Chipped Good (containing transport requirements) and Monitor. These interactions are depicted as send/receive activities with small triangles.

In each diagram, both the context of the business case and the functional actions modelled in the RSTree, as specified by the RST relations, play a crucial role.

- It starts with the *Motivation*, as resilient supply chain management is accepted as challenge due to dynamic adjustment. For instance, including the monitoring as subject and detailing its behavior sequence is considered within the scope of the communication provider, documenting the manager's purpose of contextual design.
- When the context of an activity is detailed in terms of the condition(s) to execute an activity or function, the *Circumstance* relation provides the relevant information.
- Each successive set of actions in SBDs specified to handle a certain situation follows the *Sequence* relation.
- When the effectiveness of a specific set of actions as part of task/role accomplishment is specified, like the Start-to-End sequence in the SBD in Fig. 8, it corresponds to *Enablement*, with additional details for a specific activity provided by information from the *Elaboration* relation.
- Recognizing particularities corresponds to an appreciation of how a specific situation needs to be handled. The *Concession* relation activities are implemented, e.g., when

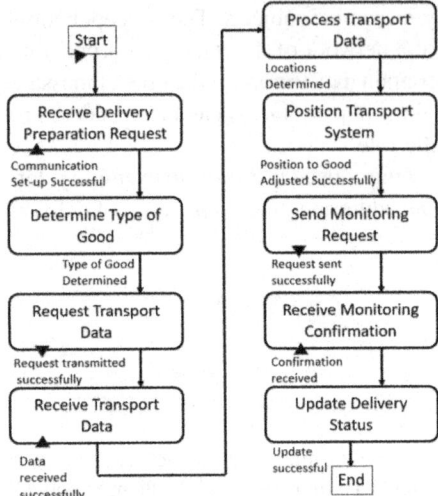

Fig. 8. Behavior Diagram of subject Project Manager.

requirements need to be detailed for transportation. The same holds for indicating substantial differences between business cases, referring to the *Contrast* relation, in our case for monitoring in static versus dynamic operational settings.

As can be seen, not each of the relations needs to be addressed in a specific business case. For instance, in the presented cases, the *Joint* relation has not been used due to the selected level of abstraction for modeling. However, for networks of actors in a platform ecosystem, adjunct activities pointing to different ways of task accomplishment could help to represent behavior accurately.

4 Discussion and Conclusion

We started out with current development of socio-technical ecosystems and aimed to answer the question, how individual work practice and perception of business operation and development can be captured for accurate modeling of business processes. Given the results, this self-knowledge can be acquired and represented in an individual way from each stakeholder's perspective from an integrated functional (role) and communication perspective [37]. Both perspectives support networked partners in sharing their role understanding in a structured way, and in developing their further collaboration given a common model. When each development step is transparent for each stakeholder role [38], organizational learning can become an interactive endeavor (cf. [39]).

Thereby, Narrative Identities encapsulate personal experiences with formal work knowledge. Both represent relevant inputs to modeling business processes, in particular in today's individual understanding of ecosystems of the platform economy. It is the personal motivation and individual design of how stakeholders (want to) participate, organize tasks and communicate with other stakeholders. Narrative Identities support meeting the respective methodological challenges when acquiring process-relevant knowledge and mapping it to business process models: Individual role carriers can tell their stories how they perceive the tasks they accomplish, and constructs from Rhetorical Structure Theory help structuring each story according to meta data including temporal relations between activities. The resulting diagrams provide insights into individually considered routines and behavior variations. This information can be captured by subject-oriented modeling, and will be featured by digital means in future settings ([cf. [40]). Further research will also include studies on more complex business cases and an adapted set of relations, based on these studies and empirical findings.

Disclosure of Interests. The authors have no competing interests to declare that are relevant to the content of this article.

References

1. Kenney, M., Zysman, J.: The rise of the platform economy. Issues Sci. Technol. **32**(3), 61 (2016)
2. Liang, Y., Aroles, J., Brandl, B.: Charting platform capitalism: definitions, concepts and ideologies. N. Technol. Work. Employ. **37**(2), 308–327 (2022)
3. Vallas, S.P.: Platform capitalism: what's at stake for workers?. In: New Labor Forum, Sage, Los Angeles, vol. 28, no. 1, pp. 48–59 (2019)
4. Piasna, A., Zwysen, W., Drahokoupil, J.: The platform economy in Europe: results from the second ETUI Internet and Platform Work Survey (No. 2022.05). Working Paper No. 2022.05, European Trade Union Institute (ETUI), Brussels (2022)
5. Thiel, C.: New Work: Der mobile Alltag Digitaler Nomaden zwischen Hype und Selbstverwirklichung. Campus, Frankfurt/Main (2021)
6. Ehlers, M.: Kommunikationsrevolution Social Media. Börsenmedien, Kulmbach (2013)
7. Dong, X., Tian, Y., He, M., Wang, T.: When knowledge workers meet AI? The double-edged sword effects of AI adoption on innovative work behavior. J. Knowl. Manag. **29**(1), 113–147 (2025)
8. Lobo, S.: Realitätsschock: Zehn Lehren aus der Gegenwart+ neu: Der Corona-Schock. Kiepenheuer & Witsch, Köln (2020)
9. Oppl, S., Stary, C.: Designing Digital Work: Concepts and Methods for Human-Centered Digitization. Springer, Cham (2019)
10. Ricœur, P.: Oneself as Another. University of Chicago Press, Chicago (1992)
11. Mann, W.C., Thompson, S.A.: Rhetorical structure theory: a theory of text organization, Los Angeles U. of Southern California, Information Sciences Institute, pp. 87–190 (1987)
12. Leng, J., et al.: Industry 5.0: prospect and retrospect. J. Manuf. Syst. **65**, 279–295 (2022)
13. Pellauer, D., Dauenhauer, B.: Paul Ricœur, Stanford Encyclopedia of Philosophy (2025). https://plato.stanford.edu/entries/Ricœur/. Accessed 20 Apr 2025
14. Tomkins, L., Eatough, V.: Hermeneutics: interpretation, understanding and sense-making. In: Cassell, C., Cunliffe, A., Grandy, G. (eds.) The SAGE Handbook of Qualitative Business and Management Research Methods, pp. 185–200. Sage, London (2018)
15. Lelièvre, S.: Introduction to "Discourse, Metaphysics, and Hermeneutics of the Self" by Paul Ricœur. Études Ricœuriennes/Ricœur Stud. **15**(2), 163–177 (2024)
16. Miyagawa, S., DeSalle, R., Nóbrega, V.A., Nitschke, R., Okumura, M., Tattersall, I.: Linguistic capacity was present in the Homo sapiens population 135 thousand years ago. Front. Psychol. **16**, 1503900 (2025)
17. Gregor, B.:. Narrare più saggiamente. B@ belonline **8**, 81–93 (2021)
18. Samuel, N.G.: Re-storied by beauty: on self-understanding in the Ricœur-Carr discussions on narrative. J. Appl. Hermeneutics, Article 1 (2015)

19. Dohnalová, M.: Ricoeur's Concept of Narrative Identity (Doctoral dissertation). Masarykova univerzita, Filozofická fakulta, Brno (2021)
20. Hołda, M.: Intersections between P. Ricœur's Conception of Narrative Identity & M. Bakhtin's Notion of the Polyphony of Speech. Forum Philosophicum 21(2), 225–247 (2016)
21. Remodo, A.: The Narrative Identity in Paul Ricoeur's Hermeneutics of the Self (2006). Accessed 22 Apr 2025. https://www.academia.edu/18073338/The_Narrative_Identity_in_Paul_Ricoeurs_Hermeneutics_of_the_Self
22. Fazakas, I.: The flesh of stories of pain and suffering towards a hermeneutics of the antepredicative. Ricœur Stud. 15(2), 111–129 (2024)
23. Romano, C.: Identity and selfhood: Paul Ricœur's contribution and its continuations. In: Davidson, S., Vallée, MA. (eds) Hermeneutics and Phenomenology in Paul Ricoeur. Contributions to Hermeneutics, vol. 2, pp. 43–59. Springer, Cham (2016)
24. Waters, T.E., Fivush, R.: Relations between narrative coherence, identity, and psychological well-being in emerging adulthood. J. Pers. 83(4), 441–451 (2015)
25. Rovetta, F.: The dual role of inner speech in narrative self-understanding and narrative self-enactment. Rev. Philos. Psychol. 15(3), 975–995 (2024)
26. Cavarero, A.: Relating Narratives: Storytelling and Selfhood. Routledge, London (2014)
27. Stary, C., Maroscher, M., Stary, E.: Wissensmanagement in der Praxis: Methoden – Werkzeuge - Beispiele. Carl Hanser Verlag, München (2012)
28. Montague, T.: True story: How to Combine Story and Action to Transform your Business. Harvard Business Press, Boston (2013)
29. Bietti, L.M., Tilston, O., Bangerter, A.: Storytelling as adaptive collective sensemaking. Top. Cogn. Sci. 11(4), 710–732 (2019)
30. Mann, W.C., Thompson, S.A.: Rhetorical structure theory: toward a functional theory of text organization. Text 8(3), 243–281 (1988)
31. Taboada, M., Mann, W.C.: Rhetorical structure theory: looking back and moving ahead. Discourse Stud. 8(3), 423–459 (2006)
32. Hou, S., Zhang, S., Fei, C.: Rhetorical structure theory: a comprehensive review of theory, parsing methods and applications. Expert Syst. Appl. 157, 113421 (2020)
33. Stede, M., Taboada, M., Das, D.: Annotation guidelines for rhetorical structure. Manuscript. University of Potsdam and Simon Fraser University (2017). Accessed 06 Apr 2025. https://www.sfu.ca/~mtaboada/docs/research/RST_Annotation_Guidelines.pdf
34. Fleischmann, A., Schmidt, W., Stary, C., Obermeier, S., Börger, E.: Subject-Oriented Business Process Management. Springer, Cham (2012)
35. Nakasone, A., Ishizuka, M.: SRST: a storytelling model using rhetorical relations. In: Proceedngs of 3rd International Conference on Technologies for Interactive Digital Storytelling and Entertainment, TIDSE 2006, pp. 127–138. Springer, Berlin (2006)
36. Stary, C.: How business process modeling can benefit from rhetorical structure theory. In: Proceedings of 15th International Conference on Subject-Oriented Business Process Management, pp. 105–124. Springer, Cham (2024)
37. Fleischmann, A., Stary, C.: Whom to talk to? A stakeholder perspective on business process development. Univ. Access Inf. Soc. 11, 125–150 (2012)
38. Fleischmann, A., Schmidt, W., Stary, C.: Subject-oriented BPM= socially executable BPM. In: 2013 IEEE 15th Conference on Business Informatics, pp. 399–407 (2013)
39. Stary, C.: Non-disruptive knowledge and business processing in knowledge life cycles–aligning value network analysis to process management. J. Knowl. Manag. 18(4), 651–686 (2014)
40. Lerchner, H., Stary, C.: Model while you work: towards effective and playful acquisition of stakeholder processes. In: Proceedings of the 8th International Conference on Subject-Oriented Business Process Management, pp. 1–10. ACM (2016)

Relating Design Rationale Representations: Concepts and Tool Support

Anke Dittmar(✉) and Peter Forbrig

Department of Computer Science, University of Rostock, Albert-Einstein-Str. 22, 18055 Rostock, Germany
{anke.dittmar,peter.forbrig}@uni-rostock.de

Abstract. The current technology-driven transformation of business processes (and everyday life) must be embedded in collaborative decision making processes. Simple design representations that require no knowledge of specific modelling languages facilitate the involvement of multiple stakeholders. However, they must be related in a structured and at the same time creative way to be an effective means in developing a shared design understanding. This paper proposes concepts for an integrated use of two design rationale representations: scenarios as concrete descriptions of situations of use and QOC diagrams as more abstract descriptions of whole design spaces. Corresponding tool support is presented which supports the intertwined creation of scenarios and QOC diagrams. The tool can easily be extended to include other design representations as demonstrated at the example of integrating personas and use cases.

Keywords: Stakeholder involvement · design rationale · design representations · creativity and sensemaking · collaborative decision making

1 Introduction

The current technology-driven transformation of business processes (and everyday life) calls for an increased awareness of the role of human involvement and creative solutions in process design. Ethical issues concerning the influence of new technologies on organizations, society, and the environment need to be discussed by the stakeholders[1]. User-oriented design approaches have a decades-long history of addressing these aspects, with an initial focus on interactive systems design but now more broadly applied. For instance, key principles in user-centred design include the active involvement of users throughout the entire system lifecycle, the use of simple design representations, multidisciplinary teams, and

---

[1] This need is also expressed in the conference call (https://s-bpm-one.org/).

© The Author(s), under exclusive license to Springer Nature Switzerland AG 2026
M. Elstermann and M. Lederer (Eds.): S-BPM ONE 2025, CCIS 2630, pp. 161–178, 2026.
https://doi.org/10.1007/978-3-032-04944-5_11

a holistic design considering "all aspects that influence the future use situation" [14]. Participatory design aims at engaging people with their personal and societal values in designing technologies that shape their future work practices or everyday life [4]. Bødker et al. [4] describe such co-design practices as "mutual learning between people and professional designers that are capable of translating the imagined futures into digital technology". Co-design activities are usually supported by design representations such as scenarios, personas, and prototypes. They are called 'simple' representations not because they are simple to create, but because they require no knowledge of specific modelling languages to be comprehensible. Hence, they help to involve multiple stakeholders by avoiding problems related to 'model-monopoly' (as described e.g. in [16]). Simple design representations facilitate a flexible interpretation by the different co-designers, and through their discussion, existing design perspectives and underlying assumptions can be revealed. The importance of developing and sharing different design viewpoints is widely acknowledged in the literature [1,12,18].

In previous work, we have argued that for informed, collaborative decision making, a co-evolution of different design representations is needed. Co-designers have to relate them in a structured and at the same time creative way to effectively develop a shared design understanding. In particular, we investigated an integrated creation and use of personas with use cases [7] and with business process models and user stories [10] to support heterogeneous teams in capturing requirements from both the organizational perspective and the users' perspectives. This paper looks at two design rationale representations: scenarios with claims [23] and QOC diagrams (Questions, Options, Criteria) [20]. Both representations support processes of idea generation, argumentation, and sensemaking, but we argue in this paper that they are less effective when used in isolation. Scenarios in this context are concrete descriptions of current and future activities. They help co-designers to switch between different perspectives and to reflect on consequences of existing or envisaged artifact use. The outcomes of their discussion are captured by claims. However, the creation of such scenarios is costly and they should be used in a deliberate way not to overwhelm the participants. QOC diagrams provide a more complete picture of design spaces, but due to the rather abstract description of design options and their assessments imagination and engaged discussion may be less supported (see Sect. 2 for details).

The paper proposes an integrated use of scenarios with claims and QOC diagrams that is guided by a conceptual mapping between these design representations. An example is developed throughout the paper to motivate and describe the integration approach. It is based on a real case and aims at demonstrating that the suggested approach leads to a more conscious use of scenarios (e.g. to encourage perspective changes) and to an increased understanding that QOC diagrams must be contextualised. Prototypical tool support is presented which supports the intertwined creation of scenarios, claims, and QOC diagrams with described relationships. The tool can easily be extended as shown at the example of integrating personas and use cases (proposed in [7]).

The rest of the paper is organized as follows. Section 2 explains the background of the suggested approach, Sect. 3 describes and illustrates an integrated use of scenarios and QOC diagrams, and Sect. 4 briefly presents a prototype for tool support. Finally, Sect. 5 discusses the potentials and limitations of the proposed integration and provides some conclusions and future work.

2 Background

External representations and models are ubiquitous in any design discipline. They express certain design perspectives or viewpoints and thus shape the direction of the design process. Visser [27] describes design activities as domain-specific generation, transformation, and evaluation of design representations. In this paper, we are interested in how multidisciplinary teams can use simple design representations in a creative and yet systematic way to imagine and reflect on future practices (including business and organisational processes). The background provided in this section is to be understood in this context.

2.1 Simple Design Representations in Multidisciplinary Contexts

Multidisciplinary work is motivated by the assumption that design problems typically require specialised knowledge and skills, but every specialised team "has the potential to miss important aspects of the design problem" [18]. Hence collaboration in multidisciplinary teams is characterised by phases of distributed work in specialised sub-teams and by phases of work in heterogeneous teams [1]. The effectiveness depends on the collaborators' willingness to question own assumptions (including those about existing power relationships) and to truly integrate their knowledge and ideas. However, it also depends on their abilities and opportunities to express their own views and understand those of others. Krogstie [16] uses the terms 'model strong' and 'model weak' participant to refer to design situations where a participant's contributions to a discussion is restricted by limited knowledge of certain ideas and modelling languages.

The question we are interested in is how equal participation in this regard can be better supported in heterogeneous teams to achieve a deeper and shared understanding of the design situation (in terms of stakeholders' needs and interests, technological possibilities, design constraints, alternative solutions etc.). A first step is that specialised sub-teams present their intermediate outcomes in a form that is easy to understand and modify by all team members despite their different backgrounds. Prototypes, personas, and scenarios are well-known examples of such 'simple' design representations that require no specific knowledge of modelling languages and notations. Other means include animations of formal models or the generation of 'folded' model versions that abstract from unnecessary details. Of course, participants can also acquire new modelling skills during a design process. In previous work [7], we argue that heterogeneous teams should additionally be enabled to use external representations of different levels of abstraction in an integrated way so that they:

- facilitate a flexible interpretation to reveal existing, perhaps conflicting design perspectives,
- evoke shared discussion and reflection on an integration of different design perspectives,
- stimulate idea generation, and
- support the documentation of design decisions for subsequent design activities (in specialised sub-teams).

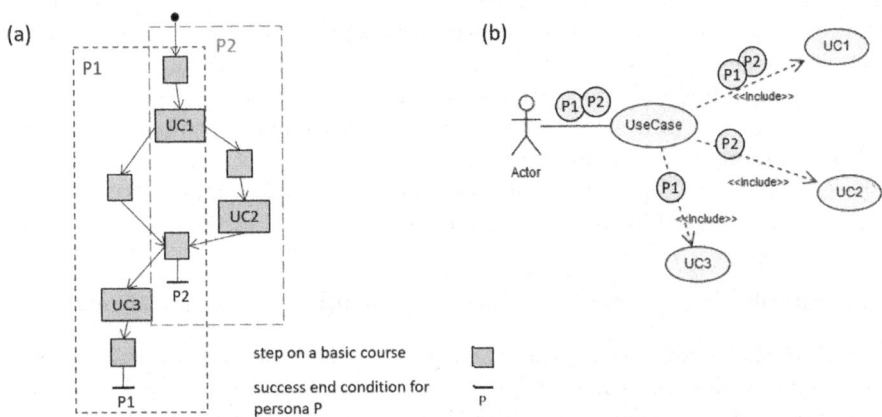

Fig. 1. Adapted use case specification: a) basic course enriched by persona-specific steps for personas P1 and P2, b) persona-specific annotations in the corresponding UML use case diagram (adapted from [7]).

An effective collaborative coupling of different design representations is challenging but can be supported by conceptual mappings. For instance, Fig. 1 illustrates in a schematic way how use case specifications can be enriched by integrating the perspective of user groups (described by personas) without losing the essential character of use cases. The focus of this paper is on design rationale representations, and hence it does not aim at providing a full overview of existing approaches to relate simple design representations. But the example in Fig. 1 is later used in Sect. 4 to demonstrate the prototypical tool support.

2.2 Modelling Current and Envisaged Worlds

As pointed out above, new business and organisational processes (including new technological artifacts) transform work or everyday life and their design must be embedded in a thoughtful analysis and reflection on the present world. Many authors from different design-oriented disciplines emphasize the need to create "two models of the world: a current one and a future one" [6]. Two examples are given in Fig. 2. The model on the left-hand side was created by interaction designers and additionally highlights that the current situation and envisaged situations have to be described at different levels of abstraction to bridge the gap between analysis and synthesis activities [8]. The diagram on the right-hand side of Fig. 2 additionally depicts for what purposes models are used when it comes to the design of information systems (sensemaking, communication, computer-assisted analysis etc.). The models of the current and future state include processes, organisation and computer systems and are perceived differently by the different stakeholders [16]. In the context of this paper, the use of design representations for human sensemaking and communication is especially relevant.

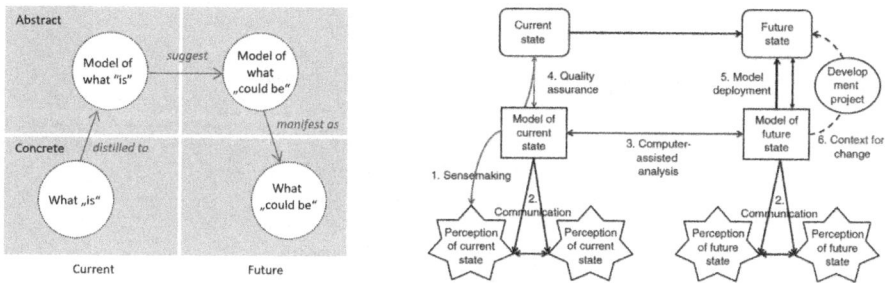

Fig. 2. Left-hand side: analysis-synthesis bridge model [8], right-hand side: different usage areas of models of current and future states [16].

It is worth noting that both illustrations in Fig. 2 (and many others in the literature) seem to support the idea of 'continuous progress'. Models of possible future worlds/states (system-to-be) describe intended improvements to (models of) the current world/state (system-as-is). In Sect. 3, we propose to distinguish between concrete and abstract representations of the current situation and envisaged future ones. But in contrast to [8], abstract descriptions of current, envisaged, and even past worlds are considered to be 'just' options in a design space.

2.3 Design Rationale Representations

Design rationale approaches aim to find good design solutions through processes of argumentation and collective sensemaking. They acknowledge that "articulating and reconciling different perspectives are central to design, and should be recognised and supported" [24]. Lee and Lai [17] distinguish between structure-oriented and psychological design rationale approaches. Approaches of the first category help to systematically explore design spaces and document design alternatives and decision making at a rather abstract level. Approaches of the second category use scenarios of current and future worlds to collaboratively explore possible consequences of future artifact use. This paper suggests an intertwined application of structure-oriented and psychological design rationale using QOC diagrams [20] and scenarios with claims from scenario-based design [23].

QOC Diagrams. The QOC notation was introduced in the early 1990ies [20] to support a systematic exploration and evaluation of design spaces. We use this notation in Sect. 3 because it is a simple semi-formal notation that is still actively used (e.g. [13]) and known by practitioners in different domains (e.g. interactive systems design [19] and software architecture [25]).

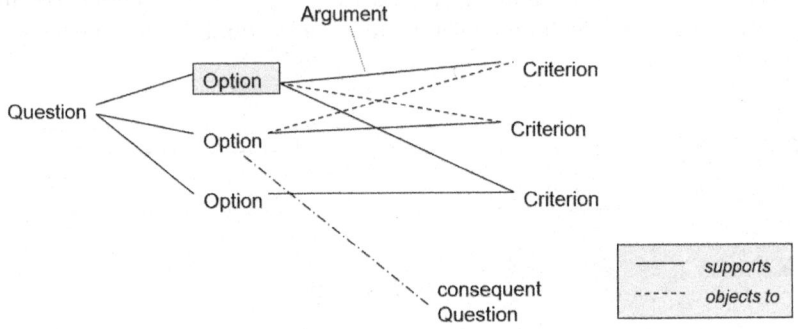

Fig. 3. Schematic QOC diagram.

A QOC diagram consists of four types of elements: (Q)uestions, (O)ptions, (C)riteria, and arguments. The diagram in Fig. 3 shows how these elements are related. Questions represent problems with no obvious or best solution that need to be discussed. They help to generate alternative solutions (options) and to structure the design space in a hierarchical way (options can lead to follow-up questions). Criteria represent goals whose achievement can be supported or hindered by an option. Such assessments are either supported or challenged by arguments based on theories, empirical data, ad-hoc theories etc. QOC diagrams can be used to manage actual discussions (rough, ill-formed QOCs) or to analyse and document discussions for later refinement (more rigorous QOCs) [24]. QOC diagrams are flexible enough to represent different viewpoints as demonstrated in the study in [2]. Diagrams with few criteria often indicate a lack of reflection on options while diagrams with few options reveal limited creativity.

Scenarios with Claims. One of the most holistic approaches for using scenarios in design processes is developed in [5,22,23]. The authors distinguish between four different types of scenarios of which two are relevant here (see Fig. 4). Problem scenarios illustrate and contextualise important aspects about the current world that were identified and analysed in empirical studies. Activity scenarios provide contextualised descriptions of alternative envisaged processes and artifacts. Problem and activity scenarios are typically written in a narrative form (alternatives are storyboards or videos). They illustrate complex issues in a vivid and comprehensible way by creating plausible characters acting in concrete (but typically fictive) situations. The description of the characters' personal motivations, relationships, goals, attitudes, conflicts etc. help people to identify with them, to understand their views and concerns, and to memorise the scenarios [26]. Thus, scenarios can be easily shared by collaborators across disciplines who interpret them based on their own (professional) backgrounds. It should be emphasized that scenarios are not design-neutral but "constructions made with a purpose" [3] which can be used, for instance, to provide information about tasks and goals of a system-as-is or to introduce ideas about a new artifact and how to use it [21]. Rosson and Carroll [23] point out that "[m]uch of the richness of a scenario is in the things that are not said". It highlights deliberately chosen themes in a way that it evokes a discussion process and facilitates collaborative reflection and imagination. Scenarios help to avoid overgeneralization by supporting the tension between reflection and action (to prevent too quick solutions), the consideration of typical and critical situations, and the consideration of alternative solutions in different situations [3].

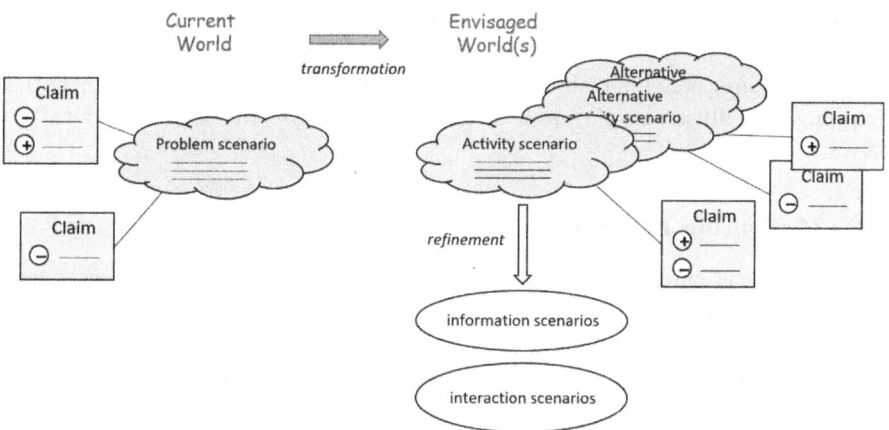

Fig. 4. Scenarios and claims in scenario-based design [22].

Problem and activity scenarios are used in combination with claims. According to [22,23], a claim refers to a feature of a conceptual or physical artifact mentioned in the scenarios and explicitly describes consequences of its use in terms of pros(+) and cons(−). Claims support the development of alternative ideas and thus lead to the creation of further scenarios. What should be covered by the set of scenarios that is created for a project is answered differently. Rosson and Carroll [23] recommend to write at least one scenario for each stakeholder, to investigate at least one or two claims for each scenario, and to write several scenarios for stakeholders with many or complex tasks. However, to keep the set of scenarios and associated claims manageable for the participants remains challenging.

Figure 4 also depicts the other two types of scenarios of the scenario-based design approach employed in this paper. Information and interaction scenarios describe business processes and user-technology interaction at the level of use cases [15]. They are used to refine the specification of a certain business process or interactive artifact and out of the scope of the paper.

3 Integrated Use of Scenarios and QOC Diagrams

As shown in the previous section, scenarios with claims and QOC diagrams both support processes of sensemaking, idea generation, and argumentation, but they do it in different ways and at different levels of abstraction. The concreteness of scenarios facilitate flexible interpretation, perspective change, imagination, and discussion as required from design representations for heterogeneous teams (see Subsect. 2.1). However, they should be used deliberately and carefully because team members may easily be overwhelmed by too many scenarios and lose the overall picture (even if the scenarios are combined with claims). QOC diagrams provide a more complete picture of a design space and are an appropriate means for documenting design decisions for subsequent design activities in specialised sub-teams. We propose to use scenarios and QOC diagrams in an intertwined way by relating them via claims. This section describes the suggested conceptual mapping and illustrates its application by an example that is based on a real case.

3.1 Motivating Example

The example is informed by events from two requirements engineering courses we taught in the summer semesters 2022 and 2023 (with 15 and 24 participants respectively). Students explored aspects of 'post-COVID' higher education[2]. Their activities included one-week diaries about own learning activities, preparation and conduction of an interview with a peer student about their learning experiences and ideas, and affinity diagramming based on the interview material. Figure 5 shows those parts of the affinity diagrams of two of the overall seven sub-groups which are related to the format of courses. In most cases, cards were grouped according to the benefits and limitations of course formats that were discussed in the interviews ('physical/in-person', 'online', 'recorded lectures', 'hybrid').

Through the affinity diagramming exercise, participants could see the similarities and differences in their experiences of the online 'Covid-semesters'. The QOC diagram in Fig. 6 documents some results from the sessions. It is based on the analysis of the resulting affinity diagrams and notes from shared discussions of all sub-groups at the end of the sessions. The cards revealed students' strong preference for recorded lectures and that perspectives from teachers and other stakeholders were rarely considered by students in their interviews. A student in one session shared his insight that those cards suggesting a hybrid course format

---

[2] In 2020 and 2021, there were online courses in our department due to the Covid-19 pandemic. The requirements engineering course was one of the few 'in-person' courses offered in summer 2022. The majority of courses are 'in-person' courses again since winter 2022/23.

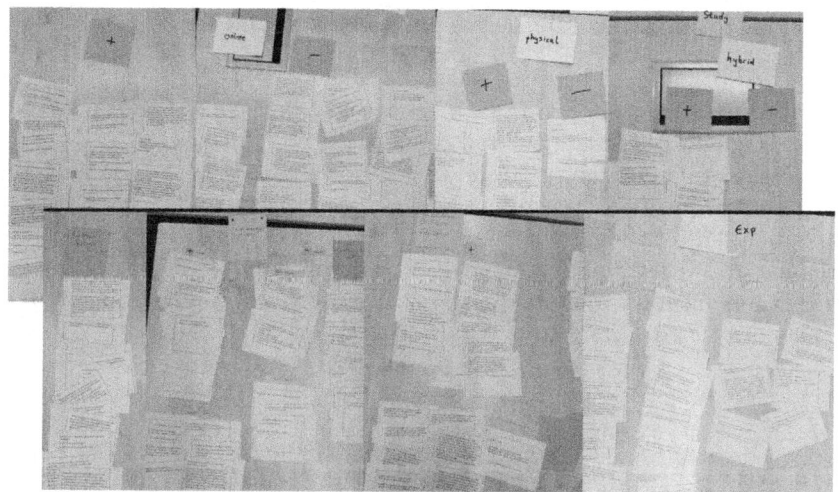

Fig. 5. Affinity diagrams from two student groups in the example.

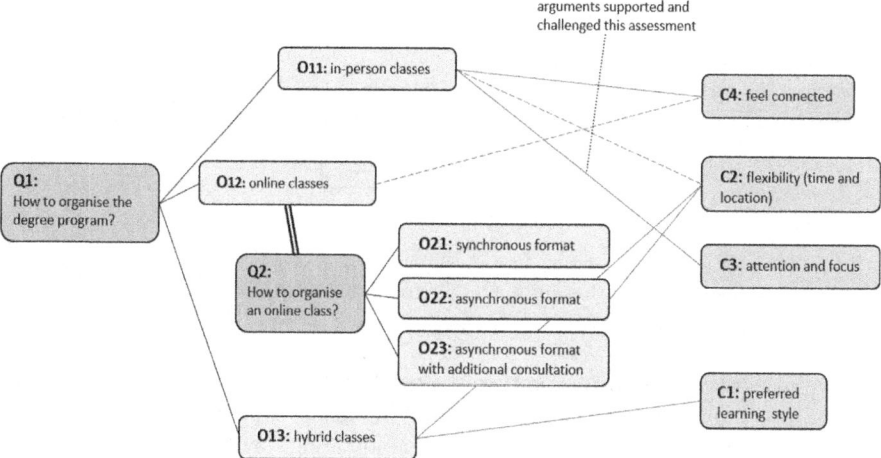

Fig. 6. Documentation of the affinity diagramming session by a QOC diagram.

for the future describe it only vaguely and mention only benefits. However, it also became obvious in the discussion that common practices such as uploading lecture material or perhaps deep-seated needs such as keeping (recording) things are sometimes difficult to question. Scenarios can help here to open up design spaces by describing new perspectives in an inspiring form.

3.2 Conceptual Mapping Between Scenarios and QOC Elements

The proposed mapping between scenarios and QOC diagrams is simple and schematically depicted in Fig. 7. Claims serve as 'connectors' between scenarios (or text fragments of scenarios) and elements of QOC diagrams. In particular, a claim refers to an option, pros and cons of a claim refer to criteria and corresponding assessments of the options. Claims are typically more context-specific than options, criteria, and arguments in QOC diagrams as they emerge from the discussion and reflection on scenarios. A criterion often represents an abstraction of points mentioned in a set of claims. However, one can also directly relate elements of QOC diagrams to parts of scenarios and omit claims.

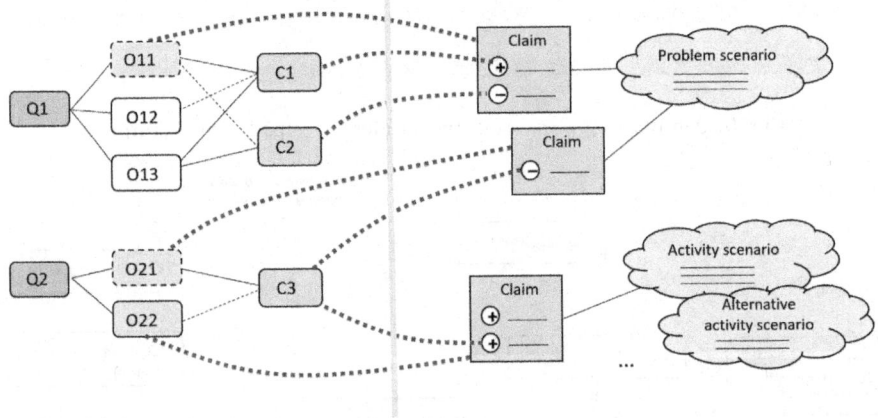

Fig. 7. The mapping: scenarios and QOC diagrams are related to each other via claims.

The integrated use of a structure-oriented and a psychological design rationale approach has several advantages. It distinguishes explicitly between descriptions of two levels of abstraction as recommended, e.g., by the analysis-synthesis bridge model (see Fig. 2). Scenarios are concrete descriptions of what is and what could be; they could also describe what was in the past. QOC diagrams are abstract representations, which in contrast to the models in Fig. 2, 'unify' descriptions of current and envisaged worlds (and even past worlds) as sets of options that can be compared and assessed on the basis of criteria. This is indicated in Fig. 7 by different edgings and colours for options. Options O11 and O21 (dashed edgings) describe the current situation as they are related to the problem scenario. Option O22 describes an aspect of an envisaged situation. Options O12 and O13 are not supported by scenarios but may describe alternative solutions for the future or something from the past. In other words, design is not understood and depicted as a kind of 'linear progress' but as intended changes with pros and cons (some of them explicitly described, some not well-understood yet). This view is illustrated in Fig. 8.

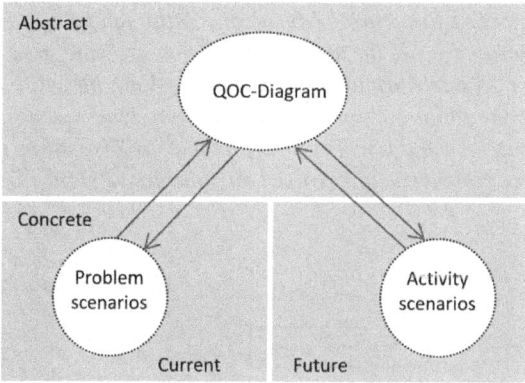

Fig. 8. Adapted analysis-synthesis bridge model.

An intertwined development of scenarios and QOC diagrams allows for a more selective use of scenarios. On the one hand, QOC diagrams provide an structural frame for scenarios that is more effective than a set of claims. They help to identify dominant and under-represented design perspectives in the design process. Scenarios can then be constructed (based on empirical data) to emotionally engage participants in perspective changes. Or, follow-up questions may arise and need to be further investigated. On the other hand, claims that emerge from the discussion of scenarios help to put elements of QOC diagrams in context. For example, contradicting arguments that support and challenge an assessment in a QOC diagram (as indicated in the example in Fig. 6 may be more or less relevant in different situations that are captured by scenarios. The mappings between scenarios and QOC elements encourage participants to switch between different levels of abstraction. They thus support creativity (both in terms of idea generation and assessment) and a systematic but contextualised exploration of design spaces.

3.3 Discussing a Scenario in the Example

In the above introduced example, the QOC diagram in Fig. 6 reveals a vague understanding of hybrid classes. In addition, the criteria mainly reflect the perspectives of students. The following scenario aims at addressing these gaps.

> *Keith opens his mailbox ... the third student now who is asking why there is no video uploaded this week. He knows that students expect him to upload recordings of the classes, but this is one of these moments where he misses Cathy's comments. Although the department does not officially offer a hybrid-flexibility model almost all colleagues provide live streaming of their classes or record them. How Cathy hated that. For her it was another step*

towards the *commodification of education*. Although he sometimes thought that she exaggerated a bit he also admired her attitude and was sad when she eventually quit her work at the university. Well, he will tell the students next week that they had an unexpected and inspiring discussion in the last lecture and that he would feel uncomfortable to distribute a recording to people who were not actively involved in that discussion.

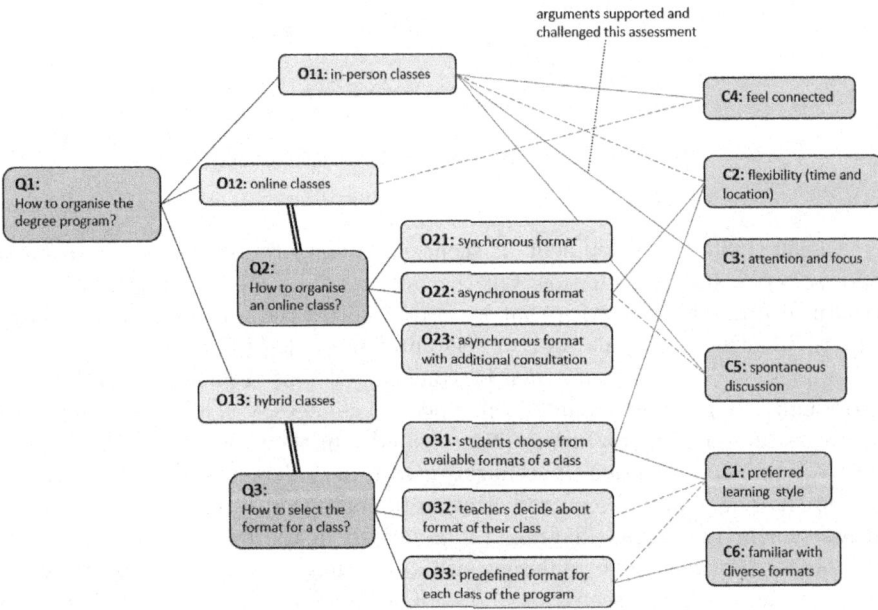

Fig. 9. QOC diagram of Fig. 6 refined by follow-up question Q3 with options and new criteria.

Let us imagine, for reasons of illustration, that the discussion of the above scenario resulted in a refinement of the diagram as shown in Fig. 9. In particular, option O13 is refined by a follow-up question that leads to alternative ideas of the hybrid class format. Two additional criteria (C5 and C6) are introduced for assessing the different design options from another perspective.

4 Tool Support

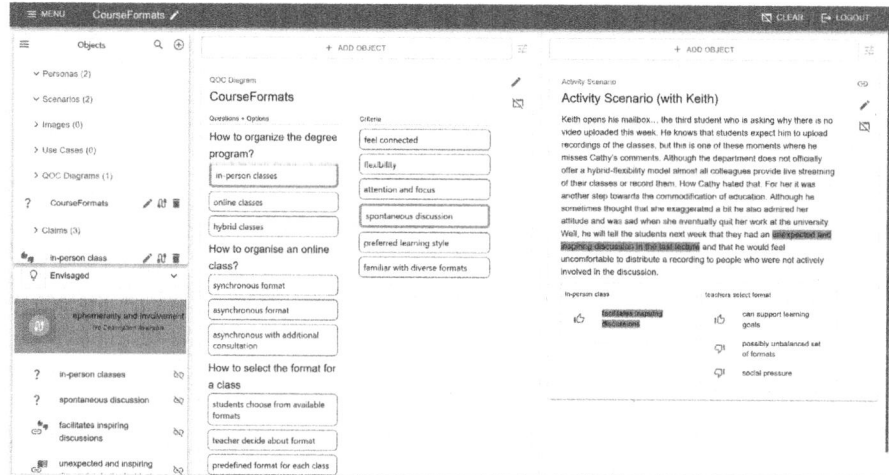

Fig. 10. Prototypical tool support for an intertwined development of QOC diagrams and scenarios with claims.

The proposed integrated use of scenarios with claims and QOC diagrams requires some form of tool support. This section briefly presents a prototype allowing users to develop and relate scenarios, claims, and QOC diagrams in the above described way. Figure 10 and 11 show screenshots of the user interface which is divided in two parts: a) two vertical panels on the left for selecting and managing design representations and mappings (connections) between them, and b) the working area consisting of two columns for displaying selected design representations. In the screenshots, the QOC diagram of the above example is shown on the left-hand side of the working area. The right column displays the example scenario with two associated claims. Selected connections are highlighted. The screenshot in Fig. 10 highlights (in red) four related elements: 1) text fragment of the scenario ("unexpected and inspiring discussion in the last lecture"), 2) associated claim 'in-person class' and its pro(+) 'facilitates inspiring discussions', 3) option 'in person-classes', and 4) criterion 'spontaneous discussion' from the QOC diagram. Figure 11 shows two other connections selected and highlighted at the same time, with different colours.

The UML class diagram in Fig. 12 specifies the structure of the different design representations in use. The class 'Connection' is introduced to manage mappings between different parts of these representations (e.g. text fragments of scenarios, claim items, options). Connections can be grouped (e.g. for describing current or envisaged worlds). As to be seen in the UML class diagram, the implemented mapping model is more generous than the conceptual mapping in Sect. 3. This decision was made for two reasons. First, users can relate the design

174   A. Dittmar and P. Forbrig

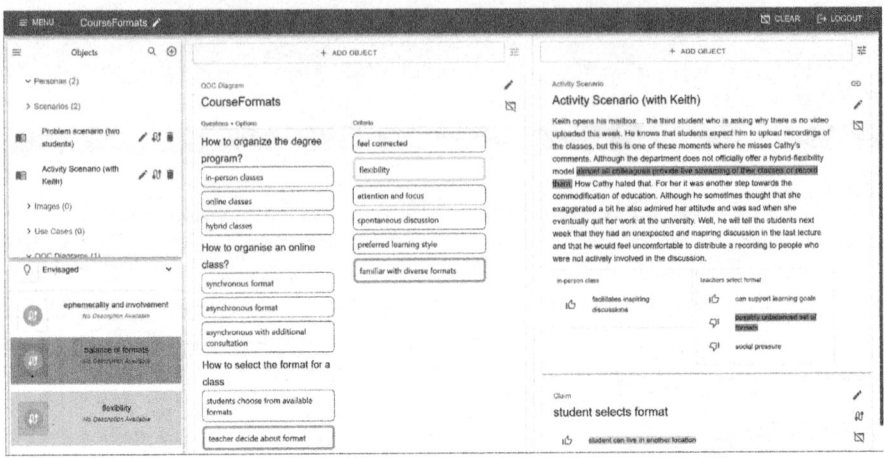

Fig. 11. Screenshot with two highlighted connections between elements of the displayed representations.

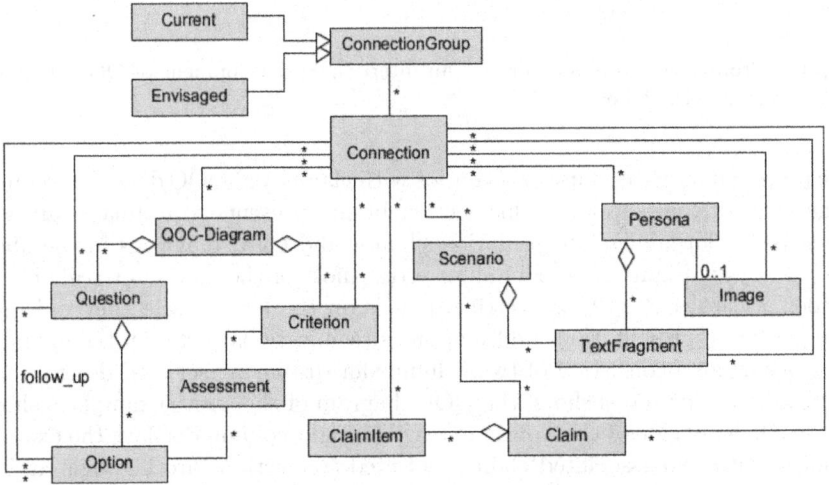

Fig. 12. UML class diagram of elements of supported design representations and mappings.

rationale representations as suggested but have more freedom in finding other useful connections. Second, the tool can be extended relatively easy to include other simple design representations and corresponding mappings.

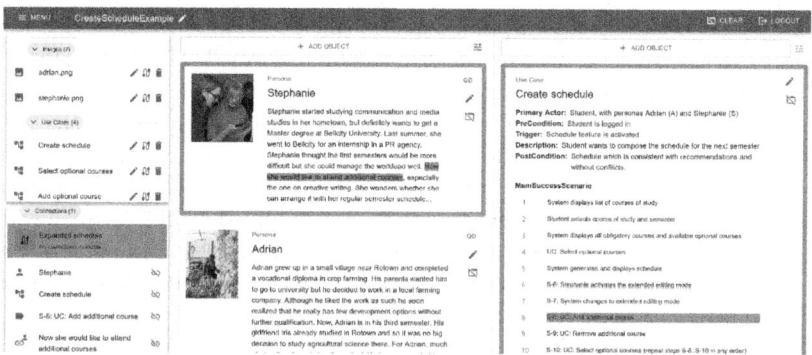

Fig. 13. Screenshot with personas on the left-hand side and use cases on the right-hand of the working area and a highlighted connection.

The current prototype additionally supports the integrated development of use cases and personas introduced in [7]. Use case scenarios are enhanced by persona-specific steps (see also the visualisation in Fig. 1). The example in Fig. 13 is taken from [7]: personas Stephanie and Adrian represent groups of students using a course management system. They help developing a more differentiated view of the use case 'Create schedule'. The screenshot shows a highlighted text fragment of persona Stephanie that led to the persona-specific (and highlighted) step 'Add additional course' in the use case.

5 Conclusions and Discussion

The paper makes a conceptual contribution. According to [11], conceptual papers do not have empirical data but their focus is on proposing new relationships among constructs and providing arguments for their usefulness. Thus, they can broaden the scope of our thinking. The paper aimed at supporting sensemaking and creativity in multidisciplinary design contexts. Starting point was the acknowledgement of the role of simple design rationale representations in describing current and envisaged worlds at different levels of abstraction. QOC diagrams and scenarios with claims are such simple representations and their proposed integration supports collaborators in developing and exploring design spaces in a systematic and at the same time creative way. This was illustrated by a carefully worked out example.

Potentials of the Proposed Integration. QOC diagrams and scenarios with claims can be related because claims share similarities with options, criteria and assessments. Their integrated use mitigates deficiencies of the single approaches. Scenarios more likely support the emotional engagement of participants in group discussions than the QOC method. Participants are better aided in changing the design perspective, contextualising ideas, and reflecting on potential risks and benefits of design choices. QOC diagrams better aid participants in structuring design spaces, integrating viewpoints, generating ideas, and documenting design decisions. All of these activities are needed for informed decision making and implementing decisions. The suggested conceptual mapping supports both the contextualised interpretation of QOC diagrams and the integration of the scenarios into the larger context. In addition, it can be seen as an attempt to overcome the idea of linear (technological) progress that is deeply ingrained in our culture. Design is understood to be a goal-directed activity aimed at improving a current state. At the same time, it is acknowledged that changes have possible negative (side-)effects; the future does not necessarily need to be better than the present. QOC diagrams abstract from concrete scenarios by putting past, present, and future options in one model.

Scope of the Representational Integration. External representations help to articulate and consider multiple design views but only if they are used in a thoughtful way. An 'explosion' of external or explicit descriptions is not manageable by co-design teams. Glinz and Fricker [12] highlight in the context of software development the value (and risks) of implicit shared understanding. Generally, design rationale representations should only address issues with no simple answers. They are not complete descriptions of requirements or designs but are used, for example, to discuss consequences of possible future technology use. We claim that the proposed integration approach results in a reduced number of scenarios (compared to the recommendation in [23]) because scenarios are now created in a more selective way to evoke discussion of identified gaps such as under-represented design perspectives or missing design alternatives. It should also be noted that a contextualised interpretation of a QOC diagram does not require scenarios for every option in that diagram. Some such short narratives may be sufficient to raise the participants' awareness of contextual aspects and to trigger situational thinking.

Limitations and Future Work. Both QOC diagrams and scenarios with claims are design rationale representations and thus their integrated use cannot resolve the limitation that "argumentation has been considered in isolation from the activity of solution construction" [9]. Fischer et al. [9] call for a unification of construction and argumentation. In other words, a combinations with other methods (e.g. long-term prototyping processes) is needed to better understand behavioural changes and other (side) effects of design solutions. Future Work also includes empirical studies on the effectiveness of the proposed approach. In this paper, scenarios were assumed to be texts, but there are other narrative forms such as storyboards which could be additionally considered in the described tool support.

Acknowledgments. The authors thank Sarah Plank and Dennis Rauch for contributing to the prototype implementation.

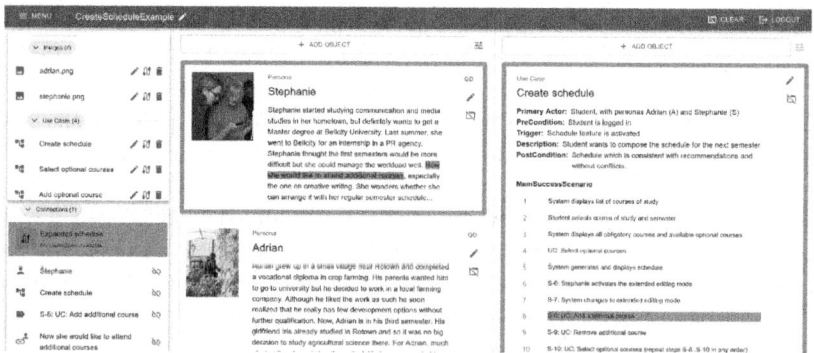

References

1. Baker, M., Détienne, F., Burkhardt, J.M.: Quality of collaboration in design: articulating multiple dimensions and viewpoints. In: 1st Interdisciplinary Innovation Conference, Telecom ParisTech (2013)
2. Bellotti, V.: Integrating theoreticians' and practitioners' perspectives with design rationale. In: Proceedings of the INTERACT'93 and CHI 1993 Conference on Human Factors in Computing Systems, pp. 101–106 (1993)
3. Bodker, S.: Scenarios in user-centred design - setting the stage for reflection and action. In: Proceedings of HICSS-32. IEEE (1999)
4. Bødker, S., Dindler, C., Iversen, O., Smith, R.: Participatory design. Synthesis Lectures on Human-Centered Informatics **14** (2021)
5. Carroll, J.M., Rosson, M.B., Chin, G., Koenemann, J.: Requirements development in scenario-based design. IEEE Trans. Software Eng. **24**(12), 1156–1170 (1998)
6. Diaper, D.: Understanding task analysis for human-computer interaction. In: Diaper, D., Stanton, N. (eds.) The Handbook of Task Analysis for Human-Computer Interaction, pp. 5–48. Lawrence Erlbaum, Mahwah (2004)
7. Dittmar, A., Forbrig, P.: Integrating personas and use case models. In: Lamas, D., Loizides, F., Nacke, L., Petrie, H., Winckler, M., Zaphiris, P. (eds.) INTERACT 2019. LNCS, vol. 11746, pp. 666–686. Springer, Cham (2019). https://doi.org/10.1007/978-3-030-29381-9_40
8. Dubberly, H., Evenson, S.: On modeling the analysis-systhesis bridge model. Interactions **15**(2), 57–61 (2008)
9. Fischer, G., Lemke, A.C., McCall, R., Morch, A.I.: Making argumentation serve design. In: Moran, T., M., C.J. (eds.) Design Rationale - Concepts, Techniques, and Use, pp. 267–293. Erlbaum (1996)
10. Forbrig, P., Dittmar, A.: Cross-pollination of personas, user stories, use cases and business-process models. In: Model-Driven Organizational and Business Agility - Second International Workshop, MOBA 2022, Revised Selected Papers. Lecture Notes in Business Information Processing, vol. 457, pp. 3–18. Springer (2022)
11. Gilson, L.L., Goldberg, C.B.: Editors' comment: so, what is a conceptual paper? Group Organ. Manage. **40**(2), 127–130 (2015)
12. Glinz, M., Fricker, S.: On shared understanding in software engineering: an essay. Comput. Sci. Res. Dev. **30**, 363–376 (2015)
13. Gregoriades, A., Sutcliffe, A.: Using task support requirements during sociotechnical systems design. Systems **12**(9), 348 (2024)
14. Gulliksen, J., Göransson, B., Boivie, I., Blomkvist, S., Cajander, Å.: Key principles for user centred systems design. Behav. Inf. Technol. **22**(6), 397–409 (2003)
15. Jacobson, I., Cockburn, A.: Use cases are essential: use cases provide a proven method to capture and explain the requirements of a system in a concise and easily understood format. Queue **21**(5), 66–86 (2023)
16. Krogstie, J.: Model-Based Development and Evolution of Information Systems: A Quality Approach. Springer Science & Business Media, Berlin and Heidelberg (2012)
17. Lee, J., Lai, K.Y.: What's in design rationale? In: Moran, T., M., C.J. (eds.) Design Rationale - Concepts, Techniques, and Use, pp. 21–51. Erlbaum (1996)
18. Mackay, W.E.: Educating multi-disciplinary design teams. Proc. of Tales of the Disappearing Computer pp. 105–118 (2003)

19. MacLean, A., Bellotti, V., Shum, S.: Developing the design space with design space analysis. In: Byerley, P.F., Barnard, P.J., May, J. (eds.) Computers, Communication and Usability: Design Issues, Research and Methods for Integrated Services, pp. 197–219. Elsevier (1993)
20. MacLean, A., Young, R., Bellotti, V., Moran, T.: Questions, options, and criteria: elements of design space analysis. Hum. Comput. Interact. **6**(3), 201–250 (1991)
21. Quesenbery, W., Brooks, K.: Storytelling for User Experience: Crafting Stories for Better Design. Rosenfeld Media, New York (2010)
22. Rosson, M.B., Carroll, J.M.: Scenario-Based Design, pp. 1032–1050. Erlbaum (2002)
23. Rosson, M., Carroll, J.: Usability Engineering: Scenario-Based Development of Human-Computer Interaction. Morgan Kaufmann Publishers Inc., Burlington (2002)
24. Shum, S.B., MacLean, A., Bellotti, V., Hammond, N.V.: Graphical argumentation and design cognition. Hum. Comput. Inter. **12**(3), 267–300 (1997)
25. Tang, A., Han, J., Vasa, R.: Software architecture design reasoning: a case for improved methodology support. IEEE Softw. **26**(2), 43–49 (2009)
26. Thier, K.: Storytelling: Eine Methode für das Change-, Marken-. Springer-Verlag, Projekt-und Wissensmanagement (2016)
27. Visser, W.: Designing as construction of representations: a dynamic viewpoint in cognitive design research. Hum. Comput. Inter. **21**(1), 103–152 (2006)

Staying Agile: A Process Lifecycle Model for Maintaining SCRUM Practices in Software Development

Katie Clark[1], Melanie Pufahl[1], and Matthias Lederer[2(✉)]

[1] Comsysto Reply, Riesstraße 22, 80992 Munich, Germany
[2] Technical University of Applied Sciences Amberg-Weiden, Hetzenrichter Weg 15, 92637 Weiden, Germany
ma.lederer@oth-aw.de
https://www.comsystoreply.de/, http://www.oth-aw.de/

Abstract. While agile methodologies are established in many software development processes, most of the research concentrates on the initial transition from traditional methods to agile practices. Relatively little attention is given to the challenge of staying agile in the development projects over the long term, especially when organizations face phases of declining agile maturity. This paper addresses that gap by presenting a comprehensive process lifecycle model that spans both the transformation phase and the subsequent periods when agile practices may deteriorate. The model integrates insights from a systematic literature review – focusing on phase models for both agile transformation and decline – with empirical data gathered from a six-year, long-running agile project. Through a focus group, concrete actions and best practices were identified that consistently helped the case project avert a loss of agility. Two cross-cutting results stand out: First, teams must actively reconnect with the core values of agility (transparency, iterative learning and customer focus) and translate them into day-to-day rituals. Second, short, well-timed external impulses (for example from agile coaches or specialized consultants) act as catalytic boundary spanners that expose blind spots and accelerate internal learning without undermining team autonomy. Taken together, the findings offer a practical guide for organizations striving to maintain agile performance and provide a robust foundation for future research into sustaining agile projects.

Keywords: Agile Software Development · Process Lifecycle · Agile Maturity · Sustainable Agility · Process Improvement · Best Practices

1 Motivation

Agile approaches such as SCRUM are widely established in software development projects [1, 2]. There is a wide variety of studies [3], guidelines [4] and case reports [5] both from theory as well as business practice. The focus is primarily on questions related to the transformation and adoption of agility. At the same time, numerous maturity models and phase models have been developed that map the maturity progress of teams or entire organizations during the transition to agile methods (e.g., see [3;6;7]). This also applies to further developments of SCRUM such as Scaled Agile Framework or SCRUM-at-Scale [8].

[9] shows, however, that research and, above all, practice are increasingly addressing the question of how agility can be maintained in the long term and thus ensure the productive engineering of software at a high level. Despite selective field reports (e.g. [10]) or studies (e.g. [11]), papers that analyze how typical regressions or "wear and tear effects" can be avoided after a successful transition are still the exception rather than the rule [9;12]. It is generally accepted in theory and practice, and is also followed in this article, that under certain conditions (e.g., changing customer requirements, rapid achievement of a marketable solution, volatile project environment), agile process models should be selected and maintained.

Against this background, in this paper we establish a lifecycle model for agile developments that focuses primarily on the sustainable "retention" of agility. This advanced SCRUM project phase is later referred to as the *mentoring* stage, in which the focus is no longer on pure adoption (transition), but on avoiding phases of decline and benefiting from the agile culture in the long term. In addition, in Sect. 3.2 we present specific techniques and measures (from now on "actions" in the wording of [13]) that can be used to counteract possible regressions in late maturity phases of the agile development process.

The methodological basis for the findings (see Sect. 2) is a combination of known agile phase models (see Sect. 3.1) as well as insights from a six-year development project (see Sect. 3.2) that has proven to be consistently agile and particularly successful. The sustainable success of the project can be quantitatively proven using classic key performance indicators in this area (e.g. velocity, product value, employee satisfaction, customer engagement, fluctuation rate, etc.). Nevertheless, this project also faced critical project phases three times. However, with targeted measures and techniques, it was possible to stabilize agility and counteract undesirable developments each time.

Considering the aforementioned aspects, two central research questions are derived:

1. *How can the lifecycle of an agile development process be systematically described over its entire course - from transition to stabilization of agile maturity? In particular: Which specific phases occur in the late process?*
2. *In the long-term, what actions have proven successful in averting negative tendencies towards non-agility?*

The aim of this article is to reduce the research gap around the *ongoing* practical *topic of agility*, to provide organizations with guidelines on how they can consolidate their agile values and principles in the long term, as well as protect them against setbacks once the transformation is complete.

2 Methodology

This study is based on two methodological building blocks: firstly, a topic-specific *Systematic Literature Review* (SLR) to identify suitable phase models for the entire agile project life cycle. This was followed by a *focus group discussion* in which experienced project participants compiled and reflected on specific practices for avoiding or preventing the deconstruction of agility.

The aim of the *literature-based analysis*, which was classically carried out according to the approach of [14] and [15] with AI support, was to find models that deal with the typical transformation to agility (i.e. the change from non-agile to agile approaches) on the one hand and explicitly consider the topic of the loss of agile maturity on the other - the latter will be the focus of this paper. As this is not only about a conventional stage-based maturity model (there are already a sufficient number of articles on this, see next section), but about descriptions of phases over time with a particular focus on possible tendencies towards decline, only those publications that present a coherent "before and after logic" for agility were included. In addition to process methodologies and published transformation models, also maturity models were taken into account if they describe clear phases of transformation or (non-)reversal of agile techniques.

In addition, the studies or models were collected to explicitly address the phase after successful adoption in order to describe potential crisis scenarios - for example, a decline in agility after a longer period. As part of the SLR, a systematic search was carried out using common IT and business-related databases (including e.g., ACM, IEEE, SpringerLink, Google Scholar). Common keywords relating to the topic (e.g. "agile maturity", "agile lifecycle", "agile phase model") and specific combinations relating to deconstruction (e.g. "decline in agile") were used as search terms. The publications underwent an AI-supported full-text review to ensure that the theoretical constructs and defined phases matched the research interest.

Ultimately, two established model approaches were combined: On the one hand, a classic transformation model for the introduction of agile approaches, and on the other hand, a model that explicitly refers to the decline and possible turnaround actions. The latter describes that actions (prompt, corrective and reorganization actions) are possible in three basic phases (inaction, faulty action, crisis phase). These two models form the basis for putting together a continuous life cycle - from transition to mentoring (see Sect. 3.1).

Then, a *focus group discussion* was conducted in order to close the content gap with regard to concrete actions to avert the threat of a "deconstruction" of agility. According to [16], this method should serve to collect practical experiences and interactions within an operational group - in this case a specific SCRUM team. In addition, the exchange between project participants creates a shared knowledge base [17], which includes a variety of perspectives. The technical realization was based on the recommendations of [18] and [19]: participants were long-standing members of the sample project who had either been actively involved in one or more destructive situations or could report on the effects. The case under investigation is a development project subcontracted by a German automotive company (Product Owner) that is staffed technically (Developer) and methodical (SCRUM Master) by an IT consultancy. According to the classic success criteria of agile development, such as those mentioned in [20] or [3], the project has been very successful for over six years. The objective metrics (e.g. velocity, product value) and soft factors (e.g. team culture, cooperation with the product owner) are extremely good. Nevertheless, the project found itself in critical project phases three times, in which the success criteria were in decline. The focus group participants were to report on how to successfully react in these states. It was ensured that people from the project's three historical crisis situations took part and were able to speak for all roles.

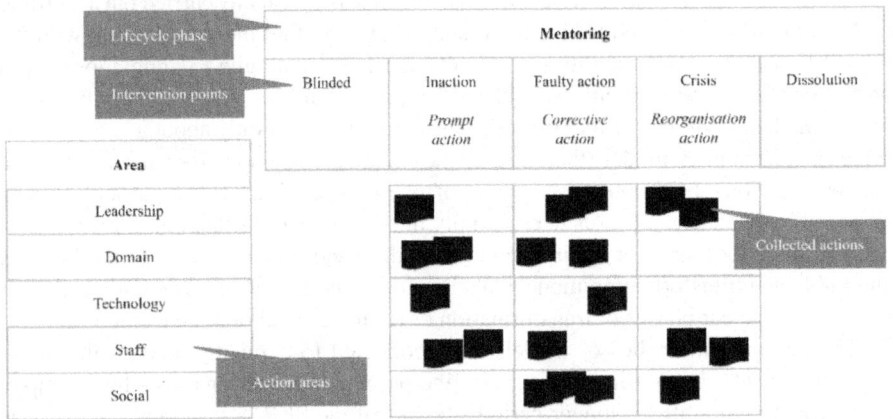

Fig. 1. Scheme for collecting actions in the focus group

The meeting took place virtually via Microsoft Teams and lasted around 70 min. After an introduction (including a review of the three crises), a stimulus was presented at the beginning, in which exemplary techniques per phase of a possible decline were presented from the literature (X axis: timeline), as described in Sect. 3.2.

Following this, the participants filled out a matrix to collect corrective actions along the area clusters defined by [9] (Y axis: leadership[1], domain, technology, personnel, social [17]). In decision theory, actions can be grouped based on these areas. When using these dimensions of actions, they therefore offer the possibility of comprehensively collecting measures and avoiding systematic errors or biases. In each field (except for the "blind phase", where people do not take any measures because they cannot notice it; and in the "dissolution phase", because the project no longer makes sense at that point), the participants entered suitable actions that, according to the focus group's assessment, could help (a) to ensure the stabilization of agile practices and (b) to reduce the deconstruction, erosion or decline of agility in the respective constellation (see Fig. 1). In a subsequent discussion and follow-up, the actions were sorted, grouped and interpreted using classic qualitative content analysis techniques, both manually and AI-based.

---

[1] Even if "leadership" cannot be a field of action in the strict agile sense because self-organization is a basic principle, leadership may still be necessary in situations of deterioration (see results by [19]). It is therefore also used as a decision science area cluster.

3 Results

In line with the research questions and methodology, the findings on the phase model are first compiled (Sect. 3.1) and then supplemented with phase-by-phase instructions for actions (Sect. 3.2).

3.1 Phase Models

There are numerous studies and meta-studies on adoption phases and practices, some of which are textbook based, some of which are based on primary data from the field, and some of which are also based on literature reviews (see Table 1). For the model of this article, original phase models resulting from the SLR are used – partly based on compilation meta studies like [21] and further research.

What many of the models have in common is the assumption that agility develops *gradually* and that teams or companies often need several iterations to reach a higher level of maturity. Implicitly or explicitly, the papers found assume that in suitable contexts and project situations (e.g., frequently changing customer requirements or unclear budget forecast), a higher level of agility goes hand in hand with higher product value. Some models include a qualitative or quantitative *assessment* with which the current status quo can be recorded and targeted improvements can then be derived. In addition, some approaches explicitly point out that maturity levels do not necessarily have to be achieved linearly or homogeneously, but can grow in *parallel* in different dimensions (e.g. processes, team culture, technical practices, management support).

Despite different focuses (e.g. on cultural vs. technical aspects), the models consistently point out that going agile should not be understood as a one-off change (transition), but as a *continuous process of change* (transformation). The final phase often represents a holding position in which work is carried out (e.g. agile consulting, mentoring) at a high agile level and disruptions or regressions are avoided.

This is where the studies and models presented in Table 2 come in, which focus on the *preservation* of already established agile working methods and/or the gradual degeneration of such practices. The corresponding approaches originate partly from general organizational and change management and partly from the empirical examination of agile degeneration scenarios. What they have in common is the realization (partly assumption, partly observation) that agile practices and values do not automatically stabilize after their initial establishment but are subject to a constant *risk of erosion*.

In contrast to Table 1, the literature on agile decline usually contains significantly fewer explicit models with clear phases. Only some of the articles found contain implicit phases or stages.

For example, [36] and [38] present a *phase model* of organizational decline. The authors describe processes of increasing ignorance of organizational problems which can ultimately lead to dissolution. Applied to this research, it means that the first signals of decline often go unnoticed, which facilitates entry into the next phase of decline. Other studies also show that a superficial adoption of agile methods can lead to *pseudo-agility* in the long term. The phenomenon of "ScrumBut" also illustrates that even formal designations such as "SCRUM" can be gradually eroded if they are not culturally anchored.

Table 1. Models for agile transformation

Name & source	Core aspects
Agile Adoption Framework [22]	• Framework for the orderly introduction of agile methods • Emphasizes the readiness of the organization and derives recommended practices from this
Agile Transformation Model [23]	• Developed a comprehensive transformation model • For the implementation, the authors recommend five illustrative steps that are task-focused
Agile Adoption and Improvement Model [24]	• Maturity model for the introduction and improvement of agile methods • Emphasizes the continuous learning and improvement process after the initial introduction
Agile Maturity Map [25]	• Agile maturity model with defined target areas, acceptance criteria and maturity phases • Focus on the how of the gradual transition to greater agile maturity
INSERT Model [26]	• "INSERT model" describes phases of an organization's agile transformation • After a start-up phase, pilot applications are recommended until an establishment phase occurs
ARTCO Model [27]	• "ARTCO model" defines five phases of agile software development. • After an analysis and training phase, an agile development project enters a coaching and results phase.
Agile Maturity Model [28]	• Five-stage model, strongly based on classic models (e.g. CMMI) • Describes objectives and typical practices per level, self-assessment via questionnaires
Agile Lifecycle Phase Model [29]	• Describe the agile transition with adaptation cycles and guiding questions • After a preparation phase, among other things, the wrong way of dealing with "threats" can push a team back to non-agile work.

(*continued*)

Table 1. (*continued*)

Name & source	Core aspects
Perceptive Agile Measurement [30]	• Focus on perceived agility instead of tool practices • The current Agile maturity level is determined with the help of a questionnaire • Used to identify weak points in the implementation
Agile Transformation Model [31]	• In the areas to be designed (team, program, and portfolio), a project goes through five phases • Provides tips on how to improve agile practices.
Agile Transformation Journey [32]	• The paper identifies typical challenges and categorizes them into five areas • They are intended to provide context-specific and organization-specific guidance for agile values, structures and practices
Agile Management Implementation Practices [33]	• Combine agile transformation with other approaches such as lean, Kanban, etc. • For some combinations, phases and practices to stay agile are available
Scrum Maturity Model [34]	• Concrete five-level model for SCRUM with defined goals per level • Tailored to SCRUM practices including measuring of effects
Progressive Outcomes Framework [35]	• Organizes agile transformation in six areas ("Outcomes") • Each area has several levels of maturity

Several studies have found that *organizational inertia* and *a lack of management support* significantly increase the risk of relapse. While the initial agile transformation is often driven by visible successes (e.g. higher productivity, improved time-to-market), after a certain period of time *routine effects* or power interests can dominate, favoring a return to previously known structures. This creates a vicious circle in which individual practices are initially reduced, later abandoned and finally replaced by traditional patterns without this being perceived as a serious loss within the company.

Looking at the recommendations and initiatives in these models, two main dimensions can be identified: *(1) the development and stabilization* of agile practices and (2) *the dismantling, erosion or decline* of these practices. While most maturity models are relatively formalized (e.g. specification of stages, criteria and assessments), some of the decline models are generic in nature or describe *concrete anti-patterns*.

A key common theme is the *multidimensionality* of agile working methods, which must be maintained: although most models are based on stages or levels that suggest an

Table 2. Models for agile deconstruction/regeneration

Name & source	Core contents
5-phase model of organizations [36]	• General stage model for organizational decline (Blinded, Inaction, Faulty Action, Crisis, Dissolution) • Shows how organizations can gradually slide into decline if warning signals are ignored
Larman's Law [37]	• Organizations tend to prevent serious change • In terms of agility, this means that a creeping return to old structures is very likely
Five Stages of Decline [38]	• General based model of corporate decline in five stages • Transferable to successful agile teams that lose their agility through negligence
Post-adoptive Agility [11]	• Focusing on the organizational aspects of post-implementation • management support and method integration seem to be particularly important
Sustainable Agile [12]	• The model gathers experiences of sustainable SCRUM application and addresses it in four thematic areas • Cultural and organizational continuity seems to be crucial
"ScrumBut" phenomenon [39]	• Analyzes deviations ("We do SCRUM, but…") that lead to a loss of quality • Provides concrete anti-patterns where teams claim to be agile but successively soften the principles
"ScrumAnd" Phenomenon [40]	• Model describes a positive phase development, i.e. development teams understand SCRUM and apply it correctly. • However, they incorporate further techniques and a continuous improvement process.
"Cargo Cult" Agile [41]	• Warning against superficial "imitation" of agile rituals without understanding the underlying principles • Shows how development practices are inappropriately implemented for individual roles and examples

(continued)

Table 2. (*continued*)

Name & source	Core contents
Long-term transformation & regression [42]	• 13-year case study of agile development in the financial sector • Phases of progress were observed; impulses ("triggers") are important to revitalize agility
Normalization Process Theory [43]	• Emphasizes that new practices only have a lasting effect if they are "normalized" in everyday life • Share ideas for embedding and sustaining agile practices over time

ascending learning curve, in practice there are often interactions and feedback effects. For example, a team may be practicing certain facets (e.g. test-driven development) at an advanced level, while other aspects (e.g. customer involvement) are still weak. Similarly, a potential decline does not necessarily occur evenly in all areas of an agile organization.

Another finding is the *significance of external and internal influences*. Some models point to changes in leadership, changes in key team members or unplanned crises as triggers for a partial or complete regression. Some papers show that even advanced agile teams can fall back into old patterns if a lack of impetus or increasing time pressure leads to neglecting basic agile principles.

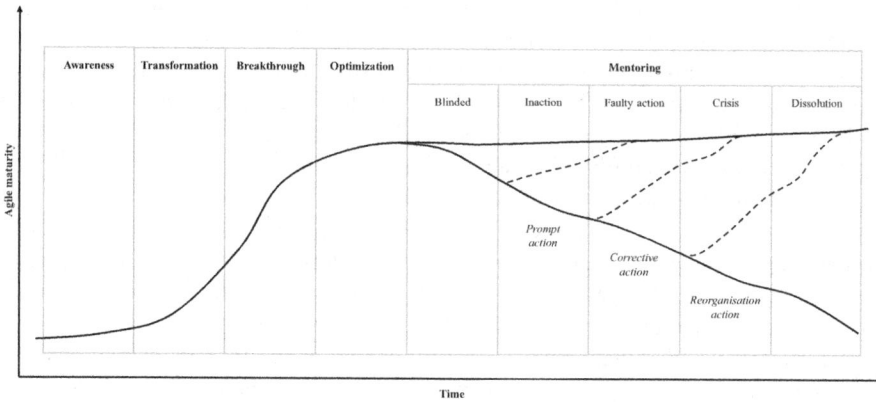

Fig. 2. Consolidated agile process lifecycle model

Against the background of the previously discussed findings, an integrated model of the agile project life cycle can be described (see Fig. 2), which includes both the build-up phases (according to [25]) and possible decline processes (according to [36]). The first model is used in this article because, like many others, it follows a typical transformation process but above all the term "mentoring" is used to describe the final phase aptly expressing the effort required to achieve stability. The second model is used because it explicitly describes three possible starting points for counteracting this process (i.e., positive mentoring) and thus provides a suitable classification for the actions to be empirically collected in the next section.

The individual development stages are plotted on the horizontal (time axis) - starting with Awareness and Transformation through to the Breakthrough and Optimization phases. This is followed by the mentoring phase, in which what has been achieved so far is stabilized and further developed. However, phases of decline can also occur during this period if warning signals are overlooked or wrong decisions are made. The vertical axis represents the degree of agile maturity, i.e. the extent to which agile principles, methods and values are anchored.

Looking more closely at the sequence of five positive stages of development [25]: Awareness marks the turning point at which an organization first recognizes the performance limits of its old processes and recognizes agile values as a possible solution. Awareness is less a phase of action than a phase of collective meaning-making; its results include a desire for change and experimentation with agile techniques. During transformation, this permission is translated into structural changes. Roles are redefined (e.g., project manager becomes product owner), cross-functional teams are formed, and events such as Planning and Review are established. Energy is high but fragile; success depends on visible quick wins. The breakthrough phase begins when these quick wins add up to a tipping point of credibility. The roles see positive results (e.g., shorter cycles, faster development) and teams experience an increase in satisfaction. In the optimization phase, the organization turns its attention from formal or large-scale changes to continuous optimization (e.g., adapting events, roles, and processes to its specific characteristics). A unique agile culture emerges. The subsequent mentoring phase serves as a stabilizing stage. It is not a plateau phase, but more like a bridge: Fig. 2 shows that different progressions are possible during this phase [22, 24, 32–34].

A team can continue to develop this maturity (upper curve), stagnate or even fall into a clear downward trend (lower curve). The decline phases described by [36] (that are Blinded, Inaction, Faulty Action, Crisis, Dissolution) are included as stereotypical negative scenarios. In the *blinded* state, the first warning signs of declining agility go unnoticed or are rationalized away. *Inaction* follows when symptoms are recognized but postponed in the hope that routine delivery will "normalize" them. The accumulated tension triggers *incorrect* measures in the negative development: for example, hasty restructuring, ad hoc changes, or blame-assigning hotfixes that treat the effects rather than the causes, thereby increasing volatility. If this remains unchecked, the project enters a *crisis* in which, for example, releases no longer work, errors increase massively, and cross-team trust disappears. Ultimately, the agile mode is de facto abandoned in the *dissolution* – either through a formal return to a plan-oriented approach, through informal resignation, or through the termination of the project as a whole [11, 36–38, 42].

These phases illustrate how an initially high-performance agile way of working can gradually lose substance. In the consolidated model, three central intervention points (Prompt Action, Corrective Action and Reorganization Action) mark the points at which targeted countermeasures can stop or even reverse the further downward trend [11, 36–38, 42]:

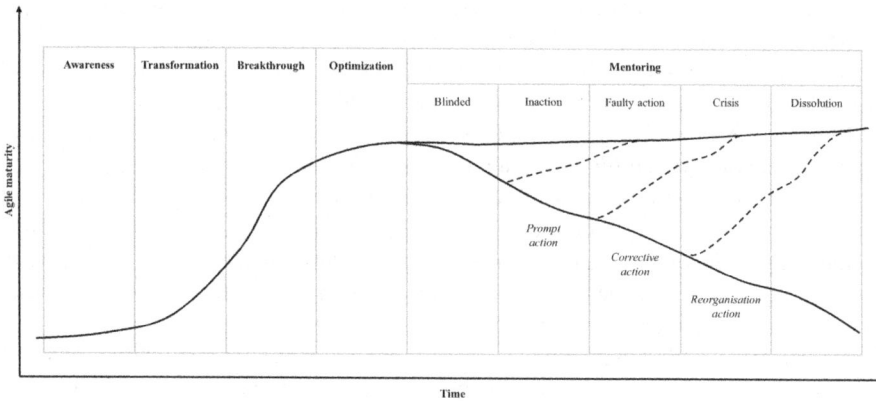

(1) **Prompt Action**: Approaches that take effect early in the decline process as soon as the first warning signs (e.g. declining discipline in events) become apparent. The focus here is on measures that participants (e.g., self-organized team members, SCRUM masters, or agile coaches) can propose and implement immediately or ad hoc to enable a quick response.
(2) **Corrective action** - measures that are taken when there are already clear undesirable developments (e.g. faulty action), and performance or motivation are visibly suffering. They are often linked to structural adjustments in SCRUM core roles, events or artifacts that are intended to correct the wrong course that has been taken.
(3) **Reorganization Action** - Interventions at an organizational level as soon as a deeper crisis becomes apparent or is expected. This may include, for example, a realignment of the project portfolio, a change in team composition, or change initiatives that often originate from people outside the team.

These three dimensions of action make it clear that the mentoring phase not only implies the further development of agility but must also actively combat the loss of already established agile values.

3.2 Phase-by-Phase Actions

The focus group discussions provide a detailed picture of which specific actions in which phase support the long-term maintenance of agility in the mentoring phase. Table 3 summarizes the results, which are based on 103 specific actions that were collected virtually during the discussions. The overview of all areas can be divided into three key success factors for "staying agile":

1. **Early visibility:** Actions that reveal trends and risks in near real time – live task tracking, radical disclosure of quality metrics, or spontaneous demo sessions – allow the team to intervene as early as the blinded phase.
2. **Learning-oriented correction:** Corrective actions have maximum leverage when they anchor learning processes in everyday work. The mentoring phase then involves joint refactoring or domain workshops that promote not only technical or procedural adjustments, but also collective reflection.
3. **Targeted but temporary transformation:** Reorganization steps are unavoidable when structural deficits lead to declining agility. Their effectiveness depends on them being scheduled, accompanied by communication, and embedded in an overarching product vision.

In the case study, the team of 12 developers, one SCRUM master and two Product Owners remained agile when it systematically navigated between low-threshold signals, focused adaptation loops and, where necessary, more far-reaching structural reforms (see Table 3). The following sections will describe the areas of action in detail and provide examples from the project case.

The evaluation shows that *leadership* has a stabilizing effect, above all when it creates a climate of high psychological safety. In the *prompt* phase, participants stated that visibly practiced tolerance for mistakes – for example, systematically reflecting on minor misconfigurations and tasks as well as their (miss-)assignment in the daily – encourages spontaneous problem reporting. It is normal for participants to clearly identify weaknesses in implementation during the review or gaps in their planning so that they can

Table 3. Summary of maintaining agility with example actions in italics

Action area\intervention points	Prompt action – early intervention	Corrective action – targeted follow-up	Reorganization – far-reaching adjustments
Leadership	Establish transparency regarding goals and progress, *for example through regular goal-oriented reviews (e.g., goal meetings with key stakeholders)*	Establish structured, bidirectional feedback and mirror leadership behavior, *for example through systematic one-to-one mentoring*	Reorganize decision-making and leadership structures, *e.g., by redefining role-based areas of responsibility at a strategic off-site meeting*
Domain	Ensure immediate feedback from users and the market environment, *e.g., through spontaneous product demos or end-user interviews*	Adjust scope management, *e.g., using feature flags, rapid prototyping, or event storming sessions*	Strategically redraw product and system boundaries; *in critical cases, cancel or recut epics and reduce dependency on third-party systems*
Technology	Encourage continuous knowledge and code sharing, *e.g., through pair reviews, "Today I learned" channels, or technical decision records*	Systematically reduce technical debt; *this includes prioritized refactoring, architecture-related spikes, or the introduction of additional test layers*	Restructure the architecture or deployment pipeline; *consolidate redundant microservices or completely automate the release process*
Staff	Make competencies visible and distribute them more widely, *e.g., via skill matrix self-assessments, task rotation, or micro proof of concepts*	Establish targeted skill development; *mentorship programs or thematically focused knowledge sharing sessions have proven effective here*	Reconfigure team setup: *Bring in coaches, set up a firefighter tandem or – in the event of persistent dysfunction – reorganize personnel*
Social	Maintain psychological safety: *informal exchange formats, non-judgmental retrospectives or consciously framing incidents as learning opportunities*	Institutionalize joint learning, *for example through blameless post-mortems or feedback workshops to strengthen interaction and trust*	Use professional conflict and culture management: *external mediation formats, explicit empowerment mandates ("PO trust") or culture coaching*

then work on improving these areas. As soon as the first signs of goal dilution appeared, the form of intervention changed to the *corrective* stage: developers meet for one-to-one discussions in a virtual office space to identify divergent expectations, followed by short-term vision reviews with business stakeholders. The Product Owner is required to explain the product vision (e.g. as a presentation at the beginning of each release) and to continuously incorporate it into discussions. This combination was described as sufficient to bring missed throughput times back to the nominal level. In isolated cases where role ambiguities persisted despite feedback and reviews, the project was forced to take *reorganization* measures. These included a targeted reshuffling of areas of responsibility and strategic project staffing.

For the *domain*, continuous, low-threshold involvement of real end users (e.g., on-site visits, interviews, insights presented by the PO) are key protective factors. Placing complete trust in the PO and taking personal interest in the system's customers ensures faster and better implementation (e.g., by User Story Mapping). In the *prompt* phase, on-the-spot demos took place regularly (e.g., even purely technical background stories such as the possibility of interface access are demonstrated), resulting in permanent feedback on small changes that prevent scope erosion from occurring in the first place. The focus group participants recommended event storming workshops as a *corrective* measure. These workshops allow contradictory business rules to be visualized together with all domain experts and checked for consistency; prototypical implementations then serve as convergence artifacts. Here, too, it was emphasized that the PO must be knowledgeable, easily available (e.g. through a virtual meeting tool), and, above all, an expert in the domain. What was striking in the case study team was that the PO is also very tech-savvy and personally committed to the project and to the team members. The boundaries become blurred in some areas of the daily work with the developers – but the roles were always clear in the events. When reorganization measures were necessary, oversized epics were abandoned and dependencies on third-party providers were encapsulated in order to maintain the product focus.

The group perceived the *technology* field of action as an "early warning sensor" for system decay. The developers perform Pair programming and peer reviews regularly in the *prompt* phase to exchange skills and make the code quality visible immediately. In addition, technical decision records were created to preserve the rationale behind technical decisions. For less formal decisions and learnings, all team members post their experience and summary in a separate communication channel in a timely and contextual manner. As complexity grew, the team sometimes moved to the *corrective* stage: The team uses technology spikes and smoke tests to experimentally address uncertainties and reduce the risk of wrong decisions. Both the developers and the PO agree that a clean code base is just as important and valuable as new business requirements. An explicit and recognized practice of "saying no to the business" – as described by the developers in the focus group – helps to legitimize necessary refactorings to stakeholders. Moreover, the agreed-upon switch of technologies (in the case study, to a cross-platform programming language) is often a particularly appropriate action. However, as soon as quality erosion affected the release pipeline itself, the team resorted to *reorganization* measures. These included rebuilding the Continuous Integration (CI) and Continuous Delivery/Deployment (CD) chain and eliminating redundant micro services, thus reducing the overall technical complexity the team had to deal with regularly.

In the area of *staff*, the skill matrix tool was described as particularly important. The matrix, which is updated regularly, serves both for self-reflection and strategic capacity planning. Early indicators (prompt) include the selection of code reviewers and pair programming partners to share knowledge and build up skills across the team. The case study also implements many classic agile working methods (e.g., developers work full-time on the project). On this basis, *corrective* interventions such as mentoring pairs and weekly knowledge-sharing sessions were established. According to participants, the effect is evident in increased code ownership across the team and a general openness to new ideas. If skill gaps remain or destructive behavior patterns emerge, the unanimous experience is that *reorganization* is necessary. In this specific case, this involved temporarily bringing in external experts to boost knowledge and remove an employee whose communication style was negatively affecting the team atmosphere. These measures were described as drastic but sustainable at the same time - Correct replacement of persons secures product value and psychological safety.

According to the participants, the *social* field forms the "crossbar" that connects all the other fields. Regular, informal exchange formats (team coffee dates) and the conscious reframing of mistakes as learning opportunities served as a prompt mechanism. Fun and even slightly childish channels, messages, and formats not only ensure a good mood every day – which has a positive effect on product quality – but also lower the barriers for asking for help. To avoid major conflicts, the developers use corrective formats such as blameless post-mortems. To maintain agility and its positive effects, it is important that the team analyzes mistakes and problems together and learns from them. Those involved emphasize that neutral moderation is crucial to prevent emotional escalations – this role is often taken on by the SCRUM Master on demand through interjections in conversations or in background discussions. In addition, learning and applying feedback techniques is particularly helpful. Persistent conflicts made reorganization necessary in individual cases: External or internal coaches conduct offsite workshops to rebuild relationships and trust.

4 Discussion

Overall, the results can be explored in greater depth along two lines of interpretation. First, it is clear that lasting agility requires a conscious reflection on the core principle of agility – that is, the idea of adaptation, learning and value-orientation that goes beyond specific agile methods and that places a complete focus on the product value. Second, the case study makes it clear that bringing in external experience during the mentoring phase can be a decisive accelerator for this re-anchoring process.

(1) The actions collected make it clear that teams can only maintain agility if they continuously translate the principles of the agile manifesto and SCRUM values into concrete decision-making and communication mechanisms. These can be highly individual and tailored but are supported transparently by everyone. Visibility creates

transparency, transparency creates opportunities for discussion, and opportunities for discussion open up learning loops. This tautological structure collapses as soon as one of the elements is neglected. In the project under investigation, transparency is not understood as retrospective reporting, but in real time: tasks, assignments, and critical notes are permanently available in a groupware system with channels. Issues were discussed in communication threads at short notice, identifying the cause and deciding on a course of action – often with a touch of humor, but always in a collegial and collective manner. Progress and satisfaction are promoted by the fact that no individual is under- or overloaded in terms of workload. The team quickly addresses inappropriate behavior in either prompt one-to-one feedback or for overarching issues, in open, facilitated, regular dialogues (e.g., Retros). In summary, it can be said that lasting agility depends less on the number of methods used (e.g., humor channels, active reporting of free capacity), but mainly on the appropriate implementation of fundamental agile values (e.g., customer focus) and principles (e.g., self-organization). Although visibility- and feedback-oriented routines might be formally established in the mentoring phase, this paper shows that SCRUM roles – especially developers, but also internal SCRUM Masters as well as Product Owners – quickly become blind to operational issues in the daily cycle. Warning signs such as condensed code ownership, creeping test instability, or shortened retro discussions need to be noticed, in order to "stay agile".

(2) Against this first aspect, the role of an external agile coach takes on particular significance. As a border crosser between the team and the organization, a coach promotes continuous self-reflection, makes implicit patterns explicit, and introduces libraries of actions that the team often cannot access under everyday pressure. In the mentoring phase, the coach acts as an "operationalized early warning system": he or she initiates prompt discussions, co-moderates corrective workshops, and, if necessary, can temporarily carry out reorganizations themselves without the team losing its delivery coherence. In the mentoring phase, agile professionals seem to be particularly important – the team can develop these organically through experience and its own dynamics. For example, the developers and the PO actively pass on their domain knowledge and technical skills as well as agile procedure competences as part of their daily work. An alternative approach seems to be the inorganic involvement of external consultants or experienced individuals. The project under investigation shows that agility is anchored internally but accelerated by external reflections. Consultants and trained agile coaches do not contribute any decision-making power in terms of content but act as a catalytic moderating force that reveals latent problems and thus enables a return to common goals. Similarly, agile consulting can focus more attention on the rapid development of organic methods – meaning actions that originate from within the team itself and are not imposed from outside. Nevertheless, external input can only be effective if the team itself has sufficient experience with healthy agility. One or two "pioneers" – like senior developers with a long project history – act as cultural resonators, anchoring new impulses and involving skeptical colleagues. In both cases, it is clear that external impulses are most effective when they do not take control, but rather open space for team reflection. From an organizational theory perspective, this phenomenon can be interpreted as "boundary spanning" and a form of agile innovation [44]. Teams in the mentoring phase are

in an intermediate stage: their process maturity already allows for self-control, but at the same time there is always a risk of agility declining. External expertise, for example in the form of agile consulting, acts as a mediator here, briefly disrupting the team's own thinking and behavior patterns or highlighting aspects based on experience, thereby averting the risk of a negative trend.

At the end of the discussion, this dual interpretation points to a tension: Agility requires both personal responsibility and the openness to allow external disruptions, for example in the form of coaching or consulting. Organizations that understand the core of agility as a permanent learning and value creation architecture must therefore operationalize two tasks: first, to cultivate a culture of genuine agility internally, and second, to open the door to external experience when the situation calls for it.

5 Closing

This paper has focused on the little-researched area of "staying agile" in software development in the long run and presented a consolidated life cycle model that integrates both the growth and decline logic of agile projects. Based on a systematic literature review and a practical focus group study, good practices within important fields of action (leadership, domain, technology, staff, social) were identified at three escalation levels for actions (prompt, corrective, reorganization).

Practices that reveal trends and risks in near real time allow teams to intervene as early as the blinded phase. Corrective actions have maximum leverage when they anchor learning processes in everyday work. Mentoring, joint refactoring, or cross-domain workshops not only serve to adapt technical or procedural aspects but also promote collective reflection. Reorganization steps are unavoidable when structural deficits become bottlenecks. Their effectiveness depends crucially on them being clearly scheduled, accompanied by communication, and embedded in an overarching agile vision; only in this way can the principles of self-organized, customer-centric development be maintained.

The discussion makes it clear that lasting agility must be understood as a balancing act between internal clarity along core agile values and external support. Those who keep the agile core – adaptation, product focus, learning orientation, value flow perspective, self-organization – alive and at the same time reflect it through targeted external impulses create robust structures that do not become rigid even in long project and product life cycles.

The empirical basis for the action examples of this paper comes from a highly successful development project in the automotive industry. Differences in industry, culture, and team size may limit generalization and transferability. Another limitation is that the results of this article are based on a single focus group and do not allow for an exact (or even quantitative) correlation between actions and the project's success metrics. In addition, the actions collected are based on self-assessments. In-depth interviews would also be possible in order to explicitly incorporate implicit actions into the developed model.

Further research should (a) empirically validate the proposed model in different domains, (b) quantify the economic benefits of the three escalation levels, and (c) investigate early warning systems that detect signals even more reliably. Of particular interest is how new technological (e.g., AI-supported assistance tools) or organizational trends (e.g., composable business) can be anchored in the life cycle model or reconciled with the example actions. If descriptive research is to be pursued further, it would be an idea to incorporate the findings of this paper more deeply into the components of SCRUM (e.g., the exact roles, the exact sequence of events). This could also result in a methodology library that could be used by the external initiators described.

In a nutshell, staying agile is not a state, but rather an ongoing effort. Teams that cultivate agile methods, design learning loops, and consciously implement structural interventions significantly increase their resilience and adaptability. The model presented in this contribution offers an initial, empirically based orientation framework for this purpose.

Acknowledgement. Transparency note in terms of [i] the general recommendation of the European Code of Conduct for Research Integrity and [ii] the domain-specific proposal according to Nature Journal in January 2023: In the planning, design, production, formulation, and revision of this research, DeepL and ChatGPT were used as tools.

References

1. Dybå, T., Dingsøyr, T.: Empirical studies of agile software development: a systematic review. Inf. Softw. Technol. **50**, 9–10 (2008)
2. Dingsøyr, T., Dybå, T., Moe, N.B.: Agile Software Development - Current Research and Future Directions. Springer, Berlin (2010)
3. Aldahmash, A., Gravell, A.M., Howard, Y.: A review on the critical success factors of agile software development. In: Stolfa, J., Stolfa, S., O'Connor, R., Messnarz, R. (eds.) Systems, Software and Services Process Improvement. Springer, Cham (2017)
4. Lacey, M.: The SCRUM Field Guide: Practical Advice for Your First Year. Addison-Wesley (2012)
5. Hajjdiab, H., Taleb, A.S.: Adopting agile software development: issues and challenges. Int. J. Manag. Value Supply Chains **2**(3), 1–10 (2011)
6. Vallon, R., da Silva Estácio, B.J., Prikladnicki, R., Grechenig, T.: Systematic literature review on agile practices in global software development. Inf. Softw. Technol. **96**(April), 161–180 (2018)
7. Hoda, R., Salleh, N., Grundy, J., Tee, H.M.: Systematic literature reviews in agile software development: a tertiary study. Inf. Softw. Technol. **85**, 60–70 (2017)
8. Edison, H., Wang, X., Conboy, K.: Comparing methods for large-scale agile software development: a systematic literature review. IEEE Trans. Software Eng. **48**(8), 2709–2731 (2022)
9. Henriques, V., Tanner, M.: A systematic literature review of agile and maturity model research. Interdiscip. J. Inf. Knowl. Manag. **12**, 53–73 (2017)
10. Upender, B.: Staying agile in government software projects. In: Proceedings of the AGILE 2005. IEEE, Los Alamitos (2005)
11. Senapathi, M., Srinivasan, A.: Sustained agile usage: a systematic literature review. In: Proceedings of the 17th International Conference on Evaluation and Assessment in Software Engineering. ACM, New York (2013)
12. Barroca, L., Keynes, M., Gregory, P., Kuusinen, K., Sharp, H., Al Qaisi, R.: Sustaining agile beyond adoption. In: Proceedings of the 44th Euromicro Conference on Software Engineering and Advanced Applications. IEEE, Prague (2018)

13. Maheshwari, S.K: Organizational decline and turnaround management: a contingency framework. Vikalpa J. Dec. Makers **25**(4), 39–50 (2000)
14. Brocke, J., Simons, A., Niehaves, B., Riemer, K., Plattfaut, R., Cleven, A.: Reconstructing the giant: on the importance of rigour in documenting the literature search process. In: Proceedings of the 17th European Conference on Information Systems. ECIS, Verona (2009)
15. Webster, J., Watson, R.T.: Analyzing the past to prepare for the future: writing a literature review. MIS Q. **26**(2), xiii-xxiii (2002)
16. Mangold, W.: Gruppendiskussionen. In: König, R. (ed.) Handbuch der empirischen Sozialforschung. Enke, Stuttgart (1973)
17. Przyborski, A., Riegler, J.: Gruppendiskussion und Fokusgruppe. In: Mey, G., Mruck, K. (eds.) Handbuch Qualitative Forschung in der Psychologie. Springer, Berlin (2020)
18. Khandwalla, P.N.: Innovative Corporate Turnaround. Sage, New Delhi (1992)
19. Lederer, M., Thummerer, J.: Organizing a self-organized team: towards a maturity model for agile business process management. In: Proceedings of the S-BPM ONE 2022. Springer, Cham (2022)
20. Serrador, P., Pinto, J.K.: Does Agile work? — a quantitative analysis of agile project success. Int. J. Project Manage. **33**(5), 1040–1051 (2015)
21. Looks, H., Fangmann, J., Thomaschewski, J., Schön, E.M.: Towards a process model for Agile transformation in e-government projects. J. Inf. Syst. Eng. Manag. **6**(1), 1–7 (2021)
22. Sidky, A., Arthur, J., Bohner, S.: A disciplined approach to adopting agile practices: the agile adoption framework. Innov. Syst. Softw. Eng. **3**, 203–216 (2007)
23. Klünder, J., Hohl, P., Schneider, K.: Becoming Agile while preserving software product lines - an Agile transformation model for large companies. In: Proceedings of the International Conference on the Software and Systems Process. ACM (2018)
24. Qumer, A., Henderson-Sellers, B., Mcbride, T.: Agile adoption and improvement model. In: Proceedings of the European and Mediterranean Conference on Information Systems. EMCIS (2007)
25. Packlick, J.: The Agile maturity map a goal oriented approach to Agile improvement. In: Proceedings of the Agile. IEEE (2007)
26. Kahra, L.: Agile transformation - how to successfully shape your transition to a more Agile organization. Springer, Berlin
27. Ndou, V., Ingrosso, A., Di Girolamo, A.: Framework for Agile transformation: guiding organizations through cultural, structural, and competency shifts in project management. Adm. Sci. **14**(11), 301–321 (2024)
28. Patel, C., Ramachandran, M.: Agile maturity model (AMM): a software process improvement framework for agile software development practices. Int. J. Softw. Eng. **2**(1), 3–28 (2009)
29. Diegmann, P., Dreesen, T., Rosenkranz, C.: In for a penny, in for a pound? A lifecycle model for Agile teams. In: Proceedings of the 53rd Hawaii International Conference on System Sciences. HICSS (2020)
30. So, C., Scholl, W.: Perceptive Agile measurement: new instruments for quantitative studies in the pursuit of the social psychological effect of Agile practices. Springer, Berlin (2009)
31. Laanti, M.: Agile transformation model for large software development organizations. In: Proceedings of the XP 2017. Agile Alliance, Cologne (2017)
32. Reginaldo, F., Santos, G.: Challenges in Agile transformation journey - a qualitative study. In: Proceedings of the XXXIV Brazilian Symposium on Software Engineering. ACM (2020)
33. Chukwunweike, J., Aro, O.E.: Implementing agile management practices in the era of digital transformation. World J. Adv. Res. Rev. **24**(01), 2223–2242 (2024)
34. Yin, A., Figueiredo, S., Silva, M.: SCRUM maturity model - validation for IT organizations" roadmap to develop software centered on the client role. In: Proceedings of the Sixth International Conference on Software Engineering Advances. ICSEA (2011)

35. Fontana, R.M., Meyer, V., Reinehr, S., Malucelli, A.: Progressive outcomes: a framework for maturing in Agile software development. J. Syst. Softw. **102**, 88–108 (2015)
36. Weitzel, T., Jonsson, A.: Five-phase model of organizational decline. Acad. Manag. Rev. **14**(2), 257–273 (1989)
37. Larman, C.: Larman's Laws of Organizational Behavior. https://effectiveagile.com/larmans-laws-of-organizational-behavior/
38. Collins, J.: How The Mighty Fall: And Why Some Companies Never Give. JimCollins (2009)
39. Elorantaa, V.P., Koskimies, K., Mikkonenb, T.: Exploring ScrumBut – an empirical study of SCRUM anti-patterns. Inf. Softw. Technol. **74**, 194–203 (2016)
40. Krishna, V.A., Basu, A.B., SCRUM: is it ScrumBut or SCRUM and. In: Proceedings of the Annual IEEE India Conference: Engineering Sustainable Solutions. INDICON (2011)
41. Havstorm, T.E., Karlsson, F., Hedström, K.: Uncovering situations of cargo cult behavior in Agile software development method use. In: Proceedings of the 56th Hawaii International Conference on System Sciences
42. Berkania, A., Causseb, D., Thomas, L.: Triggers analysis of an agile transformation: the case of a central bank. Procedia Comput. Sci. **164**(2019), 449–456 (2019)
43. Carroll, N., Conboy, K.: Applying normalization process theory to explain large-scale agile transformations. In: Proceedings of the 14th International Research Workshop on IT Project Management. IRWITPM, Munich (2019)
44. Tushman, M.L.: Special boundary roles in the innovation process. Adm. Sci. Q. **22**(4), 587–605 (1977)

A Systematic Literature Review on Business Process Automation Frameworks and Technologies

Lisa Rüeck[1], Thomas Auer[2](✉), Stefan Rösl[2], and Christian Schieder[2]

[1] METAPOTT GmbH, Huyssenallee 68, 45128 Essen, Germany
lisa.rueeck@METAPOTT.com
[2] Technical University of Applied Sciences Amberg-Weiden, Hetzenrichter Weg 15, 92637 Weiden, Germany
{t.auer,s.roesl,c.schieder}@oth-aw.de

Abstract. Business Process Automation (BPA) is a core element for digital transformation in companies. However, companies still face challenges as the knowledge is fragmented, and there is a lack of structured guidance on implementing BPA effectively. Therefore, we conduct a Systematic Literature Review (SLR) that explores the current state of research on frameworks, key factors, and technologies in the context of BPA. The aim is to provide an abstract introduction to the necessary components for successful BPA implementation and to illustrate the scope and diversity of BPA. We analyzed 40 studies from 2019 to 2024, identified 24 frameworks, extracted 32 key success factors, and revealed the most used technologies in the BPA environment. In detail, we highlight the relevance of a strong data culture, strategic leadership, change management, targeted technology investment, and a measurable, structured implementation process. Compared to existing literature, our work offers a holistic perspective on BPA by combining frameworks, key factors, and technology insights.

Keywords: Business Process Automation · Automation Frameworks · Intelligent Automation Technologies

1 Introduction

Digital technologies have continuously developed over the last few decades, triggering fundamental changes in business processes and value creation [1]. Artificial intelligence (AI), machine learning (ML), and cloud computing affect significant transformations in business processes across various industries. Business process automation (BPA), which involves the automation and optimization of processes, is a core element of digital transformation in companies [2]. It is becoming increasingly important due to its advantages, including cost reduction and improved service quality [3]. To fully exploit process automation, a holistic approach is required. This encompasses both the selection of appropriate technologies and the creation of a suitable implementation environment. A significant challenge is the fragmented knowledge base about BPA, coupled with the absence of guidance on the systematic selection and implementation of suitable technologies within organizational contexts [4].

The main objective of this research is to provide an abstract introduction to the necessary components for a successful BPA implementation and to illustrate the scope and diversity of BPA. To investigate this topic, the authors have conceptually structured their approach around three research questions (RQs) outlined in Table 1.

Table 1. Research Questions.

Research Question	Description and Motivation
RQ1: What frameworks are available for successful BPA?	We intend to identify and compare existing frameworks to guide organizations in their automation procedures
RQ2: What are the key factors that need to be considered for successful BPA?	We extract key factors from the frameworks to provide companies with guidelines
RQ3: What technologies are commonly categorized as automation technologies in the context of BPA?	We identify technologies that fall under BPA to give companies an overview

This study conducts a systematic literature review (SLR) following the proposed methodology from vom Brocke et al. [5]. Academically, this study synthesizes BPA research, highlighting existing frameworks, identifying research gaps, and proposing future research directions. Practically, it offers actionable insights by presenting proven frameworks and technologies for effective BPA implementation. The paper is structured as follows: Sect. 2 covers the theoretical background and related work. Section 3 outlines the methodology and data collection process. Section 4 presents the results, followed by the discussion in Sect. 5 and the conclusion in Sect. 6.

2 Theoretical Background and Related Work

This section defines BPA and its associated frameworks, emphasizing strategic approaches and key factors for successful implementation. Finally, the section explores related work to our research.

2.1 Business Process Automation

BPA refers to using various technologies [6] to modify, to improve [7], or even fully automate processes end-to-end [8]. The goals of BPA are to reduce task execution times [7], increase efficiency and productivity, reduce costs [9], and enhance customer experience [1]. The use of AI capable of drawing cognitive conclusions and making judgements is also referred to in the literature as "intelligent automation" [8]. Hyperautomation has established itself as a trend term that defines the automation in an organization that can be automated without human intervention [10]. This paper focuses on the concept of end-to-end automation of business processes. The term "Business Process Automation" is used as it is the most common and widely utilized term in literature.

In this research, frameworks are understood as structured approaches or systematic models and methods that encompass best practices, technologies, and processes to support the successful implementation of BPA. From the structure of these frameworks, key factors for BPA implementation can be identified, addressing the second RQ. This study focuses on frameworks that consider the broader business context, particularly strategic and organizational dimensions, implementation processes, and the selection of suitable technologies. Frameworks with a primarily technical orientation, such as those focused on RPA bot implementation or middleware integration into existing IT landscapes, were excluded, as they need to align with the research's emphasis on strategic and organizational factors.

2.2 Related Work

Within the research, seven review papers were identified, all related to the field of BPA. One of the most comprehensive is that of Moreira et al. [7], which focuses on SMEs. This study classifies processes for their suitability for automation and identifies tools, technologies, challenges and success factors. The study by Kam et al. [16] has a similar structure and covers operational and strategic benefits, implementation considerations, management aspects, and challenges. However, neither study covers the full spectrum of automation approaches.

Further studies [17–21] primarily focus on automation technologies, particularly robotic process automation (RPA). These works provide valuable insights into technologies, their benefits, challenges, and implementation aspects, but they lack a comprehensive analysis of the framework conditions. Finally, Agnihotri et al. [21] focus only on the identification of research gaps and their RQs in distribution technologies.

To the best of our knowledge, we have not found an SLR in the field of BPA that identifies and compares existing frameworks for BPA in companies, regardless of their size; that highlights the key components for successful BPA, and that provides a comprehensive overview of BPA technologies. With this SLR, the authors aim to document relevant knowledge and key aspects of BPA.

3 Research Method

In order to identify and analyze relevant literature on BPA frameworks and associated technologies, we conducted an SLR, a well-established method for uncovering research gaps and comprehensively assessing and interpreting findings relevant to our RQ and topic of interest [5]. To ensure rigor, our SLR follows the guiding principles proposed by vom Brocke et al. [5]. These principles are organized into five steps, which can be divided into three phases: I) preparation, II) data collection, and III) analysis. The structure of the SLR approach is shown in Fig. 1.

The preparation (phase I) includes the definition and framing of the review scope (step 1) and conceptualizing the topic (step 2) to create a clear search string for querying the databases. The data collection (phase II) involves conducting the literature search

Fig. 1. Phases and Steps of the SLR.

(step 3), following predefined search strategies to gather relevant entities. The analysis phase (phase III) comprises the analysis of the collected literature (step 4), along with the development of a research agenda (step 5) to identify key insights, and future research. The preparation (phase I) and data collection (phase II) are detailed in the following subsections, while the analysis (phase III) is elaborated in Sects. 4 and 5.

3.1 Preparation

To clarify the scope of the review, we adopted the taxonomy of literature reviews, which provides a structured approach for the classification and categorization [23]. Using this taxonomy improved the transparency and focus of our literature review, positively impacting the subsequent search process [5]. The six primary characteristics of our review and their corresponding categories are summarized in Table 2.

Table 2. Characteristics of the Literature Review According to Cooper [23].

Characteristic	Categories			
(1) Focus	Research Outcomes	Research Methods	Theories	Applications
(2) Goal	Integration		Criticism	Central Issues
(3) Organisation	Historical		Conceptual	Methodological
(4) Perspective	Neutral Representation		Espousal of Position	
(5) Audience	Specialised Scholars	General Scholars	Practitioners/ Politicians	General Public
(6) Coverage	Exhaustive	Exhaustive and Selective	Representative	Central/ Pivotal

The review focuses on research outcomes, specifically examining BPA frameworks and technologies. It aims to integrate findings, identify gaps, and provide a basis for future research. The unbiased synthesis of the existing BPA literature results in a neutral perspective. The review targets specialized scholars and practitioners, focusing on frameworks, technologies, and key implementation factors through conceptual organization. It should be noted that the review is not intended to be exhaustive; rather, it is representative, focusing on a limited sample in line with the inclusion and exclusion criteria set out in Table 3. Further, these criteria tailor the literature search to ensure the identification of pertinent literature aligned with the predefined RQ. To address the current relevance of the topic, this search concentrates on contributions published between 2019 and 2024. The focus was on English and German articles and conference papers that have passed through a peer-review process.

Table 3. Exclusion and Inclusion Criteria.

Exclusion Criteria	Inclusion Criteria
Other languages than English/German	Related to the RQ
Duplicated references	Published in journals or conference proceedings
Publication year before 2019	Title/Abstract related to BPA
Paper cannot be accessed	Title/Abstract related to automation technologies

In order to conduct the review effectively, keywords and their synonyms were derived from the RQ in line with the previously defined scope of the research. Supported by a preliminary ad-hoc search of relevant articles, these keywords, their synonyms, and acronyms were identified. The finally developed search queries (SQ), incorporate these terms along with logical operators such as "AND" and "OR". Terms like "business process automation," "intelligent automation," and "hyperautomation" (SQ1) reflect evolving terminology in the field of BPA. "Automation technology" and its variations (SQ2) address the technical components. Where necessary, the queries were tailored to fit the specific terminology requirements of individual databases, ensuring a comprehensive and targeted literature search.

3.2 Data Collection

The databases we used for the data collection were IEEE, Ebsco Host, Emerald Insight, AIS, and Science Direct. Adjustments were made to the search string based on the literature database's preferences due to limitations and syntax differences. The entire literature search process is illustrated in Fig. 2. The initial search with the SQ in the selected databases yielded more than 40.000 potential contributions. After several iterations, we concluded that it was important to apply the SQ to the titles of the articles to find relevant papers to answer our questions effectively. Next, all papers had to fulfill the predefined inclusion and exclusion criteria from Table 3. After removing duplicates and other review studies, we conducted an additional for- and backward search via google scholar. This procedure includes another twelve articles to our knowledge base. The described search process resulted in a total of 40 contributions that were identified as a publication of interest for our research.

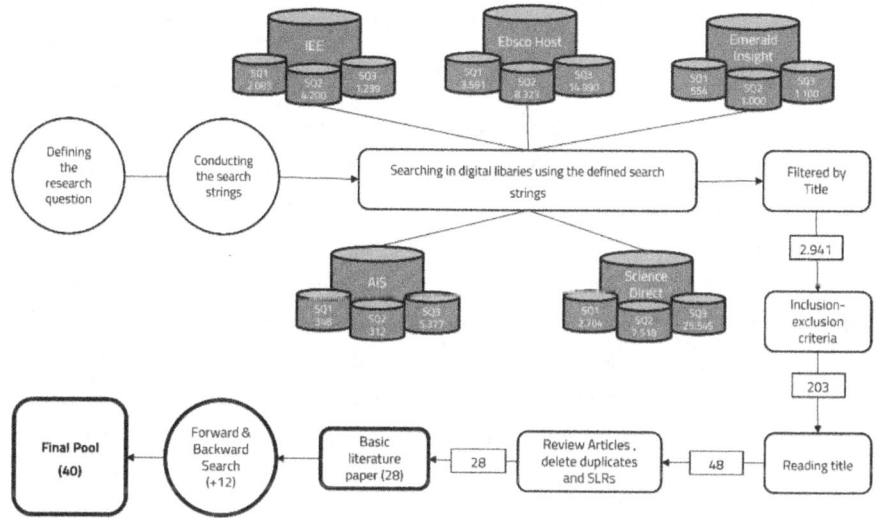

Fig. 2. Research Process.

4 Key Findings

This section is part of the analysis phase (phase III) and presents the key findings derived from the identified literature. The final pool of 40 publications forms the basis and the section is structured into three subsections, each addressing one RQ.

4.1 RQ1: What Frameworks Are Available for Successful Business Process Automation

As noted, comprehensive automation frameworks that support companies in successfully implementing BPA are lacking. Therefore, this section lists all roadmaps, processes, guidelines, methods, or frameworks for automation. We identified 24 frameworks for BPA (see Table 4). These cover different areas of focus: 50% focus on strategic aspects, 25% on technology selection and application, and 25% on IT infrastructure and integration. Nine of the models were published in 2023 or later, which indicates the increasing timeliness of the topic. A key finding of the analysis is the high importance of RPA, which is the focus of seven of the 24 studies. The aim is on identifying and selecting suitable processes for RPA, as discussed, for example, in the work of Raluca et al. [25], Riedl and Beetz [26], and Plattfaut et al. [27].

Table 4. Identified BPA Frameworks

Reference	Type	Technology	Methodology	Focus
[28]	Framework	Sales Automation	Literature	Strategic
[29]	Framework	RPA	Interviews	Strategic

(*continued*)

Table 4. (*continued*)

Reference	Type	Technology	Methodology	Focus
[30]	Guideline	Hyperautomation	Literature	Strategic
[31]	Guideline	Automation in general	Literature	Strategic
[32]	Guideline	RPA & CA	Interviews	Strategic
[33]	Guideline	Automation in general	Case Company	Strategic
[4]	Model	BPA	Delphi Study	Strategic
[34]	Method	Automation in general	Literature/Interviews	Strategic
[35]	Process	Robotic	Literature	Strategic
[25]	Stages	RPA	Case Study	Strategic
[3]	Matrix	Automation in general	Literature	Strategic
[36]	Matrix	Automation in general	Literature	Strategic
[35]	Approach	Robotic	Literature	Technology
[37]	Framework	Chatbots	Practical	Technology
[38]	Framework	AI	Literature	Technology
[26]	Model	RPA	Literature/Interviews/ Evaluation/Design/ Case studies	Technology
[27]	Model	RPA	Case studies	Technology
[39]	Morphology	Automation in general	Literature	Technology
[40]	Framework	Hyperautomation	Literature	IT
[41]	Framework	Intelligent automation	Literature	IT
[14]	Framework	Intelligent automation	Practice Process	IT
[35]	Model	Hyperautomation	Literature	IT
[42]	Method	RPA	Literature	IT
[43]	Architecture	RPA	Literature	IT

At the same time, there is an increasing focus on newer trends, such as hyperautomation and intelligent automation (IA), which enable broader technological approaches and more comprehensive integrations, as is evident in the studies by Sudharson and Tiago. Although the identified frameworks address important aspects of BPA, such as business organization, technology selection, and IT integration, there is often a lack of comprehensive guidelines for successful implementation. Only Lacity and Willcocks [32] provide a broad spectrum of principles to help organizations and digital leaders on their journey to implementation. However, the research focuses on IA programs using RPA and cognitive automation (CA). Other studies also focus on selecting sub-aspects or technologies. For example, Raluca et al. [25] focus on selecting processes for RPA, and Birkbeck and Rowe [31] focus on the human aspect. Another finding is the limited practical relevance of the frameworks: more than 50% (15 out of 24) are based solely on literature research without practical validation.

The SLR examines the frameworks of Riedl and Beetz [26], Costa et al. [34], and Lacity and Willcocks [32], as they are frequently cited. Riedl and Beetz [26] describe a three-step selection process for RPA processes with pre-selection, prioritization (feasibility, potential, and organization), and financial evaluation. Costa et al. [34] offer a systematic process evaluation, which is divided into six steps: 1. determination of the process characteristics, 2. creation of a comparison, 3. determination of the weighting of the criteria, 4. evaluation of the various processes, 5. determination of the positive and negative ideal solutions, 6. determination of the final ranking. On the other hand, Lacity and Willcocks [32] developed 39 design principles, which are divided into eight subject areas, including Strategy, Sourcing, Process Selection, and Maturity. While Riedl and Beetz [26] and Costa et al. [34] provide methodical selection procedures, Lacity and Willcocks [32] offer a comprehensive management framework. In summary, many of the frameworks examined have hardly been cited or systematically compared with each other. Differences, overlaps, and added value have not been considered.

4.2 RQ2: What Are the Key Factors that Need to Be Considered for Successful Business Process Automation (BPA)?

Since this research team does not refer to IT-specific topics in the context of BPA, the following section focuses on the frameworks that are assigned to the areas of 'strategy and organization' and 'technology selection and application'. In further analysis, only the frameworks that do not refer to a specific technology are used to identify general key factors. This ensures a consistent perspective and a comparison of the structure and key aspects of the different frameworks. To answer the second RQ, 7 of the 24 references were subjected to a detailed analysis as part of the present study, examining their framework conditions, guidelines, matrix, and topics of interest. In doing so, James [30], Birkbeck and Rowe [31], and Aleksandre et al. [33] provide general recommendations for action, which were compared and assigned to categories. Abdelwahab and Helal [3] offer a framework for priority candidates for automation. Costa et al. [34] provide a fixed process for selecting processes for automation. Milind et al. [36] show the correlation between process complexity and automation intelligence. Martinek-Jaguszewska and Rogowski [4] provide a maturity model divided into technology, process, implementation, and strategy. First, the recommendations for action were identified from the frameworks and assigned to a fixed category. Subsequently, the recommendations from James [30], Birkbeck and Rowe [31], and Aleksandre et al. [33] were analyzed and assigned to existing categories. If no suitable category was available, a new category was defined. The results of the categories and assigned recommendations for action can be found in Table 5 and reflect the key aspects that companies should consider if they want to implement BPA successfully.

Table 5. Success categories and key aspects for successful BPA.

Category	Key Aspects	Reference
Data	Establish a robust data culture	[30]

(continued)

Table 5. (*continued*)

Category	Key Aspects	Reference
Change Management	Transform knowledge	[33]
	Recruit knowledge facilitators	[33]
	Provide psychological safety	[31]
	Dissemination and communication of new technologies	[31]
	Training and education.	[31]
Realization	Assigning automation opportunities	[33]
	Divide task	[33]
	Implement automation	[33]
	Control tasks	[33]
	Appropriate reconfiguration of workforce	[31]
	Responsive and flexible to new ideas	[31]
	Identify your objectives	[30]
	Establish ownership	[30]
	Focus on continuous improvement	[30]
	Explore new use cases	[30]
Technology and Process	Complex process/intelligent-cognitive automation: Sensory digitization, NLP, ML, expert systems	[36]
	Complicated process/basic intelligent automation: Sensory digitization, NLP	[36]
	Simple process /basic automation: Screen scraping and recording, smart workflows	[36]
	Automation technology	[4]
	Coverage of automated business processes	[4]
	Investment in technology.	[31]
Process Priority	Lowest Priority: lower value, higher complexity	[3]
	Medium Priority: Higher Value, higher complexity	[3]
	Medium Priority: Lower value, lower complexity	[3]
	Highest Priority: Higher value, lower complexity	[3]
Process Selection	6 steps for selecting processes for automation: Determine process characteristics, construct pair-wise comparison of characteristics, determine the weights of the criteria, evaluate different processes, determine positive and negative ideal solutions, determine final rank	[34]
Strategy	Automation strategic alignment	[4]
	Business goals of automation	[4]

(*continued*)

Table 5. (*continued*)

Category	Key Aspects	Reference
	Automation leadership	[4]
Implementation	Organizational structure of automation implementations.	[4]
	Measuring the automation results	[4]

In summary, the research identified the following key aspects for successful BPA in companies: a strong data culture, proactive change management, a well-thought-out implementation, targeted technology investment, structured prioritization and selection of processes to be automated, strategic leadership and implementation that is organizationally embedded and measurable.

4.3 RQ3: Which Technologies Are Commonly Categorized as Automation Technologies in the Context of Business Processes Automation?

The complexity of the technologies varies depending on the application scenario. This ranges from automation in different systems to APIs and complex ML algorithms. Whether technology is best suited for the automation of a process depends on many factors. To answer this question accurately in the future, this research provides an overview of the technologies associated with BPA in literature. Our research highlights both simple and complex technologies, applications, and platforms. Figure 3 summarizes the most frequently mentioned technologies in the literature concerning BPA.

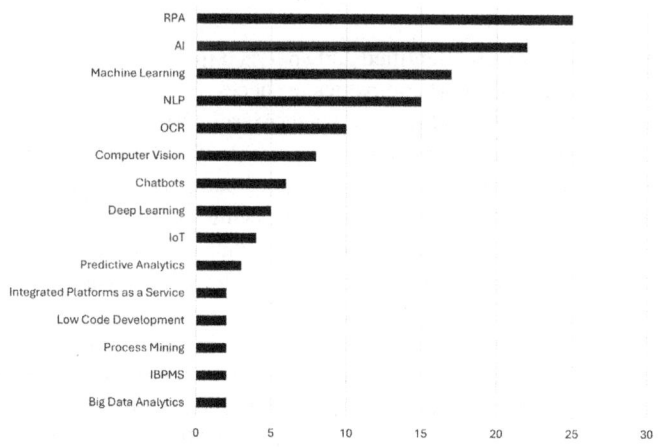

Fig. 3. Technologies.

A key finding of this research is that RPA is mentioned most frequently in literature. A total of 168 mentions of technologies were counted, of which RPA was mentioned 25 times, followed by 22 mentions of AI. This underlines the relevance and importance of these technologies for BPA. ML, natural language processing (NLP), optical character recognition (OCR), computer vision, chatbots, and deep learning (DL) are listed below, which many researchers associate with AI [1, 44, 45]. Considering this, AI is arguably the technology most frequently discussed in the literature on BPA. The research revealed some initial approaches but no consistent categorization or grouping that comprehensively covered all technologies and their different designations. For example, George et al. [1] define six main categories of technologies in hyperautomation: RPA, AI, analytics, lowcode/nocode, digital workforce, and cloud platforms, with each of these technologies having further subordinate technologies. Niedzielski et al. [46] focus on the definition of hyperautomation and present an Euler diagram showing the technologies that fall under this term: RPA, AI, low code platform development, virtual agents, intelligent business process management systems, and OCR. Both papers explicitly mention RPA and AI and are discussing lowcode/nocode.

Hoang et al. [47] paper offers a more comprehensive categorized list of technologies, tools, and applications related to offerings from automation providers. The technologies listed include RPA, workflow automation, iPaas, and IPA. In addition, the literature refers to the interaction between RPA and AI in the context of IA and hyperautomation. However, it should be noted that no scientific papers define the term technology precisely. Likewise, only a few definitions of the technologies mentioned in the papers are found, which makes a clear categorization difficult. Furthermore, other technologies are assigned to the comprehensive technology AI, such as NLP, which makes structuring even more difficult. We identify this observation as a research gap that points to the need for a specific definition of the term 'technology' in the context of BPA, including a clear assignment and listing of the technologies that are to be understood by it.

5 Discussion

First, 40 scientific papers were identified and analyzed in this SLR. A total of 24 frameworks were identified that support companies in successfully implementing BPA. A key finding is that most of the publications analyzed are from 2023 or later and have increasingly focused on topics such as hyperautomation [30, 35, 40] and IA [14, 41]. Most of the frameworks, including Raluca et al. [25], Plattfaut et al. [27], and Schlegel et al. [29], focus only on RPA. This underlines the growing importance of BPA in general and highlights the need for comprehensive models that are designed to be technology-independent. It is also striking that about half of the frameworks are purely theoretical and have no practical application [36, 42].

Second, 32 key aspects crucial for the successful implementation of BPA could be identified from seven overarching frameworks. However, these frameworks lack several key elements. For example, James [30] refers to a robust data culture but does not address data protection. Aleksandre et al. [33] and Birkbeck and Rowe [31] list aspects that can be assigned to change management but do not list any roles or competencies required in the context of BPA. Aleksandre et al. [33] also point out the need to control tasks, but no specific KPIs are listed for monitoring and checking automated processes.

Third, the study examined which technologies fall under BPA. The results show that RPA is mentioned most frequently, which can be explained by the fact that it is particularly suitable for repetitive and recurring tasks [12, 13]. Since technologies such as NLP,

OCR, and DL can also be assigned to AI [1, 44], it can be seen that AI plays also a fundamental role in the implementation of BPA. This makes it clear that cognitive abilities and the ability to perform complex tasks are becoming increasingly important. While RPA is particularly suitable for repetitive and rule-based tasks, comprehensive automation in hyperautomation requires technologies with cognitive abilities [1]. However, there was no uniform definition and categorization of BPA technologies. For example, OCR [48] and Computer Vision [15] are sometimes understood to mean the same thing, but different terms are used. This highlights the need for a uniform BPA-oriented definition of technologies.

6 Conclusion

In summary, BPA is a core element of digital transformation in companies [2]. The current challenge is the fragmented knowledge base about BPA, coupled with the lack of guidance for the systematic selection and implementation [4]. Our research aimed to identify existing frameworks and develop recommendations for companies to successfully establish BPA in their organization. Accordingly, in this research paper, an SLR was conducted to assess the current state-of-the-art of BPA by identifying and analyzing 40 relevant publications. Our findings revealed 24 frameworks and 32 key aspects in eight categories for successful BPA. The main contribution of this study is to provide a structured overview of BPA frameworks, key aspects, categories, and the technologies used. It offers both researchers and practitioners a basis for their future decision-making. Furthermore, our analysis of key aspects from theoretical literature shows that the successful implementation of BPA depends on a combination of technological, organizational, and strategic elements. This includes a strong data culture, strategic leadership, thorough change management, targeted technology investments, and a structured, measurable approach for the process implementation. Many of these key aspects are not addressed or only mentioned briefly across the reviewed frameworks.

While this SLR provides insights into the current state of research on BPA, several limitations must be acknowledged. First, the search was restricted to publications from 2019–2024 in English and German, which may have excluded earlier foundational studies or relevant research in other languages. Second, while theoretical synthesis provides valuable theoretical contributions, further empirical studies are required to validate and refine the proposed key factors and categories.

Future research should build on the findings of this study and address some of the gaps identified. First, further practical recommendations for action should be identified to expand the range of guidelines available to organizations. These recommendations should also be prioritized to create a structured and strategic roadmap to help companies implement BPA effectively. Furthermore, the study revealed a significant gap in the clear classification and definition of technologies related to BPA. Future work should develop a concise taxonomy and criteria for identifying and categorizing these technologies to provide clarity for researchers and practitioners. Addressing these areas will advance the field of BPA and equip companies with the tools and strategies needed to fully leverage automation for their strategic and operational goals.

References

1. George, A.S., George, A.S.H., Baskar, T., Sujatha, V.: The rise of hyperautomation: a new frontier for business process automation (2023). https://doi.org/10.5281/zenodo.10403036
2. Rach, M.: The future of marketing and sales automation. In: Hannig, U., Seebacher, U. (eds.) Marketing and Sales Automation. Management for Professionals, pp. 431–446. Springer International Publishing, Cham (2023). https://doi.org/10.1007/978-3-031-20040-3_27
3. Abdelwahab, M.B.M., Helal, I.M.A.: Advanced techniques for business process automation: insights and challenges. In: 2023 Intelligent Methods, Systems, and Applications (IMSA), pp. 303–308. IEEE (2023). https://doi.org/10.1109/IMSA58542.2023.10217503
4. Martinek-Jaguszewska, K., Rogowski, W.: Development and validation of the business process automation maturity model: results of the Delphi study. Inf. Syst. Manag. **40**, 169–185 (2023). https://doi.org/10.1080/10580530.2022.2071506
5. vom Brocke, J., Simons, A., Bjoern, N., Kai, R., Anne, C., Ralf, P.: Reconstructing the giant: on the importance of rigour in documenting the literature search process. In: ECIS 2009 Proceedings (2009)
6. Leopold, H., van der Han, A., Hajo A., R.: Identifying candidate tasks for robotic process automation in textual process descriptions. Enterp., Bus.-Process Inf. Syst. Model., 67–81 (2018)
7. Moreira, S., Mamede, H.S., Santos, A.: Business process automation in SMEs: a systematic literature review. IEEE Access **12** (2024). https://doi.org/10.1109/ACCESS.2024.3406548
8. Kanakov, F., Prokhorov, I.: Analysis and applicability of artificial intelligence technologies in the field of RPA software robots for automating business processes. Procedia Comput. Sci. **213**, 296–300 (2022). https://doi.org/10.1016/j.procs.2022.11.070
9. Santos, F., Pereira, R., Vasconcelos, J.B.: Toward robotic process automation implementation: an end-to-end perspective. Bus. Process. Manag. J. **26**, 405–420 (2020). https://doi.org/10.1108/BPMJ-12-2018-0380
10. Somayya, M., Rajesh, M.H., Rajeev, K.R.: The next generation intelligent automation: hyperautomation. J. Inf. Syst. Technol. Manag. – Jistem USP (2022)
11. Pfannstiel, M.A.: Einleitung „Technologien und Technologiemanagement im Gesundheitswesen". In: Pfannstiel, M.A. (ed.) Technologien und Technologiemanagement im Gesundheitswesen. Potenziale nutzen, Lösungen entwickeln, Ziele erreichen, pp. 1–19. Springer Fachmedien Wiesbaden GmbH, Wiesbaden (2024). https://doi.org/10.1007/978-3-658-43860-9_1
12. Osman, C.-C.: Robotic process automation: lessons learned from case studies. IE, 66–71 (2019). https://doi.org/10.12948/issn14531305/23.4.2019.06
13. Liermann, V., Li, S., Waizner, J.: Hyperautomation (Automated Decision-Making as Part of RPA). In: Liermann, V., Stegmann, C. (eds.) The Digital Journey of Banking and Insurance, Volume II, pp. 277–293. Springer International Publishing, Cham (2021). https://doi.org/10.1007/978-3-030-78829-2_16
14. Williams, O.C., Olajide, F.: Towards the design of an intelligent automation framework for business processes. In: 2022 5th International Conference on Information and Computer Technologies (ICICT), pp. 13–17. IEEE (2022). https://doi.org/10.1109/ICICT55905.2022.00010
15. Devarajan, Y.: A study of robotic process automation use cases today for tomorrow's business. Int. J. Comput. Tech., 12–18 (2018)
16. Ng, K.K., Chen, C.H., Lee, C.K., Jiao, J.R., Yang, Z.X.: A systematic literature review on intelligent automation: aligning concepts from theory, practice, and future perspectives. Adv. Eng. Inform. **47**, 101246 (2021). https://doi.org/10.1016/j.aei.2021.101246

17. Siderska, J., Aunimo, L., Süße, T., von Stamm, J., Kedziora, D., Aini, S.N.B.M.: Towards intelligent automation (IA): literature review on the evolution of robotic process automation (RPA), its challenges, and future trends. Eng. Manag. Prod. Serv. **15**, 90–103 (2023). https://doi.org/10.2478/emj-2023-0030
18. Filippi, E., Bannò, M., Trento, S.: Automation technologies and their impact on employment: a review, synthesis and future research agenda. Technol. Forecast. Soc. Chang. **191**, 122448 (2023). https://doi.org/10.1016/j.techfore.2023.122448
19. Sharma, R., Bharadwaj, S., Dutt, S., Tomar, M.: Robotic advancements in business process automation using artificial intelligence: an investigative study. In: 2022 11th International Conference on System Modeling & Advancement in Research Trends (SMART), pp. 1141–1143. IEEE (2022). https://doi.org/10.1109/SMART55829.2022.10046772
20. Wewerka, J., Reichert, M.: Robotic process automation -- a systematic literature review and assessment framework (2020)
21. Agnihotri, R., Chaker, N.N., Dugan, R., Galvan, J.M., Nowlin, E.: Sales technology research: a review and future research agenda. J. Pers. Selling Sales Manag., 307–335 (2023). https://doi.org/10.1080/08853134.2023.2260108
22. Sharma, C., Bharadwaj, S.S., Gupta, N., Jain, H.: Robotic process automation adoption: contextual factors from service sectors in an emerging economy. J. Enterp. Inf. Manag. **36**, 252–274 (2023). https://doi.org/10.1108/JEIM-06-2021-0276
23. Cooper, H.M.: Organizing knowledge syntheses: a taxonomy of literature reviews. Knowl. Soc. **1**, 104–126 (1988). https://doi.org/10.1007/BF03177550
24. Webster, J., Watson, R.T.: Analyzing the past to prepare for the future: writing a literature review. MIS Quarterly **26**, xiii–xxiii (2002)
25. Raluca, B., Diana Maria, C., Adrian, A.M., Emil, L.C.: Unpacking the digital the digital transformation of work: framings and (Re)configurations with robotic process automation technology (2024)
26. Riedl, Y., Beetz, K.R.: Robotic process automation: developing a multi-criteria evaluation model for the selection of automatable business processes. In: Twenty-fifth Americas Conference on Information Systems (2019)
27. Plattfaut, R., Koch, J.F., Trampler, M., Coners, A.: PEPA: Entwicklung eines Scoring-Modells zur Priorisierung von Prozessen für eine Automatisierung. HMD, 1111–1129 (2020). https://doi.org/10.1365/s40702-020-00670-3
28. Storbacka, E., Storbacka, K.: Building a revenue engine – scaling up sales automation. NIM Mark. Intell. Rev. **14**, 31–35 (2022). https://doi.org/10.2478/nimmir-2022-0014
29. Schlegel, D., Rosenberg, B., Fundanovic, O., Kraus, P.: How to conduct successful business process automation projects? An analysis of key factors in the context of robotic process automation. BPMJ **30**, 99–119 (2024). https://doi.org/10.1108/BPMJ-06-2023-0465
30. James, L.: Is hyperautomation worth the hype? Eng. Technol. **17**, 22–25 (2022). https://doi.org/10.1049/et.2022.0105
31. Birkbeck, A., Rowe, L.: Navigating towards hyperautomation and the empowerment of human capital in family businesses: a perspective article. JFBM **14**, 727–734 (2024). https://doi.org/10.1108/JFBM-09-2023-0157
32. Lacity, M., Willcocks, L.: Becoming strategic with intelligent automation. MSQE **20**, 169–182 (2021). https://doi.org/10.17705/2msqe.00047
33. Aleksandre, A., Esko, P., Tapani, R.-K., Antti, S.: Organizational implementation of intelligent automation as distributed cognition: six recommendations for managers. In: ICIS 2019 Proceedings (2019)
34. Costa, D.S., Mamede, H.S., Da Silva, M.M.: A method for selecting processes for automation with AHP and TOPSIS. Heliyon (2023). https://doi.org/10.1016/j.heliyon.2023.e13683

35. Kuftinova, N.G., Ostroukh, A.V., Maksimychev, O.I., Odinokova, I.V.: Road construction enterprise management model based on hyperautomation technologies. In: 2021 Intelligent Technologies and Electronic Devices in Vehicle and Road Transport Complex (TIRVED), pp. 1–4. IEEE (2021). https://doi.org/10.1109/TIRVED53476.2021.9639114
36. Milind, G., Rehan, S., Wasana, B.: Exploring the nexus between intelligent automation and process complexity. In: Proceedings of the Pacific Asia Conference on Information Systems (2022)
37. Bergner, A.S.: Adaptive sales automation - ChatBots as personalized and scalable sales agents, 50–57 (2020)
38. Rodriguez, M., Peterson, R.: Artificial intelligence in business-to-business (B2B) sales process: a conceptual framework. J. Market. Anal., 1–12 (2024). https://doi.org/10.1057/s41270-023-00287-7
39. Gotzen, R., Schuh, G., Stich, V., Conrad, R.: Classification of software-based automation technologies: derivation of characteristics through an empirical investigation. In: 2021 IEEE International Conference on Engineering, Technology and Innovation (ICE/ITMC), pp. 1–9. IEEE (2021). https://doi.org/10.1109/ICE/ITMC52061.2021.9570264
40. Sudharson, D., Bhuvaneshwaran, A., Kalaiarasan, T.R., Satheesh kumar, D., Sushmita, V., Jyothi Lakshmi, N.: A multimodal AI framework for hyper automation in industry 5.0. In: 2023 International Conference on Innovative Data Communication Technologies and Application (ICIDCA), pp. 282–286. IEEE (2023). https://doi.org/10.1109/ICIDCA56705.2023.10099581
41. Coito, T., et al.: A novel framework for intelligent automation. IFAC-PapersOnLine **52**, 1825–1830 (2019). https://doi.org/10.1016/j.ifacol.2019.11.501
42. Yatskiv, S., Voytyuk, I., Yatskiv, N., Kushnir, O., Trufanova, Y., Panasyuk, V.: Improved method of software automation testing based on the robotic process automation technology. In: 2019 9th International Conference on Advanced Computer Information Technologies (ACIT), pp. 293–296. IEEE (2019). https://doi.org/10.1109/ACITT.2019.8780038
43. Özkan, G., Esgin, E.: SOPRANO: seamless sales order management robotic process automation experience at SAP. In: 2023 Innovations in Intelligent Systems and Applications Conference (ASYU), pp. 1–6. IEEE (2023). https://doi.org/10.1109/ASYU58738.2023.10296770
44. Anica-Popa, L.-E., Vrîncianu, M., Petrică Papuc, I.-M.: AI – powered business services in the hyperautomation era. In: Proceedings of the International Conference on Business Excellence, vol. 17, pp. 1036–1050 (2023). https://doi.org/10.2478/picbe-2023-0094
45. Braatz, Y., Klaiber, M.J.: End-to-end automation frameworks for mapping neural networks onto embedded devices and early performance predictions: a survey. In: 2021 Smart Systems Integration (SSI), pp. 1–4. IEEE (2021). https://doi.org/10.1109/SSI52265.2021.9467015
46. Niedzielski, B., Buła, P., Yang, M.: Hyperautomation as a vital optimization tool in organizations: cognitive approach with the use of Euler circles. JEBDE **3**, 61–73 (2024). https://doi.org/10.1108/JEBDE-02-2023-0004
47. Hoang, V., Henrik, L., van der Han, A.: What is business process automation anyway? In: Hawaii International Conference on System Sciences, pp. 5462–5471 (2023)
48. Kavitha, R.: Hyperautomation-beyond RPA: leveraging automation to transform the manufacturing industries. In: 2023 International Conference on Computer Communication and Informatics (ICCCI), pp. 1–5. IEEE (2023). https://doi.org/10.1109/ICCCI56745.2023.10128636
49. Vorndran, J.: Benefits and limitations of sales tax automation **38**, 27 (2020)

50. Schöpf, A.: Daten und Automation bei KMUs in Sales und Marketing - Zwei Use-Cases aus der Praxi, 28–33 (2020)
51. Borg, S.W., Young, L.: Continuing the evolution of the selling process: a multi-level perspective. Ind. Mark. Manage. **43**, 543–552 (2014). https://doi.org/10.1016/j.indmarman.2014.02.013

Empowering Experts in Data-Driven Process Design: A Reference Model for Sales

Matthias Lederer[✉], Steevan Christopher Menezes, and Kris Dalm

1Technical University of Applied Sciences Amberg-Weiden, Hetzenrichter Weg 15, 92637 Weiden, Germany
`ma.lederer@oth-aw.de`

Abstract. This article develops a reference model for decision modeling using Decision Model and Notation (DMN) based on the example of sales processes. While Business Process Modeling and Notation (BPMN) is widely used to visualize sales processes, the underlying decision logic rarely remains formalized. To close this gap, the DMN reference model shows initial results of decision points with reusable decision tables along the seven phases of the sales cycle (prospecting, preparation, approach, presentation, objection handling, closing, and follow-up). These can be used by practitioners as a blueprint for modern data-driven sales approaches (e.g., automation, artificial intelligence, omnichannel marketing). Further research will focus on expanding the phases and models and measuring the positive impact on decision-oriented performance improvements.

Keywords: sales processes · decision modelling · Decision Model and Notation (DMN) · Business Process Modeling and Notation (BPMN)

1 Motivation

The use of data in marketing processes has been widely discussed for years and many applications already appear to be widely accepted and used today. The typical forms (e.g. digital marketing, marketing automation, customer journey, user experience marketing) utilise the fact that extensive operational and analytical data is collected at many points of contact with customers and is therefore available for analytics and decision-making (Chaturuedula et al., 2019; Ehsan et al., 2021; Vilone & Longo, 2021).

Modelling such decisions offers business and IT users the opportunity to build a suitable bridge between strategic, operational and tactical decisions. If decision models are developed, they can be used for implementation in IT (similar to how process models with BPMN are used today). For example, Six et al. (2022) shows how BPMN can be used for modelling sales processes - with a particular focus on supporting the manual decisions of experts along a sales or customer journey. BPMN provides a common language for modelling the control flow. The OMG has also developed the DMN standard for this purpose. Many people involved in decision management, such as business experts (e.g. sales staff who describe the sales rules and monitor their implementation) and IT specialists (who implement rules in automation solutions), can easily understand DMN.

The two OMG visual modelling standards can be used individually but were created to complement each other as indicated in Fig. 1 (Weske, 2019; Saba et al., 2021; Vilone & Longo, 2021; OMG, 2024). The visual models used by the DMN standard are verifiable and standardized and serve both as operational input for the decision automation engines and as human-readable documentation. DMN enables non-programmers or experts from sales departments to create and verify executable decision logic. This means that they are a suitable way for sales managers to collaborate on the design and improvement of processes that are then executed in a highly automated manner with the help of AI. Just as BPMN has democratized the control flows in sales processes, DMN is therefore potentially able to promote participation in AI in sales processes and thus also support the acceptance of this disruptive change (Settembre-Blundo et al., 2021; Saba et al., 2021; OMG, 2024; Weske, 2019).

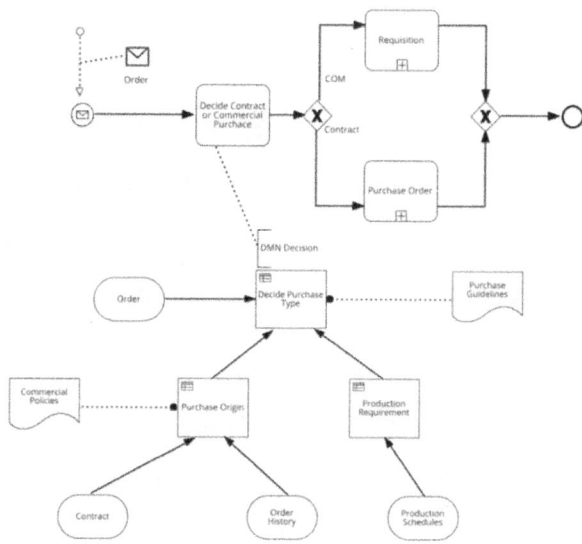

Fig. 1. Connected DMN and BPMN models (Debevoise et al., 2014)

A recognized way to make the application of standards (here DMN) for a use case (here sales processes) known and usable for researchers and practitioners is to sketch a reference model. This paper therefore develops a DMN reference model for sales processes to (a) lay the foundations described above for experts to participate in the digital transformation of sales processes. (b) In addition, the framework is intended to serve as an illustrative example of decision modelling of sales workflows.

2 Method

According to Ahlemann & Gastl (2007), the creation of a reference model consists of (a) the construction and (b) the application of the reference model. In this article, (a) is pursued first, while an evaluation or test of the model in the narrower sense is withheld from further research.

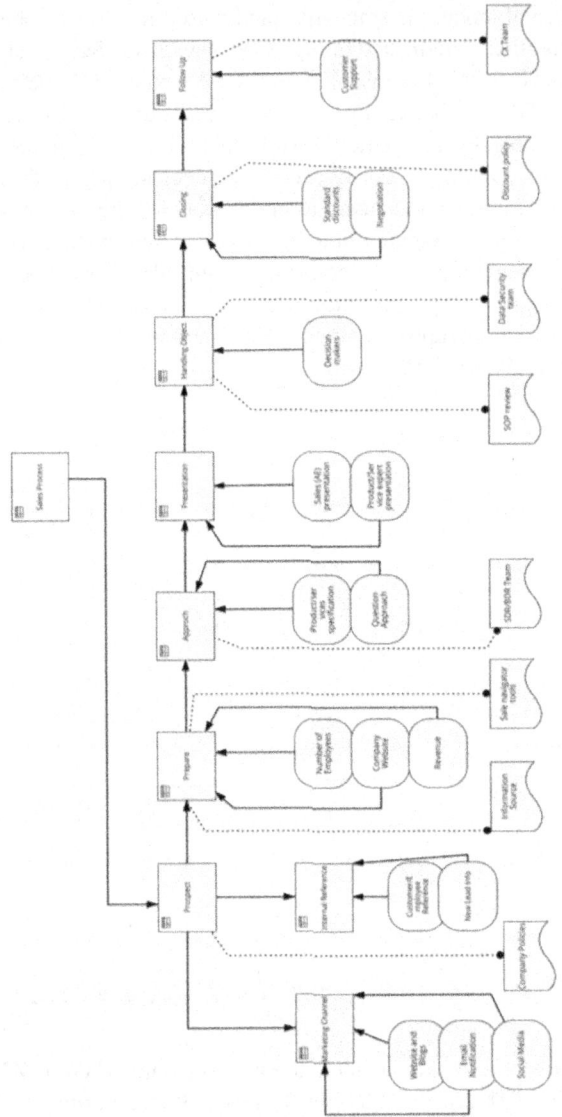

Fig. 2. Seven steps of the reference model with decision requirements (OMG, 2024; Debevoise et al., 2014; Six et al. 2022)

In order to develop the reference model, this work-in-progress article follows methods recognised in the information systems discipline that support the construction of the reference model (Ahlemann & Gastl, 2007). Specifically, the approaches of Schütte (1998), Ahlemann & Gastl (2007) and Becker et al. (2001) are followed, which included interviews in four different marketing organisations and a literature review according to the approach of Wetterich & Plänitz (2021) and Sulaiman et al. (2016) as a data basis.

3   Excerpt from the Reference Model

Figure 2, shows the seven-stage sales process as a DMN (OMG, 2024; Debevoise et al., 2014). In keeping with the idea of a work in progress, only the first phase will be described – details on the other phases should be up to further research.

Prospecting, the first phase of the sales process, aims to identify and generate new potential customers or "leads". This is a crucial first step in any sales process, often involving synchronised work between marketing, sales and product teams. A customised marketing campaign can serve as a springboard for this. In the age of digitalisation, prospecting has expanded far beyond traditional methods. It no longer involves just face-to-face networking or cold calling, but fully utilises the power of the internet. Online research on professional social networks such as LinkedIn or other forums such as Quora has proven to be effective in keeping track of potential customers, understanding their buying behaviour and weighing up their fit with the products or services on offer. Table 1 shows an example of how the decisions to be made in the reference model can be made explicit (Ye, 2023; Ingram et al., 2006; Malshe & Sohi, 2009; OMG, 2024; Debevoise et al., 2014; Six et al. 2022).

In addition to online research, sales teams can work with marketing teams to create targeted prospect lists and create messages that are tailored to their buying behaviour. This can help to streamline the sales process and increase the likelihood of success - Table 2 shows a further illustration of possible decisions based on the customer's criteria and the way in which the customer came into contact (Soini, 2014; Mishra & Mishra, 2009).

Table 1. Prospecting Decision Logic Table as Marketing Channel (excerpt)

	Inputs						Outputs
U	Website and Blogs		Email Notification		Social Media		New Output
	{Read the Website and Blogs, Follow the website and Blogs, Not Read or Followed}		{Email Notification Read, Email Notification Responded, Email Notification Spammed}		{Followed on LinkedIn, Not Followed on Social Media}		{Potential Customer, Not Potential Customer}
1	=	Read the Website and Blogs	=	Email Notification Read	=	Followed on LinkedIn	Potential Customer
2	=	Read the Website and Blogs	=	–	=	Followed on LinkedIn	Potential Customer
3	=	Read the Website and Blogs	=	Email Notification Read	=	Not Followed on Social Media	Potential Customer

(*continued*)

Table 1. (*continued*)

	Inputs			Outputs
U	Website and Blogs	Email Notification	Social Media	New Output
	{Read the Website and Blogs, Follow the website and Blogs, Not Read or Followed}	{Email Notification Read, Email Notification Responded, Email Notification Spammed}	{Followed on LinkedIn, Not Followed on Social Media}	{Potential Customer, Not Potential Customer}
4	=	–	= Email Notification Read	= Followed on LinkedIn	Potential Customer
5	=	–	= –	= –	Not Potential Customer
6	=	Follow the website and Blogs	= Email Notification Responded	= Followed on LinkedIn	Potential Customer
7	=	Follow the website and Blogs	= Email Notification Responded	= –	Potential Customer
8	=	Follow the website and Blogs	= Email Notification Responded	= Not Followed on Social Media	Potential Customer
9	=	–	= Email Notification Responded	= Followed on LinkedIn	Potential Customer
10	=	Not Read or Followed	= Email Notification Spammed	= Followed on LinkedIn	Not Potential Customer
11	=	Not Read or Followed	= –	= Not Followed on Social Media	Not Potential Customer
12	=	Not Read or Followed	= Email Notification Responded	= Followed on LinkedIn	Potential Customer
13	=	Not Read or Followed	= Email Notification Read	= Followed on LinkedIn	Potential Customer

Prospecting can also take place at business events or conferences. Sales representatives use these opportunities to make contacts that could develop into potential leads or referral sources. Another important aspect of prospecting is generating referrals. Sales teams can ask existing customers or colleagues for referrals. Based on trust and a good relationship, this can lead to new and interested leads. Prospecting is therefore an essential and versatile first step in the sales process that has a strong influence on the following phases. It is an ongoing process that requires regular maintenance and adjustment in order to adapt to changing market conditions and consumer behaviour - which is why additional criteria are also considered for the decision-making models depending on the company's focus (Soini, 2014; Mishra & Mishra, 2009; Malshe & Sohi, 2009; Debevoise et al., 2014; Six et al. 2022).

Table 2. Prospecting Decision Logic Table as Customer Reference (excerpt)

U	Inputs				Outputs
	Customer/Employee Reference		New Lead Info		New Output
	{Subsidiary Company, General Reference, Previous Organisation, Professional Network, Spammed Reference}		{Website, Email Address, Social Media, The Champion}		{Potential Customer, Not Potential Customer, Nurture the Prospect}
1*	=	Subsidiary Company	=	Website	Potential Customer
2	=	Subsidiary Company	=	The Champion	Potential Customer
3	=	General Reference	=	Email Address	Potential Customer
4	=	General Reference	=	Social Media	Potential Customer
5	=	Previous Organisation	=	Email Address	Potential Customer
6	=	Previous Organisation	=	The Champion	Potential Customer
7	=	Professional Network	=	Social Media	Potential Customer
8	=	Professional Network	=	Email Address	Potential Customer
9	=	General Reference	=	–	Not Potential Customer
10**	=	Subsidiary Company	=	–	Nurture the Prospect
11	=	Spammed Reference	=	–	Not Potential Customer

(*continued*)

Table 2. (*continued*)

	Inputs				Outputs
U	Customer/Employee Reference	New Lead Info			New Output
	{Subsidiary Company, General Reference, Previous Organisation, Professional Network, Spammed Reference}	{Website, Email Address, Social Media, The Champion}			{Potential Customer, Not Potential Customer, Nurture the Prospect}
12	=	Spammed Reference	=	Email Address	Not Potential Customer
13	=	Professional Network	=	–	Nurture the Prospect
14	=	Previous Organisation	=	–	Nurture the Prospect

In the subsequent phases, the **preparation** phase uses internal CRM data, market reports, and social media signals to derive buyer firmographics, competitive pressure, and pain points; typical DMN decisions here include *lead qualification* (good/bad prospect) based on revenue, number of employees, and web activity. **Approach** links this information with contact and interaction data (email opens, website visits) and uses rules to decide whether to trigger a *demo invite, free trial*, or pure *nurturing*, with the channel (phone, email, social media) being selected dynamically based on preference attributes. In the **presentation**, product configuration data and customer-specific use cases are fed into a decision table that determines which features are emphasized, which pricing option is shown, and whether an expert is called in. When **handling objections**, the conversation log (e.g., speech-to-text) is checked against rule sets to automatically suggest the next line of argument or additional evidence (ROI proof, compliance document). Closing uses price lists, discount matrices, and contract terms as inputs for a decision table that determines the optimal offer (standard discount vs. special conditions) and the necessary approvals. **Nurturing** combines usage and support data to select rules via DMN for *renewal reminders, up/cross-selling*, or escalation to customer success, thereby managing customer loyalty in a data-driven manner (Davies, 2022; Ingram et al., 2006; Fischer et al., 2022; Debevoise et al., 2014; Six et al. 2022; Malshe & Sohi, 2009; Soini, 2014).

4 Closing

This work-in-progress paper presents a DMN reference model in sales processes. The model provides a structured and comprehensive basis for the development and implementation of data-driven sales processes, as the decisions to be made in a (BPMN) process model are recorded in exemplary tables. These contain decision-relevant attributes and characteristics that can help to improve sales performance, increase customer satisfaction and maximize sales. It is important to note that the presented DMN reference model for AI in sales processes is not a universal solution for all companies and industries. In addition to further research (e.g., on the development for more phases and refinement in further academic work), users are also advised to tailor the specific requirements and circumstances of each company when implementing the model. There is also a need to validate the model in different companies and industries to further verify its effectiveness and applicability.

In a nutshell this work in progress demonstrates the potential for DMN in sales processes to make data-driven decisions transparent – the reference model provided is an invitation to now take the next transparent step.

Acknowledgement. In the planning, design, production, formulation, and revision of this research, DeepL and ChatGPT were used as tools (transparency note in terms of [i] the general recommendation of the European Code of Conduct for Research Integrity and [ii] the domain-specific proposal according to Nature Journal in January 2023).

References

Ahlemann, F., Gastl, H.: Process model for an empiracally grounded reference model construction. In: Fettke, P., Loos, P. (eds.) Reference Modeling for Business Systems Analysis. IGI Global (2007)

Becker J.: Referenzmodel. In: Mertens, P., et al. (eds.) Lexikon der Wirtschaftsinformatik. Springer (2001)

Damoiseaux, J.: An exploration of a data-driven decision-making framework leveraging the decision model and notation (DMN) standard: DMN-D3M. Eindhoven University of Technology (2023)

Davies, C.: The ultimate guide to creating a sales process (2022). https://blog.hubspot.com/sales/sales-process-

Debevoise, T., Taylor, J., Sinur, J., Geneva, R.: The MicroGuide to process and decision modeling in BPMN/DMN: building more effective processes by integrating process modeling with decision modeling. CreateSpace Independent (2014)

Ehsan, U., Liao, Q.V., Muller, M., Riedl, M.O., Weisz, J.D.: Expanding explainability: towards social transparency in AI systems. In: Proceedings of the 2021 CHI Conference on Human Factors in Computing Systems (2021)

Fischer, H., Seidenstricker, S., Berger, T., Holopainen, T.: Artificial intelligence in B2B sales: impact on the sales process. Artif. Intell. Soc. Comput. **28**, 135–142 (2022)

Gartner. Gartner Magic Quadrant for Sales Force Automation Platforms (2023a). https://www.gartner.com/en/documents/4710499

Gartner. Gartner Magic Quadrant for CRM Lead Management (2023b). https://www.gartner.com/en/documents/3989183

Ingram, T.N., La Forge, R.W., Avila, R.A., Schwepker, C.H., Williams, M.R.: Sales management - analysis and decision making. Thomson (2006)

Malshe, A., Sohi, R.S.: What makes strategy making across the sales-marketing interface more successful? J. Acad. Mark. Sci. **37**, 400–421 (2009)

Mishra, A., Mishra, D.: Customer relationship management: implementation process perspective. Acta Polytechnica Hungarica **6**(4), 83–99 (2009)

OMG. Decision Model and Notation Version 1.6 (2024). https://www.omg.org/spec/DMN/1.6/Beta1/PDF

Saba, D., Sahli, Y., Hadidi, A.: The role of artificial intelligence in company's decision making. In: Hassanien, A.E., Taha, M.H.N., Khalifa, N.E.M. (eds.) Enabling AI Applications in Data Science. Springer (2021)

Schütte, R.: Grundsätze ordnungsmäßiger Referenzmodellierung. Springer (1998)

Six, T., Lederer, M., Schmidt, W., Nirschl, M.: Business process management bridging marketing and IT: transformation model for customer journey maps and BPMN. In: Proceedings of the S-BPM ONE 2022. Springer

Soini, S.: Developing a toolkit for supporting the sales process in an IT company. Helsinki University (2014)

Sulaiman, N., Mahrin, M., Yusoff, R.: Influential factors on the awareness of agile software development methodology: a systematic literature review. J. Internet Comput. Serv. **17**(5), 161–172 (2016)

Vilone, G., Longo, L.: Notions of explainability and evaluation approaches for explainable artificial intelligence. Inf. Fusion **76**, 89–106 (2021)

Weske, M.: Business Process Management. Springer (2019)

Wetterich, C., Plänitz, E.: Systematische Literaturanalysen in den Sozialwissenschaften. Budrich (2021)

Ye, L.: The Ultimate Guide to Sales Qualification (2023). https://blog.hubspot.com/sales/ultimate-guide-to-sales-qualification?hubs_content=blog.hubspot.com%2Fsales%2Fprospecting&hubs_content-cta=qualify%20your%20prospects

Employee Retention as a Success Factor: Data-Based Optimization of HR Processes in the Consulting Industry

Theresa Zopke[1(✉)], Michael Hein[2], and Ana Moya[1]

[1] International School of Management, Otto-Hahn-Straße 19, 44227 Dortmund, Germany
Theresa.zopke@gmail.com

[2] Datatoolbox, Stiftsplatz 9, 40213 Düsseldorf, Germany

Abstract. The consulting industry faces the challenge of retaining qualified personnel in the long term to maintain its performance. This study examines how data-based analyses of job interviews can help predict employee retention and make HR processes more efficient. Based on 565 data sets from a consulting firm, concepts correlating with employee retention are identified using text mining and the CHAID decision tree method, and are assigned to the Big Five personality factors. The results show that agreeableness and extraversion, in particular, have predictive significance. Furthermore, the analysis reveals considerable optimization potential along the entire HR lifecycle: insights from personnel selection are hardly systematically transferred to downstream processes such as talent management, onboarding and offboarding. The study concludes with concrete recommendations for a lifecycle-oriented, data-based HR design in consulting firms.

Keywords: HR analytics · employee selection · OCEAN model

1 Introduction

In today's volatile economic landscape, the consulting industry occupies a paradoxical position as both victim and beneficiary of systemic uncertainties. While organizations increasingly rely on external expertise to navigate complex challenges, consulting firms face mounting pressure to optimize their primary value creation mechanism: human capital management. The industry's intellectual capital-intensive nature transforms personnel selection from an operational task into a strategic imperative, where misalignment between selection processes and organizational needs can trigger cascading failures in client relationships and market positioning.

This study tries to address the consulting sector's dual challenge of maintaining service excellence amidst high talent turnover. Our central hypothesis posits that process-driven optimization of recruitment creates self-reinforcing retention mechanisms, thereby securing medium-to-long-term organizational performance. This research demonstrates the effectiveness of the data-driven approach in managing knowledge-intensive processes where human interactions are the primary value creation mechanism. It offers a blueprint for transforming recruitment from a cost center into a strategic retention driver.

2 State of Research

The scientific discourse on personnel selection procedures centers around diagnostic validity, predictive accuracy, and fairness. The use of structured interviews is regarded as an effective means to minimize subjective biases and to enhance the comparability of applicants. The assessment of personality traits—particularly along the Big Five (OCEAN model)—has been shown in numerous studies to be a valid predictor of job performance and person–job fit.

Meta-analytic findings demonstrate a particularly high relevance of the dimensions conscientiousness and extraversion for occupational performance in consulting-related roles [3]. More recent studies employing machine learning algorithms also suggest that the automated analysis of language and textual data from application processes may offer a more valid access to personality and aptitude than traditional questionnaires [4].

Moreover, in corporate practice, it is often overlooked that insights gained during personnel selection are rarely used systematically beyond the point of decision-making. Information on personality, strengths, and development potential is seldom transferred to downstream HR processes such as onboarding, talent development, performance evaluation, or offboarding. This omission significantly reduces the effectiveness of subsequent personnel measures. A data-driven analysis and targeted utilization of this information across the entire employee lifecycle offers substantial potential: it enables tailored development, strengthens employee motivation, and sustainably reduces turnover rates.

The case study investigates, based on free-text analyses from interview evaluations, which factors—particularly those related to the Big Five—correlate with longer employee retention. A data-driven approach is applied that integrates both interview data and machine learning methods.

3 Case Study

The analysis is based on 565 applicant records from a medium-sized consulting firm. Collected data included both structured personnel information and free-text entries from first and second interviews, each differentiated by two interviewers per session. The target variable of the study is the employee retention duration within the company.

Using text mining and the CHAID decision tree method, concepts that significantly correlate with employee retention were identified. These concepts were assigned to the Big Five personality traits using a language model. The subsequent segmentation of influencing factors enables differentiated insights into relevant predictors of employee retention.

Influence of Promotion History:

Employees who have received at least one promotion exhibit a significantly higher likelihood of remaining with the company. Interestingly, however, a very rapid initial promotion (within less than one year) is, on average, associated with a shorter retention duration compared to a delayed first promotion.

Significance of entry level:

Junior Consultants tend to exhibit a longer retention duration compared to Consultants. The longest tenure was observed among individuals who began their careers as

Junior Consultants and advanced to the positions of Senior Consultant or Manager. This highlights the positive effect of internal development pathways (Fig. 1).

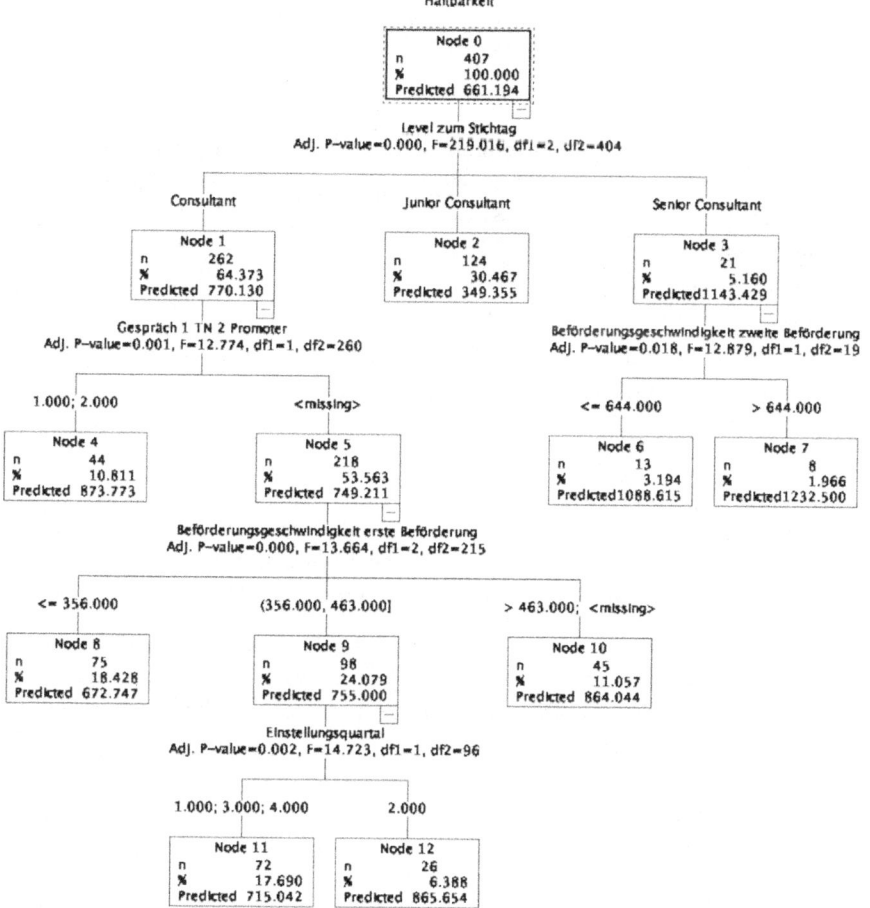

Fig. 1. Output for the target variable "retention" when the entry level is set to Junior Consultant

1. Influence of interview evaluations (Promoter Score):
    The subjective assessment by interviewers ("promoters") proves to be relevant in several respects: Applicants who received positive evaluations show a higher likelihood of being promoted but tend to leave the company earlier. Applicants with neutral evaluations tend to remain with the company for a longer period. Missing or inconsistent promoter assessments are associated with shorter retention durations.
2. Text Mining and personality traits:
    Out of 1,666 analyzed text modules, 569 valid statements were identified and assigned to the Big Five personality dimensions (Fig. 2):

- Agreeableness: Represented in 81–86% of the statements; the most frequently mentioned factor
- Extraversion: Represented in 11–23% of the statements; e.g., positive body language, proactive communication, self-confidence
- Openness & Conscientiousness: Clearly subordinate in frequency
- Neuroticism: Hardly represented

Big Five factor	Frequency 1.interview	Frequency 2.interview
Agreeableness	81%	86%
Extraversion	23%	11%
Conscientiousness	4%	5%
Openness	4%	4%
Neuroticism	0,3%	0,5%

Fig. 2. Frequency of the Big Five factors in the concepts that contribute as independent variables to long retention

3. Interaction of personality traits

One third of the extraverted statements were simultaneously associated with agreeableness. This combination was particularly evident among employees with long retention durations and solid development trajectories.

In summary, employee retention correlates significantly with specific personality traits, career paths, and interview assessments. The analysis also highlights the untapped potential of systematically transferring insights gained during the personnel selection process into subsequent HR processes.

4 Practical Implications

The findings have direct relevance for HR practice in consulting firms. They suggest that the targeted analysis of applicant evaluations can contribute to assessing employee retention potential. Structured interviews should be used not only for assessing professional qualifications but also for evaluating personality traits. The evaluation should follow defined criteria (e.g., adjective clusters based on the Big Five). Evaluation forms should be mandatory and standardized to avoid gaps and biases in assessment. Personnel selection processes should not be solely focused on immediate performance but rather on long-term fit. HR analytics can be employed to systematically analyze existing data sources, such as free-text entries from applicant evaluations, and to improve them based on data-driven insights. Onboarding and retention strategies should be aligned with the identified personality profiles. Offboarding, in particular, presents an often underutilized opportunity for validating and refining selection criteria. Analyzing exit interviews or reasons for resignation in connection with the original interview data can help identify patterns and develop more precise predictive models for retention. Personnel development, in turn, benefits when known personality traits are specifically used to design individualized learning paths and career plans. Overall, lifecycle-oriented HR processes must be more closely integrated in the future. Only in this way can the full potential of data-driven personnel decisions be realized.

5 Conclusion

The data-driven analysis of interview evaluations offers significant potential for advancing personnel-related decision-making in the consulting industry. The following research directions present themselves as next steps:

- Validation in other industries: How do the identified factors apply in sectors with lower levels of client interaction?
- Validation in other consulting firms: What role does corporate culture play, especially with regard to the expression of the Big Five personality traits?
- Expansion to include external influencing factors: To what extent do economic cycles, labor market pressures, or corporate culture affect retention?
- Integration into operational systems: How can analytical results—such as through decision support tools—be incorporated into real-time decision-making?
- Linkage with HR lifecycle models: What measures can be implemented to systematically transfer insights from the selection phase into development, retention, and offboarding processes?

In the long term, the combination of structured interview methodology and modern data analysis promises a significant increase in predictive accuracy and, consequently, in the quality of personnel selection decisions. The consulting industry may serve as a model sector in which data-driven HR optimization can be implemented particularly efficiently.

References

1. Wollsching-Strobel, P., Werkmann, S., Sternecker, P.: Einleitung. In: Wollsching-Strobel, P., Werkmann, S., Sternecker, P. (eds.) Consulting am Wendepunkt, pp. 1–8. Springer Fachmedien, Wiesbaden (2024)
2. Wollsching-Strobel, P., Werkmann, S., Sternecker, P.: Wer neue Wege gehen will, braucht Beratung. In: Wollsching-Strobel, P., Werkmann, S., Sternecker, P. (eds.) Consulting am Wendepunkt, pp. 121–140. Springer Fachmedien, Wiesbaden (2024)
3. Barrick, M.R., Mount, M.K.: The big five personality dimensions and job performance: a meta-analysis. In: Personnel Psychology, vol. 44, no. 1, pp. 1–26 (1991)
4. Satra, M., Mungi, F., Punamiya, J., Kelkar, K.: Personality prediction system to improve employee recruitment. In: Kautish, S., Chatterjee, P., Pamucar, D., Pradeep, N., Singh, D. (eds.) Computational Intelligence for Modern Business Systems. Disruptive Technologies and Digital Transformations for Society 5.0., pp. 295–308. Springer, Heidelberg (2024)

Many Rules, Many Roles, Few Bytes
The Public Sector IT Project Paradox

Matthias Kurz(✉)

Neuss, Germany
sbpm-one-2025@matthias-kurz.info

Abstract. Public IT projects often face high failure rates due to complex legal requirements and numerous stakeholder roles. This report compiles a list of legal requirements and roles specific to the school administration of a federal state that add complexity to software development projects. It will demonstrate that successful projects in this context require expertise beyond domain knowledge and technical skills.

Keywords: IT Projects · legal requirements · complexity · public sector

1 Introduction

Professional media in the IT sector indicate a high probability of failure for IT projects. It is specifically alleged that IT projects in the German public sector fail at particularly high rates [1, 2]. If this assertion holds true, it would be deeply concerning, given that the digitization of public administration is a central objective.

This practical report aims to offer a potential explanatory contribution to this phenomenon by showcasing the legal requirements and roles relevant in public sector software development projects of the school administration of North Rhine-Westphalia (NRW). During these projects, software is developed for schools, municipalities, districts and/or state level administration.

The report will demonstrate that due to the multitude of regulations and roles, domain expertise and technical skills are not sufficient for successful projects in the school administration. Unless explicitly stated, these regulations and rules are relevant only for this type of project and therefore not relevant in software development projects of the private sector. The report could serve as a basis for a more systematic and scientifically grounded analysis of this phenomenon.

The report is based on observations from long-time public sector employees who have been involved in numerous IT projects in software development projects of the school administration (SWDPSA) of NRW. The legal requirements and roles are extracted from [3].

This paper does not represent the views of the employer or of the State of North Rhine-Westphalia. The findings do not relate to individual persons, projects, or offices.

The author wishes to express his great respect for the colleagues who work with great dedication to digitizing the school administration, despite occasional adversities.

The legal requirements and roles are divided into the following phases according to a typical project lifecycle: (1) Analyzing requirements, (2) Creating contract documents, (3) Checking prerequisites, (4) Awarding the contract, and (5) Accepting the solution. These phases identified in [3] serve as the fundamental structure of this paper.

2 Methodology

For the identification of the legal requirements and roles in SWDPSA, qualitative expert interviews with school-administration staff who had participated in software-development projects were conducted. Experts were eligible if they had at least three years of experience in such projects. To protect participants, all interviews were anonymized and treated confidentially.

The semi-structured interview guide began with a brief introduction – thanking participants, presenting the research question ("Which legal requirements are critical in school-administration software projects?"). The initial question elicited each expert's current role and years of experience in SWDPSA. The second question asked experts to name and rate the relevance of legal topics encountered. Next, the experts were presented a literature-derived list of legal requirements organized by project phase, asking experts to rate any topics they had not already mentioned. Any newly cited requirements were incorporated into subsequent interviews. The session concluded with thanks and an offer to share results upon study completion.

Responses were analyzed via qualitative content analysis of the recording, emphasizing factual reporting over interpretation. Data on professional roles and experience were tabulated (see Table 1).

More information about the methodology can be found in [3].

Table 1. Roles and experience of the interviewed experts

Expert Roles	Experience in IT Projects
3 Head of IT	27 years
2 IT Project Manger	24 years
2 IT Consultant	21 years
1 IT Security	21 years
1 Head of the Legal Department	9 years
	6 years
	4 years
	4 years
	3 years
N = 9	$\sum$ = 119 years

3 Analyzing Requirements

Before the actual software development begins, the requirements for the software are identified based on the project's objective. These requirements describe the functional scope of the software to be developed. Naturally, the focus of the requirements analysis is on determining business requirements. However, the following requirements will focus on the legal aspects of software development specific to the school administration of NRW.

3.1 Data Protection

Data protection is the protection of personal data to prevent misuse and surveillance. The most important legal basis is the GDPR, an EU regulation that overrides national law but contains opening clauses for national regulations. The federal government has implemented this in the BDSG.

Although data protection regulation affects private companies as well, for SWDPSA there are more specific regulations to consider: (1) The Datenschutzgesetz NRW (Privacy Protection Law, DSG NRW), (2) data protection rules from §§ 120–122 SchulG NRW, and (3) the regulations VO-DV I (for students) and VO-DV II (for teachers). Conflicts between SchulG NRW and GDPR are not impossible, and in case of conflict, the SchulG NRW must be interpreted in conformity with Union law or not applied.

3.2 Information Security

Information security ensures the availability, integrity, and confidentiality of information in IT systems. The IT-Planungsrat (IT Planning Council) coordinates standard setting in Germany, and the IT-Grundschutz (IT Baseline Protection) of the BSI is the most widespread set of rules for the public service. It comprises four standards and a compendium with specific requirements.

SWDPSA have to implement the IT-Grundschutz. In future, it is likely that the NIS2 directive, which strengthens cybersecurity in the EU, has to be considered by an increasing number of public sector organizations – including the school administration.

While there is an increasingly dense regulatory framework for private companies providing critical infrastructure services, most private companies have much lighter rules for IT security than the school administration.

3.3 Accessibility

Accessibility means that information processing systems can be used by people with disabilities without particular difficulty. The UN Convention on the Rights of Persons with Disabilities calls for equal access to information technologies but is abstract. More specific is EU Directive 2016/2102 for websites and mobile apps, which has been implemented in Germany through the Gesetz zur Gleichstellung von Menschen mit Behinderungen (BGG) and Barrierefreie-Informationstechnik-Verordnung (BITV 2.0).

In the public sector of NRW, the BGG NRW and BITV NRW implement a regulation similar to BGG and BITV 2.0. It is recommended to strive for accessibility according to EN 301 549 and WCAG for new software as this makes it likely to comply with BGG NRW and BITV NRW. The Accessibility Monitoring Office of North Rhine-Westphalia (Überwachungsstelle für Barrierefreiheit NRW) regularly tests web applications for accessibility.

While ensuring conformance with WCAG may be a business case for private companies due to an increased potential audience, it is not a legal requirement.

3.4 Standards of the IT Planning Council (IT-Planungsrat)

The federal states have their own legislative powers, which can lead to different IT regulations. Article 91c II GG enables joint mandatory IT standards between the federal government and the federal states. The IT-Planungsrat (IT Planning Council) coordinates these standards in accordance with the IT State Treaty (IT-Staatsvertrag). An example of such a mandatory standard is resolution 2019/53 on DIN SPEC 91379 for personal names. These standards are mandatory for the public sector only.

3.5 Specialized Law (Fachrecht)

In SWDPSA, the specific Specialized Law (Fachrecht) must also be considered. As legislation in the education sector is a matter for the federal states, the Fachrecht is typically state-level legislation. In North Rhine-Westphalia, the School Act for the State of NRW (SchulG NRW) regulates the legal foundations, supplemented by numerous ordinances and decrees. The Ministry for Schools and Education (MSB NRW) publishes a consolidated list of laws and regulations (Bereinigte Amtliche Sammlung der Schulvorschriften NRW, BASS) online to make the legal situation more accessible.

3.6 Technical IT Equipment in Schools

The School Act NRW (Schulgesetz NRW) mandates that municipalities are responsible for providing the IT equipment of schools. As there is little legislation standardizing the IT infrastructure of schools across the various municipalities, the IT equipment varies widely between schools. To ensure compatibility, SWDPSA often create web applications, as they have fewer technical requirements.

3.7 Retention Obligations and File Management (Aufbewahrungspflichten Und Aktenführung)

Authorities are obliged to keep files. State-level administration must keep electronic files. The principles of orderly file management must be observed, and software creating record-worthy documents should have an interface to store these documents in the state-wide e-file solution. While various laws – such as tax laws – mandate orderly record keeping for private companies as well, the E-Government Law (EGovG NRW) mandates electronic record keeping for the school administration.

3.8 Substitution of Written Form (Schriftformersatz)

In SWDPSA, the written form (Schriftform) can be a challenge. Although administrative law is generally not bound to the written form, there are numerous administrative rules that require the written form. The written form is often an obstacle in digitalization projects, as it causes media breaks. Instead of the rarely used qualified electronic signature, other electronic procedures are now permitted as a replacement for the written form, in particular through secure identity verifications in forms provided by authorities. In SWDPSA, for example, the national e-ID (BundID) can be used for such identification. Although state-level regulation may be changed as part of a SWDPSA, in practice there is often not enough time. This sometimes leads to unnecessarily complex processes and software.

3.9 Identification Means and Trust Services (eIDAS)

The eIDAS Regulation (EU) No. 910/2014 aims to promote the internal market and ensure a high level of security for electronic identification means and trust services. It regulates the electronic identification of persons and trust services such as electronic signatures and certificates in digital solutions of the public sector. For software development projects of the school administration, the recognition of identification means of other EU member states is particularly relevant, provided they are notified and have reached the security level "High". The BundID offers a compliant identification solution for SWDPSA.

3.10 Accessibility of Administrative Services

The Onlinezugangsgesetz (OZG) obliges the federal government and the federal states to offer administrative services electronically. It aims to provide online administrative services for the public. The OZG promotes the joint use of user accounts and data exchange between federal levels. For SWDPSA, this means they should ensure OZG compliance, particularly by using centrally provided modules such as Verwaltungsportal and BundID.

4 Creating Contract Documents

The development of software for the school administration is regularly carried out by service providers, as the school administration does not have sufficient resources for software development on a larger scale. Before the contract is awarded, however, concrete contractual regulations must be made and put in writing in the form of contract documents.

4.1 Service Description (Leistungsbeschreibung)

The Service Description (Leistungsbeschreibung) is the core of the project and part of the contract documents. It must describe the expected software comprehensively and precisely. It builds on the requirements analysis and focuses on business requirements, while technical details often remain open. Contractor and client jointly concretize the Service Description into the specification after the contract is awarded, before development begins. While the Service Description is not inherently specific to SWDPSA, it must be created with special care as it is extremely difficult to change once the contract has been awarded.

As it is difficult to create a comprehensive Service Description for a new software, it is advisable to add clauses for further development of the software. That way, unforeseen but crucial requirements can be implemented in the software. Of course, this means allocating sufficient budget for implementing these additional requirements.

4.2 EVB-IT

For IT procurements in the public sector, the Ergänzenden Vertragsbedingungen für die Beschaffung von IT-Leistungen (EVB-IT) were developed, which serve as model terms and conditions. EVB-IT consists of model contract forms and general terms and conditions for different types of IT projects. The use of the EVB-IT reduces the risk of overlooking important legal aspects in contracts and provides a proven, balanced basis for IT procurements. Their use is mandatory for SWDPSA.

Agile software development is gaining popularity in software development projects. However, EVB-IT traditionally assumes a comprehensive Service Description, while agile software development focuses on the flexibility to respond to new requirements. There are attempts to adapt the EVB-IT contracts to agile software development. However, these attempts are not yet sufficiently mature for larger projects. Projects may elect to use an EVB-IT Dienstvertrag – an agreement for contracting developers – rather than contracting for the delivery of a complete software product and subsequently applying agile methodologies. However, accurately forecasting the total development effort required to complete the software remains exceedingly challenging for project managers.

5 Checking Prerequisites

In the project phase Checking Prerequisites, various roles check whether individual legal requirements have been adequately identified and implemented in the contract documents.

5.1 Data Protection Officer (Datenschutzbeauftragter)

In SWDPSA, the involvement of the Datenschutzbeauftragter (Data Protection Officer) is common, although there is no direct legal state-level obligation. However, the respective offices may have specific rules mandating the inclusion of the Datenschutzbeauftragter. Data protection officers have a similar role in the private sector.

5.2 Informationssicherheitsbeauftragter (Information Security Officer)

The information security guidelines of the individual offices often prescribe the implementation of the IT-Grundschutz and mandate consulting the respective organization´s Information Security Officer (Informationssicherheitsbeauftragter, ISB). Since the development of new software is generally relevant to information security, the ISB must be involved before the contract is awarded. Again, Information Security Officers in the private sector have a similar role.

5.3 Personalvertretung (Staff Council)

In SWDPSA, Personalräte (Staff Councils) must be involved, similar to staff counciles (Betriebsräte) in the private sector. There are local Personalräte (Staff Councils) as the first point of contact and higher-level representations such as Bezirkspersonalräte (District Staff Councils) and Hauptpersonalräte (Central Staff Councils). If software is used in several offices or statewide, the Hauptpersonalrat Verwaltung (Central Administrative Staff Council) must be involved. Depending on certain characteristics of the software project, the involvement of the Personalrat (Staff Council) can take the form of hearing, participation, or co-determination rights. Co-determination provides the Staff Councils with substantial influence on projects and is particularly relevant in SWDPSA. If the software is to be used at schools, some or all eight Central Staff Councils of the affected school types are to be consulted.

While larger private companies often have staff councils with similar rights, SWDPSA have to consider an especially complex network of staff representation (with potentially 6000 Staff Councils and eight Central Staff Councils) representing different but overlapping parts of the workforce.

5.4 Schwerbehindertenvertretung (Representation of Disabled Employees)

The Schwerbehindertenvertretung (Representation of Disabled Employees) must be involved in SWDPSA if the interests of severely disabled or equivalent employees are affected. They have the right to be heard and consulted in all matters concerning this group of employees. Similar to the Central Staff Councils, the eight Central Representations of Disabled Employees of the different school forms have to be consulted if the software is to be used at schools.

5.5 CIO NRW

The CIO NRW steers and coordinates the IT of the state administration. Ministries must coordinate information technology projects, such as SWDPSA with the CIO NRW at an early stage.

Coordinating software development projects with the CIO is common in the private sector. Therefore, this role is not specific for SWDPSA.

5.6 Budget

According to the State Budget Code of North Rhine-Westphalia (Landeshaushaltsordnung, LHO NRW), expenditures are generally only permissible for the planned purpose and in the planned budget year. Therefore, funds must be allocated in the budget plan in good time before SWDPSA start. If deadlines are delayed, existing budgetary funds risk expiring and no longer being available for the remaining project.

While needing enough funds for software development is not unique to SWDPSA, losing parts of the funds if they are not spent in the planned volume in the planned year is less common in the private sector.

6 Awarding the Contract

After the legal requirements for software have been checked and implemented in the contract documents, the contract for software development can be awarded.

Procurement law consists of two areas: the upper threshold area and the lower threshold area. The upper threshold area applies if the estimated contract value exceeds the threshold values specified in the Act Against Restraints of Competition (Gesetz gegen Wettbewerbsbeschränkungen, GWB), which results from EU directives. In larger SWDPSA, the threshold value of €221,000 is typically exceeded.

The legally secure awarding of contracts for the development and operation of a new solution is of utmost importance, especially in the upper threshold area, as bidders there enjoy extensive legal protection. Errors in the awarding process lead at least to considerable delays – and possibly to the failure of the project. Due to the complexity and dynamics of this area of law, the awarding of contracts in the upper threshold area is often accompanied by specialized procurement law firms.

7 Accepting the Solution

The acceptance of the fully developed solution has significant legal consequences, as it marks the beginning of the limitation period for claims for defects. Therefore, the acceptance should be carried out carefully, and a comprehensive functional test within 30 days is advisable. As accepting an incomplete solution may waive future defect claims, the software should be checked thoroughly. This applies to the private sector as well.

8 Conclusion

The dense web of EU, federal, and state regulations – from GDPR and IT Grundschutz to accessibility directives and procurement thresholds – creates a highly specialized legal landscape that software teams must navigate at every project phase. Coordinating with many stakeholders – data protection and information security officers, multiple tiers of staff councils and disability representatives, budget authorities, legal advisors, and even the CIO NRW – turns requirements gathering and contract award into a complex choreography. As a result, successful school administration IT projects demand not only deep technical and domain expertise but also rigorous legal acumen and extensive cross functional collaboration.

Changing these rules is out of scope for typical software development projects of the school administration (SWDPSA), as most rules exist in a regulatory framework comprising of the state level, national level, and supranational level (EU). Only in the case of the Fachrecht (e.g., Schulgesetz NRW), changing these rules can be feasible (and is necessary in some cases).

Therefore, project managers must be empowered to confront this complexity. One means of doing so is to engage specialized external expertise. This is particularly relevant in the field of procurement law, where specialized law firms oversee the tendering process. Furthermore, project managers should be prepared for the multifaceted challenges of SWDPSA, which can be accomplished through targeted training programs or the provision of comprehensive guidelines.

References

1. Mischler, G.: Woran Behörden scheitern, Golem.de (2025). https://www.golem.de/news/digitales-desaster-woran-behoerden-scheitern-2501-190937.html, Accessed 10 June 2025
2. Krämer, C.: Kleinstaaterei lässt IT-Projekte scheitern (2011). Manager Magazin, https://www.manager-magazin.de/politik/deutschland/a-802446.html, Accessed 10 June 2025
3. Kurz, M.: Rechtsrahmen für Softwareprojekte der Schulverwaltung NRW: Ein juristischer Leitfaden für die Schulverwaltung des Landes Nordrhein-Westfalen, BoD, Hamburg (2021)

Author Index

A
Auer, Thomas 198

B
Bönsch, Jakob 91, 103

C
Clark, Katie 179

D
Dalm, Kris 214
Dittmar, Anke 161

E
El Bobbou, Sleiman 91
Elstermann, Matthes 3, 35, 69

F
Fleischmann, Albert 19
Forbrig, Peter 161

G
Geiger, John 91

H
Hein, Michael 223
Heß, Simon 103

K
Kannengiesser, Udo 52
Krämer, Andreas 35

Kurz, Matthias 228

L
Lederer, Matthias 179, 214
Lizak, Timo 103

M
Menezes, Steevan Christopher 214
Moya, Ana 223

O
Okello, Leon Patrick 103
Ovtcharova, Jivka 91

P
Piller, Christoph 115
Pufahl, Melanie 179

R
Rösl, Stefan 198
Rüeck, Lisa 198

S
Schaller, Thomas 19
Schieder, Christian 137, 198
Schmid, Saskia 137
Stary, Christian 146

Z
Zopke, Theresa 223

Made in the USA
Monee, IL
03 May 2026